Best wishes,
Clem Allison

Seeing Beyond

· · · · · · · · · ·

Awakening to the Reality of a
Spiritually Interconnected, Evolving World

CLEMENT ALLISON

ISBN: 978-0-9971739-0-1 (trade paperback)
ISBN: 978-0-9971739-1-8 (e-book)

Cover design by Pete Garceau
Book interior by Morgana Gallaway

This edition was prepared for printing by The Editorial Department
7650 E. Broadway, #308, Tucson, Arizona 85710
www.editorialdepartment.com

To my late parents, Les and Hellen Allison,
whose love of books and thirst for knowledge became my touchstone.

CONTENTS

ACKNOWLEDGMENTS

It is certainly true that no one accomplishes anything worthwhile in this life without help, encouragement, and inspiration from others. Here I wish to mention a few of the many who have influenced my life in ways that have led to this book.

First, I am indebted to those whose leadership, integrity, and wisdom have provided opportunities for my intellectual and spiritual growth. They include the late Reverend Dr. Roy Blakeburn, whose passion for social justice, courage to speak the truth, and unconditional love and understanding of those in need, continues to guide and inspire me. I am also indebted to Dr. Robert Knott, the former president of Tusculum College who skillfully and thoughtfully guided the Tusculum College community in new and innovative directions. My interest in early Christian and biblical history can be traced, in large measure, to the invitation he extended to me and other faculty colleagues to teach a course in the Judeo-Christian roots of American democracy in the early 1990s.

By the same token, I wish to pay tribute to the late Dr. Arnold Thomas, who, on a leap of faith, asked me to come join the Tusculum College faculty in 1966. It was because of his initial mentoring that I was able to go on and pursue the academic career I loved for the next thirty-four years. The support and encouragement that Arnold and his wife, Ruth, gave me freely were invaluable. Among these and other former Tusculum colleagues to whom I am indebted is Dr. David Hendricksen, whose extensive knowledge of the Scriptures and biblical research has provided me with a broad base of information about writers of the New Testament and what they had to say that is relevant to our modern world.

When it comes to members of our local community, I am grateful for the opportunity I have had to meet each Sunday morning with the open-minded, free-thinking members of Greeneville's First Presbyterian Church to discuss and debate a variety of social issues and engage the intellectually and spiritually stimulating views of modern Biblical scholars. These discussions have provided an invaluable testing ground for my own ideas.

In addition, I owe much to Ron Stone of Portland, Oregon, who has generously shared his spiritual insights and impressive knowledge gained from years of study and research. Our discussions about our common interest in the evolution of human consciousness and the prospects for the development of a more integral, ecologically friendly world in the new millennium have been enormously helpful to me.

I also wish to express my sincere appreciation to The Editorial Department for providing me with such talented and immensely helpful editors as Beth Jusino, Marcia Ford, Julie Miller, and Doug Wagner. Because of their honest assessments, attention to details, and wise recommendations, my manuscript evolved into one that is far more polished and focused than it was initially. I especially want to thank The Editorial Department's Director of Client Services, Jane Ryder, for not only selecting such great editors to work with me but also for her patience, cheerful spirit, kind words of encouragement, and sound advice. How fortunate I was to have such extraordinary help and support!

Likewise, I am indebted to The Editorial Department's Logistical Coordinator, Liz Felix and her highly skilled and talented production staff for preparing my manuscript for publication. I cannot emphasize enough how cooperative and helpful Liz and her entire production staff were throughout the whole publishing process. Among those staff members, I particularly want to thank Pete Garceau for his amazing ability to capture the essence of this book in his outstanding cover design and Morgana Gallaway for sharing her extensive knowledge about the various publishing options available to authors today.

I also owe much to Esther Bell, CEO of Global Intellectual Property Asset Management, PLLC, for her expert advice regarding various copyright issues and for her enthusiastic support of my writing efforts from beginning to end.

Finally, I wish to pay special tribute to my wife, Beverly, who has been my best friend, confidante, and trusted adviser for the last fifty-eight-years. I could not have produced this book without her patience, keen insights, and support during the many months of my researching and writing. I am equally indebted to our daughters, Carrie and Jennifer, for their generous support and encouragement. Their intellectual achievements and genuine care for the welfare of others have truly been an inspiration to Beverly and me.

INTRODUCTION

Personal Reflections and Motivations

Before I begin, let me be clear. I am not a theologian and I have never been a member of a clergy associated with any religion. Instead, as a progressively oriented, growing Christian, my voice comes from the pews rather than from the pulpit. For me, being a Christian means following the example of Jesus's life and his teachings as I understand them from the New Testament and a variety of scholarly biblical references even while admitting to my many shortcomings in trying to put into practice what I have learned along the way. In more specific terms, I consider him to be my moral guide. In my view, he embodied the true nature or essence of God.

My hope and assurance are found in Jesus's words in John 14:12: "Very truly, I tell you, the one who believes in me will also do the works that I do and, in fact, will do greater works than these." With these words, Jesus seems to acknowledge humanity's God-given potential and purpose to "seek and to find". (Matthew 7:7)

So I accept Jesus's call to seek new ideas and possibilities even if they should happen to challenge conventional religious beliefs and assumptions. Jesus also made it clear that our potential as individuals and as a people can be found only in and through human relationships characterized by compassionate caring and service to others: "Truly I tell you, just as you did it to one of the least of these who are members of my family, you did it to me" (Matthew 25:40).

Nevertheless, in many parts of the world today, the needs of the poor and powerless continue to go unmet in the face of narrow political and economic interests. For this reason, calls for social justice, equal rights, and protection of all aspects of the world's environment are on the increase and becoming more persistent. The world appears to be poised either for a significant evolutionary leap forward in the light of what appears to be a global spiritual awakening, or for a period of catastrophic destruction resulting from the failure of the world's leaders to respond positively and constructively to this awakening.

I wrote this book, then, not only as a profession of faith but as an effort to stimulate and disturb the reader enough to view our changing world from a new spiritual perspective with great promise and potential.

Toward this end, I am less impressed with the institutional aspects of Christendom and its various "boundaries" as defined by the officially proclaimed beliefs of Catholics or Protestants and their numerous subgroups than with the ways individual Christians or those of other faiths—or no faiths—live their lives in relation to others. Like an increasing number of other nontraditional, non-exclusivist Christians, I have come to a point in my life when I can no longer accept, without question, some of the major doctrines, creeds, and beliefs of orthodox Christianity that tend to dominate the more conventional forms of Catholicism and Protestantism today. Needless to say, my views tend to differ from most mainstream, conservative Christians—but more about that later.

I came to be a Christian the way many Christians do: I was born and raised by Christian parents, and they, along with my older brother and I, attended our local Presbyterian church on a regular basis as I grew to young adulthood in the 1940s and '50s. I then went on to earn a degree at a Methodist college, marry the girl of my dreams, and help her raise our twin daughters while we all attended another Protestant church on a more or less regular basis.

During those years I didn't make a serious effort to learn much beyond the basic tenets of other religions, although a fair number of my friends, both then and now, are followers of other faiths. In some ways, my situation was like that described by Harvey Cox in his book *The Future of Faith*. At one point, Cox refers to a metaphor used by the Danish philosopher Soren Kierkegaard, who said that when we become old enough to reflect on our lives, "we find ourselves on a ship that has already been launched."[1] Cox goes on to say:

> As we become aware of the mysteries of world, self, and other, they always arrive suffused with the specific languages, emotions, and thought patterns of a particular cultural tradition. And these supply the theories, myths, and metaphors with which we respond. Living *with* the mystery is something we all have in common. But *how* we live with it differs. To extend Kierkegaard's metaphor, we sail on one launched ship among many, large and small, that often seem to be crisscrossing, colliding and heading in different directions.[2]

I have been sailing on a "Christian ship" all my life, but it wasn't until the last decade of my teaching career as an art professor at Tusculum College in the 1990s that I began to think about what it really means to be a Christian in broader, more self-reflective terms.

During those same years, my father passed away, my mother suffered a stroke, and one of our daughters battled and overcame cancer. Such events can prompt one to consider matters of time, mortality, and spirituality. This was certainly the case for me, especially after I had a brief glimpse into another level of reality at my parents' home on the evening of May 31, 1990, where my father had died a few hours before.

That evening, not long after my mother, my niece, and I had gone to bed, my niece suddenly noticed a pulsating white light in my parents' bedroom. When she alerted me, I stood silently with her in the doorway to the bedroom as the small bursts of pure white light came and went at a heartbeat pace. The light moved slowly and silently from a distance of about a foot or two below the ceiling in front of my niece and me to a spot over my father's bed, and then to one over his dresser, before moving back in front of us. After a few minutes, the pulsating light moved toward the master bathroom and disappeared.

The whole extraordinary episode lasted less than ten minutes, during which we never spoke a word. Since the light moved to places associated with my father, I am convinced it was his way of expressing joy and peace to us from the "other side." This experience strengthened my conviction not only that life continues in spiritual form after physical death but that the material and spiritual worlds are continuously intertwined.

Later, during the mid-1990s, I was given the opportunity to teach a college-level course called Jerusalem, on the Judeo-Christian roots of American democracy, that all our students at Tusculum College were required to take in addition to their academic-major requirements. I was one of a handful of faculty members who agreed to do so on request, and the experience turned out to be especially enlightening for me. (Another group of faculty members taught a parallel course, Athens, on the Roman Republican roots of American democracy). While I had the benefit of a broader range of life experiences than my younger students, we all gained new insights together from a reexamination of the biblical writers and the impact they had on those who shaped early American democracy.

But why would I "wander" outside of my academic area of the arts and have the audacity to write a book on the subject of religion and spirituality? While the decision to do so may seem odd to some, the relationship between the arts and the many forms of religious expression that have existed throughout the ages actually runs quite deep. In my case, the affinity centers on the creative process itself.

Through most of my life as an artist, it has been clear to me that the experience of creating a painting, a handmade print, or other work of art is, at its best, a spiritual experience. When the mind of the artist releases and becomes especially receptive to the higher or divine consciousness, imaginative leaps and new, unexpected possibilities often present themselves. Conversely, the creative experience can be the catalyst for those sudden "aha" moments. I am sure most visual or performing artists, composers, creative writers, and playwrights know exactly what I'm talking about. Actually, I believe that all human beings, whether we happen to be artists or not, are God's co-creators, especially when we open ourselves to a spiritual source of all love and understanding.

Taking all this into consideration, I became increasingly aware of a disconnect between, on one hand, the writings of the New Testament and those of other, lesser-known Christian authors written relatively soon after the death of Jesus and, on the other, the imperial, hierarchical nature of Christianity that emerged in the fourth and fifth centuries, especially in the wake of Emperor Constantine's conversion to Christianity in 312 CE. In the coming chapters, I will refer to this form of post-Constantine Christianity as orthodox Christianity.

After more than two hundred years of persecution by the Roman state, the early bishops of the church welcomed the prospect of making Christianity the official religion of the Roman Empire upon the orders of a newly Christianized emperor. Early Christian communities had countered anti-Christian persecutions by consistently offering peaceful, love-based alternatives to the oppressive power of the pagan Roman state, but the bishops of the newly Christianized Roman state found themselves able to promote their hierarchical beliefs "from the inside" with the aid of imperial decrees, as well as enforcement powers against heretic dissenters who had the audacity to question the new imperial Christianity. Efforts to promote social justice through the power of love and individual, faith-based spiritual enlightenment were soon replaced by efforts to ensure order and consistency by imposing "official" beliefs. Harvey Cox explains it this way:

> Whether it was a love marriage or a mutual seduction, plainly both parties entered into it freely. If the liaison between church and the empire was some kind of unnatural act, at least it was consensual, but a large share of the fault lies with the hierarchs of the Christian community, who had become infected with what a psychoanalyst might term "empire envy."[3]

Although these events occurred long ago and we live in a very different world today, most Christians cling to and defend many of the creeds and doctrines formulated in those early centuries and maintained with minor variations for the next sixteen hundred years. Those doctrines often contain phrases and images that have little credibility or meaningful relation to the twenty-first century. Consider such examples from the Apostles' Creed as "in Jesus Christ His [God's] only Son our Lord" and "who [Jesus] was conceived by the Holy Ghost, born of the Virgin Mary." The claim that Jesus was the only Son of God was actually meant to challenge the first century Roman notion that the emperor was the Son of God, but it also suggests that no other human being is worthy of being a true son or daughter of God. Likewise, the creed's claim that Jesus was conceived by the Holy Ghost strongly implies that he was not fully human. On the other hand, modern research concerning the historical Jesus paints a different picture.

I agree with Bishop John Shelby Spong when he says it is time Catholics and Protestants alike reopen the discussions that raged among thoughtful Christians during the early history of Christianity in light of modern theological and scientific discoveries.[4] In Part 1 of *Seeing Beyond*, then, I show some of the more obvious "imperial" or orthodox aspects of Christianity to be at odds with a more inclusive and progressive spirit represented by a growing minority within many churches today. In my opinion, the various doctrines, creeds, and long-standing beliefs we will examine in Part 1 have resulted in what could be called a hierarchical theology of separation and final judgments. These qualities are a contrast to the theology of oneness or inclusion that more or less characterized Christianity before its unholy marriage to the imperial Roman State—and that might better serve the world today.

Apparently, I'm not alone in this call for a reawakening. An increasing number of sincere, spiritually aware Christians are either moving in new directions as subgroups within established mainline churches, as described by Hal Taussig in his book *A New Spiritual Home: Progressive Christianity at the Grassroots*, or are leaving the organized traditional church altogether out of a sense of frustration with what is perceived to be a systemic resistance to change.[5] Likewise, in her book *Christianity After Religion: The End of Church and the Birth of a New Spiritual Awakening*, Diana Butler Bass makes this observation about a growing amount of dissatisfaction among the Christian faithful:

> New surveys and polls pointed to an erosion of organized Christianity in nearly all its forms, with only "nondenominational" churches showing a slight numerical increase. It began to appear that vital churches might well be only islands of success in the rising seas of Western unbelief and the high tides of cultural change are leaving traditional religion adrift. All sorts of people—even mature, faithful Christians—are finding conventional religion increasingly less satisfying, are attending church less regularly, and are longing for new expressions of spiritual community.[6]

To me, this phenomenon is just one sign of a new desire to reach beyond religious boundaries and divisive images that minimize or deny the spiritually interconnected nature of our world and the universe. Furthermore, it indicates a gravitational return to a more diverse and spirit-filled form of Christianity that existed between the death and resurrection of Jesus and the advent of orthodox Christianity in the fourth century CE. In a sense, then, the way forward to a new, more integral Christianity necessarily involves going "back to the future."

Having said all this, I also recognize that many Christian churches today actively reach out to those in their local communities and beyond who are suffering from sickness, poverty, loneliness, and intolerance. Then, too, I realize that many churches provide loving and caring environments within which human relationships can grow and be shaped in ways consistent with Jesus's ministry of compassion and passionate advocacy for social justice. Both examples reveal the genuine nature of Christianity, free of judgments, preconditions, and creedal dogmas.

Therefore, I wish to be clear that my criticisms of orthodox Christianity are not aimed at these positive aspects of Christian life and service that are clearly at work in many Catholic and Protestant churches today. Instead, my focus in Part 1 is on the traditional orthodox doctrines that tend to be more exclusive, literalistic, and out of touch with modern scientific knowledge.

In Part 2, we will examine the growing amount of evidence within the fields of quantum physics, biblical research, medicine, evolutionary psychology, ecology, economics, and politics that point to the existence, since the beginning of time, of a spiritually interconnected, divinely inclusive world. In my opinion, this increasing breadth of knowledge is part of a significant spiritual awakening, not only within the Christian community but also in other religions and across the spectrum of human life in all parts of the world. We will see, for instance, that subatomic, interchangeable particles and waves are not only the common building blocks of everything that constitutes the physical universe but have always been influenced by human consciousness. In addition, we will examine what is so significant about the rising number of near-death experiences and their importance in understanding the connections between the physical and spiritual realms of existence.

I also address the fact that human consciousness is evolving from its present self-conscious state toward a more holistic, or cosmic, level of consciousness, largely through the process of repeated earthly reincarnations of the soul. Finally, Part 2 explores how some of the dramatic and unsettling changes we are experiencing around the globe suggest a world in a monumental state of transition from our present ethnocentric (tribal) level of human consciousness to a more "worldcentric" (inclusive) one.[7]

Taken together, these last five chapters serve to show that we are very possibly on Earth at this time for the purpose of participating in one of the most significant changes in the evolution of human consciousness. Rather than seeing these developments as separate, unrelated issues, I maintain that they are interconnected parts of a global spiritual awakening governed by Divine grace and intention.

PART 1

*A Critical Look at Various
Christian Doctrines and Beliefs*

CHAPTER 1

Beyond Theism: Reexamining the Nature of God

EARLY JUDAIC CONCEPTS OF GOD

The idea that a single all-knowing, all-powerful God created the world first emerged in Western civilization over twenty-five hundred years ago in the sixth century BCE as part of a Judaic reform movement after the release of the Jews from many years spent in Babylonian captivity. The reform's purpose was to replace the older conventional Hebrew idea that a pantheon of gods governed the world. The post-exilic Jewish priesthood had come to recognize that worship of multiple gods had become overly complex and morally corrupt. Modern theologians generally refer to this historic shift in understanding the nature of God as a change from polytheism to monotheism.[1]

However, it is worth noting that the priestly leaders of the ancient Judaic reform, who introduced this monotheistic model of the Divine, actually did so by combining the names of two earlier Hebrew gods having different characteristics. Henceforth, the name given to God was Yahweh-Elohim. Yahweh had already been known as the warrior god of armies associated with the Jewish kingdom of Judah. The name Elohim, on the other hand, was a reference to El-Elohim, the God of Israel, to the north of Judah, and of Abraham before that. What is particularly interesting is that the term El-Elohim meant "God of Gods," or seemingly the greatest of a *family* of gods. Support for this idea is even suggested by Genesis 1: 26: "Then God said, "Let *us* make humankind in *our* image, according to *our* likeness." In effect, the combination of the two names created ambiguity, if not an outright contradiction, regarding the purity of early Judaic monotheism.[2]

A SEPARATION OF THE HUMAN AND DIVINE

But one thing seems clear about each of the two "faces" of early Judaic monotheism. What they shared in common was an image of an omniscient, omnipotent, human-like male being that exists beyond the world and chooses to intervene in its affairs from time to time as its Supreme Creator and Ruler. In other words, early Judaic monotheists envisioned a god who was mainly transcendent (above or separate from the world) and occasionally immanent (present or actively involved in the world). God's occasional intervention in the physical world that he supposedly created out of nothing (the "void") long ago was, therefore, deemed to be supernatural.

This way of perceiving God suggests that a clear boundary exists between the Divine (God) and humanity (the physical world). Even though the New Testament refers at times to the Holy Spirit of God as being "in" or "within" Christians, the Scriptures never support the idea that such persons either are or can become divine. Some theologians have even referred to this division as an "ontological distinction or discontinuity" between humanity and God.[3] Equally important is the fact that this way of understanding God essentially dominated Judaism after the sixth century BCE and eventually became a central part of orthodox

Christian theology, especially during and after the fourth century CE, when the foundations of orthodox Christianity were firmly established.

THE CHRISTIAN COMPROMISE

The notion of an inherent "ontological distinction" between humanity and God was compromised significantly when the Christian doctrine of the incarnation was officially established by Orthodox Church fathers in the fourth century CE. This doctrine asserted that in one person and one person only—namely Jesus—was God in the flesh. In other words, in this one exceptional case, the human and divine natures were united, making Jesus uniquely divine.

Furthermore, the belief in the existence of only one God (monotheism), which had been central to Christianity, was essentially challenged by the doctrine of the Trinity, first introduced by the early church in the third century CE. The doctrine, which still enjoys wide acceptance among Christians, claims that God became "three different, distinct, and coeternal Persons—not personalities, not roles, not aspects, not functions, not modes, but Persons."[4] Those persons, of course, are the Father, Son, and Holy Ghost commonly named in most Christian churches today. (This doctrine, as it applies to the divinity of Jesus, will be explored later in Chapter 2.)

Since the doctrine of the Trinity promotes the existence of three distinct divine entities having nearly equal authority and status, one can understand why some Jews and Muslims believe that the doctrine represents at least a partial revival of polytheism.[5] After all, the concept of a Trinitarian god was well known throughout the pagan world before Christianity. For instance, the ancient Babylonians worshipped a god having three heads and used the equilateral triangle as a symbol of such a "trinity in unity."[6] Likewise, as early as the fourth century BCE in

Greece, Aristotle stated, "All things are three, and thrice is all: and let us use this number in the worship of the gods; for, as the Pythagoreans say, everything and all things are bounded by threes, for the end, the middle and the beginning have this number in everything, and these compose the number of the Trinity."[7]

An even earlier flirtation with polytheism occurred when the Judaic priests of the sixth century BCE came to think of evil as a being named Satan. Early Christian writers endorsed this personification of evil, and Satan became a "bad god" whose evil power competed with God's power of good.[8] Prime examples are found in the New Testament Gospels of Mark (1:12-13), Matthew (4:1-11), and Luke (4:1-13), which tell the story of Jesus's encounter with Satan in the wilderness. Even today, the belief in the existence of a lesser god of evil called Satan is still professed by many traditionally oriented Christians.

Many Christian churches today continue to promote the fourth century doctrines of the incarnation and the Trinity, thereby clinging to the view that, on one hand, God came to Earth for a while as Jesus and, on the other, that Jesus was God's only son. In either case, the popular belief that most Christians hold is that God and the risen Jesus answer our prayers from a place some distance apart from humanity and the world.

THEISM: THE IMAGE OF GOD ADOPTED BY THE EARLY CHRISTIAN CHURCH

By the time Christianity had become the state religion of the Roman Empire under Emperor Constantine in the early fourth century CE, the Christian image of God as an all-knowing, all-powerful creator of the universe, external to the world, had also begun to assume the characteristics of an imperial ruler and lawgiver. This may have been due to the fact that Constantine was deeply involved in the affairs of the newly recognized orthodox Christian Church and provided a convenient model that the Christian faithful could understand. In fact, the images of royalty associated with absolute monarchies would have been quite familiar to Christians throughout Europe for the next fourteen hundred years. Along with the image of God as monarch came the idea of God as the ultimate source of authority: the enforcer of laws, the ultimate judge, and, consequently, an object of fear as well as a source of occasional acts of forgiveness and grace. This particular way of understanding God, in combination with the idea of an external transcendent being who is occasionally present in the world, has been known as theism by theologians ever since the English philosopher and theologian Ralph Cudworth introduced the term in the seventeenth century.

Cudworth did so as a way of distinguishing what he considered to be a theistic concept of God from another form of monotheism known as deism.[9] Deists, including Thomas Jefferson and Benjamin Franklin during the eighteenth century, proclaimed that since God created a perfect, self-sufficient world, he saw no need to be present or to intervene in the affairs of humanity. In other words, deists understood God to be beyond the world, not present in it.

The popular monarchical image of God so typical of theism leads to what Marcus Borg describes as a "performance model" of the Christian life.[10] First, the idea of God as king automatically places human beings in the position of being lowly subjects who owe the king loyalty and obedience. Second, many Christians believe that the Old Testament book of Genesis claims that we are inherently sinful as a result of the fall from God's favor in the Garden of Eden and that such a violation of God's law deserves punishment. Along with this theistic view goes the popular Christian assumption that since God loves us despite our miserable state, he provided a way for us to escape the punishment we deserve by sending his "only" son, Jesus, to suffer a cruel death on the cross as an ultimate act of atonement for humanity's inherited disobedience.

In other words, Jesus served as the scapegoat sacrificed to honor God's law so that humanity could avoid what appeared to be its certain fate. (A more complete discussion of atonement will be presented in Chapter 2.) Ironically, Jesus, whose life and ministry contrasted sharply with the elevated status of a king and the realities of Roman imperial rule, was ultimately referred to as Christ "the king," who will come again to judge all of us at the so-called Last Judgment when the world ends. This monarchical image of Jesus is closely associated with theism.

Also associated with theism is a preoccupation with sin and guilt. As Borg explains, "Repentance becomes contrition for sin, redemption becomes redemption from sin, liberation becomes liberation from sin, and salvation becomes salvation from sin."[11] The overall effect is that one thinks of himself or herself primarily as a sinner who needs to repent and receive forgiveness. Even when forgiven, we cannot escape our inherent sinful state as humans, and so we remain undeserving in the eyes of God the king. This predicament inevitably leads to guilt.

So, the monarchical image of God that most often comes with theism usually leads to a life of always trying to measure up to God's law. In the minds of many theists, our hope of entering heaven and being "saved" depends largely on how well we "perform" in meeting God's "requirements" in life.[12] In this sense, humanity always sees itself on trial before God and Jesus, who will "come to judge the quick and the dead."

There are also negative human consequences that can come from theistic perceptions of nature, society, and gender. Since theists assume God is separate from the natural world and the universe, then God is *not in nature* and nature is *not in God*.[13] By extension, theism suggests that nature is less sacred or holy than God. Perhaps it is easier to understand, then, why many Christians believe nature exists only in terms of its value to humans—the emphasis is too often placed on the material rather than intrinsic value of nature. Is there a connection, then, between theism and the exploitation of nature by humans? If it's not a direct and inevitable connection, theism at least makes that possibility greater.

SOCIAL CONSEQUENCES OF THEISM

When it comes to the societal aspects of theism, the connection between the monarchical model of God and the long history of absolute monarchical governing systems is obvious. The monarchical form of government—which dominated the world before, during, and after Christianity became imperial—fostered hierarchical social orders. It placed absolute power in the hands of male autocrats, power that was not meant to be questioned or compromised.

Today, the world has changed radically in its types of governing systems, yet the Vatican in particular still fosters a monarchical system, with its palace complex, ornate royal trappings, and royalist court filled with cardinals who function in elevated positions reminiscent of an earlier time's royal princes. A similar case could be made for the hierarchical and ceremony-laden aspects of the Anglican and Episcopalian churches today, at least in terms of outward appearances. Comparatively speaking, however, the Anglican and Episcopalian churches have made greater strides toward modernity than the Catholic Church, with its continuing male-dominated culture.

The theistic model of God has also contributed to the domination and exploitation of women. The male image of God, so typical of theism, is clearly linked to patriarchal dominance in politics and the family. Repeated references to God's supposed maleness in the theistically oriented religions of Judaism, Christianity, and Islam have legitimized male dominance over women for centuries. When it comes to Christianity, the most obvious example today is the priestly top-down structure of the

Catholic Church. However, the more conservative Protestant churches also continue to endorse a patriarchal-dominant attitude in words and actions, either overtly or in subtle ways.

Another example of the ancient tradition of male domination that Christian theism failed to change is the framework that sees nature as female while perceiving God as male. Since theism understands God and nature to be separate entities in descending order, it inherently ensures an inferior status for women. To put it another way, theism tends to view men as closer to God while more closely associating women with "Mother Earth." Taken together, these potentially harmful value distinctions between men and women still exist in varying degrees within Christianity (as well as within the Judaic and Islamic faiths) even though modern feminist theology has done much to expose the negative aspects of these lingering orthodox Christian biases. It is yet another way that orthodox Christian theism has contributed to a theology of separation.

PANENTHEISM: AN ALTERNATIVE TO THEISM AND DEISM

But theism and deism are not the only ways of perceiving God that have long histories. A third imaging of God, known as panentheism, also has ancient origins. The term *panentheism* is derived from the Greek words *pan-en-theos*, meaning "all-in-God." Taken as a whole, the phrase implies that everything is in God and God is in everything. [14] Although German philosopher Karl Christian Friedrich Krause first used the term *panentheism* in 1829, panentheistic beliefs can be traced as far back as the twenty-eight-hundred-year-old Hindu *Upanishads* in the East as well as to the Greek philosophers Plato and Plotinus in the West. [15]

By the same token, early Muslim Sufi mystics, such as Bayazid Bistami, Mansur al-Hallaj, and Jalaluddin Rumi, all promoted a panentheistic image of Allah. Panentheism has Judaic roots as well. Maimonides,

Jewish Kabbalah mystics, and eastern European Hasidic teachers such as eighteenth century Rabbi Israel ben Eliezer all envisioned God in this way.[16] Likewise, some early Christians espoused a panentheistic understanding of God before the fourth century CE, when orthodox bishops managed to move the church away from this more mystical understanding of God toward a more anthropomorphic, theistic image perfectly suited to a growing authoritarian church hierarchy.

Nevertheless, Christian panentheism continued to survive beyond the fourth century despite being reduced in status to a minor theological undercurrent within the later history of Christianity. Some devout Christians dared over time to openly present their panentheistic beliefs as an alternative to the dominant theistic views of the Catholic Church hierarchy in particular. Prominent among them were ninth century Irish-Catholic theologian John Scottus Eriugena, thirteenth century German theologian Meister Eckhart, and early twentieth century theologian and Jesuit priest Pierre Teilhard de Chardin. [17]

More recently, Paul Alan Laughlin interpreted panentheism this way: "God/The Ultimate is the inner spiritual essence of everything ... and then some."[18] In broader terms, this statement means that God's spiritual existence *above and beyond* the universe and God's eternal presence *in* the universe are *equal* in importance. This idea opposes theism's emphasis on God as an external, transcendent being who is occasionally present in the world. As an analogy, one could say we human beings are fish within the ocean that is God. Victoria LePage provides what is perhaps a more complete analogy in an article she wrote for the Theosophical Society in America, "The God Debate: Monotheism vs. Panentheism in Postmodern Society": "The panentheistic view is that everything existent is alive, there is no such thing as dead matter; the world lives in God and influences God in the same organic way that the cells of our body influence us, it is a true two-way relationship."[19]

But what is the nature of this panentheistic, two-way relationship between God and humanity if, as panentheists believe, "everything is in God"? LePage also makes it clear that the relationship is a deeply personal one:

> The heart of the panentheistic exposition lies in the twin concepts of divine holism and divine love, which imply a voluntary self-limiting on God's part, a voluntary self-transformation. So does a mother interact with the child in her womb in such a way that both are undergoing a growth and an evolution together, in mutual love, while remaining distinct entities.[20]

Dr. Timothy Conway elaborates on this two-way relationship between God and humanity in his 1995 article for Enlightened-Spirituality.org, "Panentheism and the Reality of God":

> It is critically important and far more wise and reasonable for our theology to regard God not just as the "Supreme person" but *also* as **the *Trans*-personal or Supra-Personal Divine**. This Transpersonal God or Reality is so absolutely more loving, compassionate, creative, playful, humorous, intimate and responsible in His/Her Divinity (the I AM THAT AM) than we are as mere "persons." Thus, it makes much more sense to speak of God as the Transpersonal One Who can also express on the "Personal" level as long as we (at our stage of spiritual development or "soul-ular evolution") take ourselves to be merely persons and have not discovered WHO WE REALLY ARE in authentic God-Realization or Self-Realization.[21]

I am sure that many of us have had personal experiences of a spiritual nature that perfectly illustrate Conway's point. In my case, I vividly recall an experience that could only be described as a personal encounter with God's embracing, uplifting love at a time when I was in a state of deep despair and anger against him: when one of our beloved daughters had just been diagnosed with cancer. Clearly, my experience was not unique. Countless parents have had to face similar frightening news. As I drove away from our daughter's apartment angrily expressing the apparent unfairness of it all, I asked God why he was so silent in response to my prayers, so unwilling to even provide some sign of his existence!

After I arrived at the motel where my wife and I were staying, my attention was drawn to a television program, already in progress, that featured the true story of parents with a young daughter in the midst of a serious battle with cancer. They spoke of "feeling" a sense of assurance that their daughter would recover despite the surgical crisis they faced. At that moment, I knew that message was meant for my wife and me. I suddenly sensed the presence of God as I never had before. The strength I thought I did not have now seemed available all at once. I felt that whatever lay before us, my wife and I would have a source of strength beyond our own means alone to see things through for our daughter's sake.

Most of all, I knew God had reached me with a sign: not that our daughter would be spared her suffering or even that she would survive but that God's loving, compassionate presence embraced us all, then and always. Still today, no one can convince me that this moment was a coincidence or that I was engaged in wishful thinking. It was real and life-changing for me.

We were among the fortunate ones whose children survived cancer, but the lesson is no less important for those whose loved ones do not survive cancer. God is not about rewards and punishments or choosing life for some and death for others. Instead, our "Supra-Personal" God of all understanding is about the transformative power of love and compassion. And these are given unconditionally to every person in the midst of every joy or crisis, even until death and beyond.

Panentheism should not be confused with another way of understanding God that has ancient origins and is known as pantheism. Frequent confusion is due mainly to the fact that until recently, panentheism has been less familiar to most people than pantheism. While the differences between these two images of God may be subtle, they are important. Although panentheists and pantheists agree that everything that exists in the universe is pervaded by divinity, pantheists believe *God is the universe* and all is God, whereas panentheists believe the *universe is contained within God.* To put it another way, pantheists tend to understand God to be simply the sum total of things that exist in the physical universe. [22]

Furthermore, since pantheists see the universe as God, they do not believe in a personal God the same way panentheists do. The pantheist lack of a personal God is addressed as follows by C. Alan Anderson and Deborah G. Whitehouse in their book, *New Thought: A Practical American Spirituality:* "God's presence is an overriding presence that cancels the possibility of the existence of anything else, of any genuine beloved, of any loving or unloving response to God. In Pantheism, human existence or any other finite existence is at best a mystery."[23] Today, however, panentheism is becoming more widely accepted among progressive Christians mainly because of the expansion of scientific knowledge and a reexamination of Jesus's life and ministry. For example, contributing greatly to this panentheistic understanding of God are Anglican bishop John A.T. Robinson's 1963 book, *Honest to God*; Roman Catholic priest Matthew Fox's 1993 book, *Original Blessing*; and the writings and teachings of theologians such as Marcus Borg and John Dominic Crossan.

The panentheistic image of God presented so far essentially promotes a theology of inclusion. First of all, it implies that God and humanity are one. If everything is in God and God is in everything, separation is nonexistent. This does not presume that humanity and God are equal but simply that we *come from* God and *are not made by* God from something other than God. Quincy Howe, professor of classics at Scripps College, essentially describes the panentheistic relationship between God and humanity by referring to God's initial act of creation as an "emanation" from God rather than a process of creating the world out of nothing as claimed by the theist tradition:

> Our traditional Christian view of creation envisions God fashioning the cosmos out of the void, something alien to himself. There is already a rather troublesome contradiction here, in that the void (which is by definition empty) is providing the stuff of creation. For both the Hindu and the Neoplatonist the formula is somewhat different. God has two modes of being: quiescent and manifesting. When he goes from quiescence to manifestation, he simply extends and diversifies his being into the myriad forms of physical and ideational creation. One such form that emanates from God is the human soul. This theory of emanation entails neither paradox nor contradiction, for if God is omnipresent and all pervasive, there cannot be anything that does not partake of his Being.[24]

Such a description is not only consistent with the concept of panentheism, but it also relates well to the so-called Big Bang theory of modern physics. The theory holds that the creation of the universe began approximately 13.7 billion years ago, either with an unimaginably powerful explosion or some sort of supernatural expansion from "an infinitesimally small, infinitely hot, infinitely dense something" that physicists call a "singularity."[25] It seems fair to say that most religions would interpret this singularity as God. Some scientists believe that before the singularity, there was nothing, but from the perspective of panentheists, there was never a time when nothing existed, since this particular theology assumes that the consciousness of God has always existed. In other words, the universe began from intelligently directed, conscious energy—energy emanating from the Divine, in all directions as with light. Accordingly, everything that exists in the universe, including human life, is an emanation of God's light energy.

Therefore, it seems reasonable to conclude that each of us is endowed with a "divine spark" that enables us to find God *within* rather than beyond and "above." In short, there is no place where God cannot be found. Again, this places panentheism closer to the mystical traditions of such eastern religions as Hinduism, Taoism, and Buddhism, the mysticism of the Christian Medieval Age, and especially the early Christian Gnostics, from before the fourth century, who claimed that God can be found "within." That panentheism incorporates elements of each of these modes of religious thought and expression illustrates how broad and inclusive its concept of God is.

BIBLICAL CONFIRMATIONS OF PANENTHEISM

Panentheistic images of God can also be found in the Scriptures. For instance, a panentheistic understanding of God seems perfectly consistent with Paul's statement in Acts 17:28: "For in him we live, and move, and have our being ... For we are also his offspring." In Luke 17:21 we find Jesus's statement "The Kingdom of God is within you." And in John 12:45 Jesus says, "Those who see me, see the one who sent me." Borg points out, "Both the Hebrew Bible and the Christian Testament speak of 'the glory of God' which the Jewish theologian Abraham Heschel defines as 'the effulgence of a living presence.'"[26] Further confirmation comes from Psalm 139 in the Old Testament:

> *You have searched me and known me;*
> *You know when I sit down and when I rise up;*

You go before me and behind me,
and lay your hand upon me;
Where can I go from your Spirit?
or where can I flee from your presence?

If theism presents a patriarchal image of God as a divine being who, for the most part, resides beyond the universe and the human world, then panentheism understands that God is not *a* spirit or person but Spirit itself, a non-material reality that pervades all that is and all that isn't. For this reason, God is accessible not just through a belief in Jesus or the church's commandments but personally and directly from within one's own heart and soul.

Likewise, if theism interprets God's creation of the universe as a single monumental event that occurred long ago, panentheism tends to regard creation as an ongoing evolutionary process that affects not only the material world and universe but human consciousness in particular. At the same time, the panentheist considers all aspects of God's continually evolving creation to be connected and inseparable. No material or non-material aspect of creation—which is to say God—exists independent of others. In the end, they are all one—in The One.

Panentheism also differently interprets salvation. Rather than considering salvation an escape from condemnation and eternal banishment by God at some future time, panentheism views salvation as an awakening, not only to the reality of God's presence but also to the power of God's love and the spiritual interconnection of all that exists—even in the midst of one's own imagined separation from God. While Christian theism closely links salvation with sin and understands sin to be a violation of God's "laws," panentheism interprets sin to be a lack of understanding and compassion and a turning away from God's loving relationship to us. Or, to put it another way, sin is a self-imposed exile from God's unconditional love. Here, Borg says it well:

> God is the lover who yearns to be in relationship to us. Rather than sin and guilt being the central dynamic of the Christian life, the central dynamic becomes relationship—with God, the world, and each other. The Christian life is about turning toward and entering into a relationship with the one who is already in relationship with us—with the one who gave us life, who has loved us from the beginning, and who loves us whether we know that or not, who journeys with us whether we know that or not. The Christian life thus has at its center becoming conscious of that relationship.[27]

For all these reasons, I believe, as many other progressive Christians do, that the panentheistic understanding of God is closest to what Jesus presented to the world. Pantheism's concept of oneness, or the inseparability of God and all of creation, is dramatically illustrated by our infinitely interconnected world, especially today. Furthermore, the interdependency and interconnectedness of all aspects of life, both physical and spiritual, are being more fully confirmed by modern research in multiple fields of study as human consciousness continues to evolve.

CHAPTER 2

Beyond Exclusivism: Reexamining the Nature of Jesus

Who was Jesus? Was he human, divine, or both? Was Jesus actually God incarnate, or was he the product of an immaculate conception and therefore the only begotten Son of God? Or was he neither? If he was the Son of God, when did he become so—at birth, at the time of his baptism, or after the Resurrection? Was he resurrected bodily or in spiritual form? Will he come again in triumphant glory? Did God send him to save the world from sin through his sacrificial death and the Resurrection? These and other questions became the subject of debate among Christian theologians, especially during the time between the death of Jesus and the crystallization of orthodox doctrines and beliefs in the fourth and fifth centuries.

Since the early centuries of Christian history, the Apostles' Creed, the doctrine of the Trinity, and various theories of atonement have been major factors for most Christians in shaping the popular image of Jesus and his mission. This chapter essentially challenges these commonly accepted images of Jesus as products of an imperial age that no longer exists. What I offer as an alternative is a more historically accurate and relevant portrait of Jesus based on recent biblical and theological research.

JESUS AS DEFINED BY THE APOSTLES' CREED

To provide a more historically accurate and relevant image of Jesus, we will examine the key statements about Jesus in the Apostles' Creed that appear here in italics:

I believe in God the Father Almighty; Maker of Heaven and Earth; and in *Jesus Christ His only (begotten) Son our Lord; who was conceived by the Holy Ghost, born of the Virgin Mary;* suffered under Pontius Pilate, was crucified, dead, and buried; He descended into hell; the third day He rose from the dead; *He ascended into heaven; and sitteth at the right hand of God* the Father Almighty; from thence *He shall come to judge the quick and the dead.* I believe in the Holy Ghost; the holy Catholic Church; the communion of saints; the forgiveness of sins; *the resurrection of the body;* and the life everlasting.[1]

This ancient confession of faith is still recited in many Protestant churches by Anglicans, Congregationalists, Lutherans, United Methodists, Episcopalians, and Presbyterians, while Catholics know the confession as the Nicene Creed.[2] Shorter, less formalized versions of the Apostles' Creed can be traced back as far as the late first century, when it was used first as a baptismal confession. Beyond that, there is no clear evidence that the creed was actually written and distributed by the original twelve apostles. Biblical scholar James Orr maintains that a legend of the apostles' authorship did not appear until the fifth or sixth centuries, thereby calling into question any earlier appearance.[3]

Given the dramatic expansion of knowledge the world has seen since 460 CE, when the creed emerged in its present form, there would seem to be a need for a more credible interpretation of Jesus's nature and mission than the creed currently offers.[4] More specifically, the creed's orthodox images of Jesus seem to promote a sense of separation between human and divine forms of existence and stress the hierarchical nature of Jesus's unique relationship with God. In short, the creed tends to justify a form of Christian exclusivism. With this claim in mind, let's now examine the language within the creed that specifically relates to the nature of Jesus.

> "... His [God's] only (begotten) Son our Lord; who was conceived by the Holy Ghost, born of the Virgin Mary ..."

This description of Jesus early in the creed seems to foremost imply that no other person is truly the son or daughter of God. Although certain prominent second and third century theologians—such as Ignatius of Antioch, Polycarp, Justin, Irenaeus, Tertullian, Hippolytus, and Clement of Alexandria—believed Jesus was both human and divine, they considered him to be divine only as the result of his miraculous conception and subsequent birth.[5] So his divinity was deemed to be unique and not shared by human beings conceived naturally.

However, this unique status for Jesus seems to conflict with the Church's oft-repeated claim that we are all "the children of God." In fact, Jesus never refers to himself as anything but "the Son of Man" in the synoptic Gospels. It is only in John's New Testament Gospel, which was the last to be written, more than sixty years after the death of Jesus, that Jesus claims Son of God status for himself. The net effect of understanding Jesus as the *only* Son of God is to elevate him above humanity, which ultimately serves to separate the two. If Jesus was not one of us, either spiritually or physically, how can we as humans truly follow and emulate him? John 14:12 quotes Jesus as saying, "The one who believes in me will also do the works that I do and, in fact, will do greater works than these." I read this statement as a confirmation that Jesus was not only genuinely human but also divine in the sense that we are all a part of God's divine Creation. In other words, we all share Jesus's divinity. Paul's statement in Acts 17:28, "For in him we live and move and have our being,'" also essentially confirms this idea.

The claim that Jesus is the only Son of God also promotes the notion that no other religion in the world has such a divine connection with God. Furthermore, some early church leaders' assumption that Jesus's divinity equaled God's eventually resulted in making official the Church's doctrine of the Holy Trinity, or triune God, at the Council of Constantinople in 381 CE—more than 350 years after the death of Jesus!

Well before this event, however, the church fathers had made several inconclusive attempts to define who and what Jesus really was. After Bishop Tertullian's initial introduction in the early third century of the general notion of a Trinitarian God consisting of the Father, Son, and Holy Spirit, the whole issue of establishing a commonly understood relationship—particularly between God the Father and the Son—became the basis for a heated debate into the fourth century.[6]

In an attempt to resolve this and other divisive issues once and for all, Emperor Constantine convened a council of the early Church's leading bishops in 325 CE at Nicaea. He was the first Roman emperor to make Christianity the official religion of the empire after becoming a Roman convert to Christianity—or so it seemed. His motivation for conversion actually had more to do with political expediency than a genuine adoption of Christian beliefs and practices. More than anything else, he wanted to maintain unity in the empire, and the serious Christological disputes splitting the Church threatened to cause unrest beyond religion's domain. Arthur Cushman McGiffert, author of *A History of Christian Thought*, puts the issue in context: "Constantine himself of course neither knew nor cared anything about the matter in dispute but he was eager to bring the controversy to a close."[7]

Because he was head of both the Roman state and, by default, the Church, Constantine became actively involved in all the council discussions among the bishops. In the course of these discussions, some of the bishops initially refused to consider elevating Jesus to the status of God because, according to Egyptologist Arthur Weigall in his 1928 book *Paganism in Our Christianity*: "It must not be forgotten that Jesus Christ never mentioned such a phenomenon [the Trinity] and nowhere in the New Testament does the word 'Trinity' appear. The idea was only adopted by the Church three hundred years after the death of our Lord; and the origin of the conception is entirely pagan."[8]

Arius of Alexandria was prominent among those at Nicaea who opposed the concept of a coequal relationship between the Father and the Son. Arius and his followers, who represented about a third of the bishops attending the council, were known as Arians or the "Arian party."[9] Arius's main protagonists in this Christological dispute were Bishop Alexander and his powerfully outspoken assistant, Athanasius, both from Alexandria. Alexander, Athanasius, and their followers made up another powerful minority of those in attendance who were referred to as the "orthodox party."[10] The rest of the bishops remained uncommitted to either Arius or Alexander and tended to waver between the Arian and orthodox viewpoints.

Those who leaned toward the orthodox opinions held by Alexander and Athanasius believed that Jesus (the Son) was co-eternal with the Father and therefore divine in the same way as the Father. Alexander also insisted that Christ had been "begotten" rather than created or "made" by the Father out of nothing, like Adam and his human successors.[11] In her book *A History of God*, Karen Armstrong describes this novel idea as a significant turning point in the development of orthodox Christianity:

> The notion that God had summoned the whole universe from an absolute vacuum was entirely new. It was alien to Greek thought and had not been taught by such theologians as Clement and Origen, who had held to the Platonic scheme of emanation. But by the fourth century, Christians shared the Gnostic view of the world as inherently fragile and imperfect,

separated from God by a vast chasm. God and humanity were no longer akin, as in Greek thought. God had summoned every single being from an abysmal nothingness, and at any moment he could withdraw his sustaining hand. There was no longer a great chain of being emanating eternally from God.[12]

In defense of his position, Alexander chose to use Jesus's statement from the Gospel of John, "I and the Father are one" (John 10:30), as his source of authority.[13] Apparently, he chose to ignore the statement that Jesus makes later in John in which he points to the possibility of an inherent divine connection between the Father and all of humanity: "That they all may be one; as thou, Father, art in me, and I in thee, that they also may be one in us: that the world may believe that thou hast sent me" (John 17:21).

The central problem for Alexander and Athanasius was Arius and his followers' insistence that the Father's divinity was greater than the Son's and that the Son could not be co-eternal with the Father. Even though Arius subscribed to the idea that Jesus was the only begotten Son of God, he insisted that, as a true Son, Jesus must have come after the Father, and so there was a time when the Son did not exist.[14] Alexander and most of the other bishops interpreted this theological position as heretical because, in their minds, Arius not only made the Son unequal to the Father but contradicted the scriptural statement, "I and the Father are one." As far as Alexander and Athanasius were concerned, Christ was either an essential part of the solely divine realm of God or merely a part of the "fragile and imperfect" non-divine world of created beings. There seemed to be no room for compromise.[15]

Nevertheless, Constantine's overpowering presence was instrumental in moving the council to adopt an early version of the Nicene Creed, largely shaped by Athanasius's more emphatic Christological language:

We believe in one God, the Father Almighty,
maker of all things, visible and invisible,
and in one Lord, Jesus Christ,
the Son of God, the only-begotten of the Father,
that is, of the substance (ousia) of the Father,
God from God, Light from Light,
true God from true God,
begotten not made, of one substance (homoousian) with the Father,
through whom all things were made,
those things that are in heaven and those things that are on earth,
who for us men and for our salvation came down and was made man,
suffered, rose again on the third day,
ascended into the heavens and will come to judge the living and the dead.
And we believe in the Holy Spirit.[16]

Actually, many of the bishops had signed the creed against their own inclinations, and differences continued to fester. Despite this final action taken by the Council of Nicaea, the effects of Constantine's heavy-handed involvement were ultimately inconclusive. As Armstrong points out: "The show of agreement pleased Constantine, who had no understanding of the theological issues, but in fact there was no unanimity at Nicaea. After the Council, the bishops went on teaching as they had before, and the Arian crisis continued for another sixty years."[17]

An important example of this continuing crisis was the uncertainty surrounding the concluding phrase in the creed, "And we believe in the Holy Spirit." As it was, the term "Holy Spirit" remained undefined, with no explanation of its true nature and meaning. This oversight eventually caused considerable problems for the early Church in the years after the council. According to Armstrong, "People were confused about the Holy Spirit. Was it simply a synonym for God or was it something more?"[18]

During the second half of the fourth century and a few years before the Council of Constantinople met in 381 CE, three theologians from Asia Minor (central Turkey) offered a more specific definition of the Holy Spirit that went beyond Athanasius's earlier vision. Basil, bishop of Caesarea; Gregory, bishop of Nyssa; and Gregory of Nazianzus all agreed that "God the Father, Jesus the Son, and the Holy Spirit were coequal and together in one being, yet also distinct from one another."[19]

However, it remained for the Council of Constantinople to officially incorporate this concept of the Holy Spirit's being "coequal and together" with God the Father and the Son in the final version of the Nicene Creed. The latter included the following passage: "And we believe in the Holy Spirit, the Lord and Giver of Life, who proceeds from the Father; who with the Father and the Son together is worshiped and glorified; who spoke by the prophets."[20]

This fourth century notion of a Holy Trinity, which came out of the Council of Constantinople—but is nowhere to be found in the Bible—continues to be honored today, not only by Catholics but also by various Protestant denominations. For instance, the Missouri Synod branch of the Lutheran Church officially says, "We teach that the one true God is the Father and the Son and the Holy Ghost, three distinct persons, but of one and the same divine essence, equal in power, equal in eternity, equal in majesty, because each person possesses the one divine essence."[21] Two other doctrinal examples come from the United Methodist Church and the Southern Baptist Convention, respectively: "There is but one living and true God, everlasting, without body or parts, of infinite power, wisdom, and goodness; the maker and preserver of all things, both visible and invisible. And in unity of this Godhead there are three persons, of one substance, power, and eternity—the Father, the Son, and the Holy Ghost"[22]; and "The eternal triune God reveals Himself to us as Father, Son, and Holy Spirit, with distinct personal attributes, but without division of nature, essence, or being."[23]

Even while the claim that Jesus is God's only begotten son, co-eternal with God and the Holy Spirit, is innocently endorsed by countless Christians in Protestant as well as Catholic worship services today, little consideration seems to be given to the religiously exclusivist nature of these statements and how they fail to relate in a credible way to our post-imperial world.

"… conceived by the Holy Ghost, born of the Virgin Mary."

In addition to at least indirectly promoting the concept of a Trinitarian God, the Apostles' Creed goes on to claim that Jesus was the product of a virgin birth. In this way, according to those early orthodox proponents of the creed, Jesus arrived "uncorrupted" by the so-called "original sin" passed down from Adam and Eve. What is also suggested is that humanity alone is not capable of producing such an individual as Jesus. The virgin-birth idea further elevates Jesus above humanity, and separates him from the world. Such an idea conflicts with Jesus's message that the Kingdom of God is found within each of us, as mentioned, for example, in Saying 3b (the sayings of Jesus) from the non-canonical Gospel of Thomas: "When you understand yourselves you will be understood. And you will realize that you are Sons of the living Father. If you do not know yourselves, then you exist in poverty and you are that poverty."[24]

Furthermore, the alleged virgin birth of Jesus is not the only one reported in history. For example, long before Jesus's time, it was commonly believed that Alexander the Great had been virgin-born, as was the case with Plato. Hindus promoted the same idea with respect to Lord Krishna. Buddhists claim the same about Siddhartha Gautama (the Buddha), and Taoists also ascribe a virgin birth for Lao Tse. Even six hundred years after Jesus, Muslims claimed that Muhammad was the product of a virgin birth. Nevertheless, Muslims generally assumed that their virgin-born leaders were extraordinary beings rather than divine.

Likewise, Muhammed, the Buddha, and Lao Tse were never considered to be God incarnate.[25]

It is also worth noting that Paul never mentions a virgin birth in his writings. Such is the case in Mark's Gospel as well, even though the written works of both men were the earliest among those of the New Testament.[26] In addition, it is a fact that in the pre-scientific, early Christian world, a woman was considered to be a "passive receptacle" for the seed of the male. It was not known then that a child receives its genetic makeup from both the mother and father, rather than just the father. Consequently, it was assumed that Jesus's divinity was not compromised by human "impurity," or in other words, "original sin." Obviously, such a belief reveals a lack of knowledge regarding the reality of a mother's genetic participation in each conception. In fact, it was not until 1724 that the female egg cell was known to exist.[27]

The belief in a virgin birth can be recognized as part of the pre-scientific, early Christian worldview, so it makes no sense to continue honoring this orthodox misconception in the modern world. If the virgin-birth idea is abandoned in recognition of Jesus's natural human conception, we are all potentially capable of rising to his example. This would seem to be the whole point, the ultimate "Good News" brought to light by Jesus's life and teachings.

On the other hand, there were others such as the early Jewish converts to Christianity known as the Ebionites who insisted, at least as far back as the year 120 CE, that Jesus was fully human by virtue of having been conceived and born "normally." From their point of view, Jesus was an ordinary man who grew to become so perfectly righteous that God chose him to be his son at his baptism.[28] Likewise, some Roman converts to Christianity who, unlike the Ebionites, had no Jewish heritage agreed that Jesus was completely human and became the "adopted" Son of God only at his baptism. These gentile converts were followers of a late second-century Christian known as Theodotus the Cobbler, who went so far as to claim that Jesus's adoption by God did not mean Jesus had become divine.[29]

This "adoptionist" explanation of Jesus's divinity also seems to be indicated in the Gospel of Mark, the earliest of the four canonical Gospels. Here there is no mention of a miraculous birth or Jesus's pre-existence, since Mark's story only begins with Jesus's baptism.[30] As Mark tells us, God proclaims Jesus to be his son in the midst of the baptism: "And just as he was coming up out of the water, he saw the heavens torn apart and the Spirit descending like a dove on him. And a voice came from heaven, 'You are my Son, the Beloved; with you I am well pleased'" (Mark 1:10-11).

The writers of Matthew and Luke tell a very similar story, but it is difficult to know what if any parts of the story in the synoptic Gospels were simply literary elaborations or whether these words from on high were actually spoken. God's statement "You are my Son, the Beloved; with you I am well pleased," could be interpreted as a divine claim of Jesus's adoption or the acknowledgment that we are all the beloved sons and daughters of God, Jesus notwithstanding.

What's more important is that this baptismal event, however it occurred, must have been profoundly transformational for Jesus. It is quite possible that he had an otherworldly, life-changing encounter with the Spirit similar to a near-death experience. The fact remains that Jesus was not only an extraordinary teacher but also a spirit-filled visionary and healer, particularly after this event.[31]

Furthermore, other "messengers of God" have also experienced powerful spiritual encounters of this kind. Biblical examples would include God's "calling" of Moses from the burning bush and, of course, Paul's encounter on the road to Damascus. Then, too, Buddha's enlightenment experience under the Bo tree at the age of thirty seems remarkably similar to Jesus's baptismal encounter with the Holy Spirit at about the same age.[32]

In fact, there are many remarkable parallels between the lives of Jesus and Buddha. Both emphasized the need to be compassionate and to love one's neighbor as one's self. Buddha was actually known as the "compassionate one." He taught about following "the path," which involved the four noble truths of Buddhism, while Jesus taught about "the way," which involved giving of one's self in service to others. Love was at the heart of both forms of wisdom. Even though Buddha was not known as a social prophet and activist for social justice as was Jesus, they were both enormously transformational figures in the world who inspired reformist religious movements known to be nonviolent and more inclusive.[33] If Jesus was worthy of being adopted by God, why would the same not have been true of the Buddha? Christian exclusivism would seem to be the only explanation.

Other adoptionist theories existed as well during the early proto-orthodox period of Christianity. For instance, some Christian Gnostics argued that at Jesus's baptism, a divine being known as "Christ" entered into him, enabling Jesus to accomplish his ministry. Then, according to this particular Christology, the divine Christ left Jesus shortly before his Crucifixion to return to the divine realm, leaving the human Jesus to suffer his own fate.[34]

There were also those such as Paul who seemed to imply that Jesus became the Son of God as late as his resurrection. For example, he is quoted as saying in Acts 13, "What God promised to the [Jewish] fathers he has fulfilled to us their children, by raising Jesus from the dead—as it is written in the second Psalm, 'You are my Son, today I have begotten you.'" On the other hand, Paul's alleged words seem inconsistent with the main message throughout Luke and Acts, which is that Jesus became the Son of God by virtue of his immaculate birth. Recent biblical research suggests that Acts 13 actually predated Paul and appears in Acts only as the result of later editing.[35]

Still other Christians, such as the Gnostic bishop Marcion, insisted that Jesus was not human at all. To them, Jesus was God himself and merely appeared to be human. Given this line of reasoning, Jesus could not have experienced the limitations and finality of human life.[36] However, Irenaeus, Tertullian, and other orthodox bishops raised strong objections to this way of understanding Jesus, since it required an act of deception on the part of God.

By the time the Council of Nicea met at the request of the newly converted Roman Emperor Constantine in 325 CE, the orthodox Christian interpretation of Jesus as the only divine *begotten* Son of God had prevailed and would remain the dominant way of interpreting Jesus for at least the next fifteen hundred years. All other Christological alternatives were branded as heretical and largely suppressed.

"He ascended into Heaven and sitteth on the right hand of God, the Father Almighty."

The Creed's third statement about Jesus continues to feature hierarchical images of a theology tied closely to a pre-scientific, imperial age.

In the first place, the idea that Heaven is located "above" is no longer relevant in our modern age of space exploration. For astronauts traveling in outer space, perceptions of what is "above" or "below" are not fixed and consistent as they are from an earthly perspective. Second, the phrase "sitteth on the right hand of God, the Father Almighty" assumes that God has human form, is male, and sits on a royal throne above the Earth. All three images are typical of a theistic God that is now yielding to a more modern and relevant panentheistic understanding.

But even more important, because Jesus is assigned to an exclusive position of divine authority at the "right hand of God," he is dramatically separated from humankind and the world. The kind of judgment implied and expected from a monarch who sits on a heavenly throne is enough to raise fears in the minds of many Christians even today.

This should come as no surprise, since many such images depended on fear for motivation—that is, fear of offending God by failing to observe and adhere to prescribed orthodox doctrines and beliefs. Ironically, these hierarchal concepts of Jesus and God the Father contradict other, more personal and intimate images found in the Scriptures and, instead, seem more closely related to the Roman imperial regime associated with that period in history.

This portion of the creed reflects the fact that by the fourth century, the Church was engaged in a codependent relationship with the imperial Roman social order rather than serving as Rome's challenger as it had during the initial stage of Christian history. The scriptural picture of Jesus as the humble but courageous and subversive advocate for the poor, outcasts, and the powerless in the face of Roman oppression now appeared to have changed in support of the status quo by virtue of the creed. In addition, the exclusive stature of Jesus is further emphasized by the next statement in the creed.

"He shall come to judge the quick and the dead."

Here the creed's writers seem to convey the idea that Jesus will return to Earth at some point in the future (sooner rather than later, according to many early Christians). "He shall come to judge" refers in particular to an orthodox Christian interpretation of Jesus as primarily an apocalyptic or millenarian prophet. This view of Jesus assumes his message was primarily about an impending cataclysmic destruction of the Earth by God in preparation for a "new world." An embellished version of this prophetic vision known as dispensationalism would later become a major feature of modern Protestant fundamentalism.

When one considers the various apocalyptic warnings Jesus gave in the synoptic Gospels, it is easy to understand why many Christians have assumed Jesus was an apocalyptic prophet. In fact, Paul predicted Jesus's return in the near future, as did the author of Revelation.[37] The following verses from the Gospel of Mark even go so far as to describe the event in vivid detail:

> But in those days, after the tribulation, the sun will be darkened, and the moon will not give its light, and the stars will be falling from heaven, and the powers in the heavens will be shaken. And then they will see the Son of Man coming in the clouds, with great power and glory. And then he will send out the angels, and gather his elect from the four winds, from the ends of the earth to the ends of heaven (Mark 13:24-27).

However, the problem remains that the Second Coming of Jesus and all the events associated with it did not occur then or since. This means either Jesus was wrong or the inclination to define him primarily as an apocalyptic prophet is incorrect. The latter conclusion has gained considerable support from biblical scholars, particularly since the 1980s.[38]

For instance, Marcus Borg points out that while Jesus talks about judgment from God at various places in the synoptic Gospels, he does so as a social prophet seeking justice on behalf of the poor and oppressed *now* rather than urging patience for a reward in heaven *later*.[39] Likewise, biblical scholar John Dominic Crossan explains that Jesus actually spoke of a "durative," or prolonged, apocalypse rather than an "instantive," destructive apocalypse. In other words, Jesus preached about the destruction of the world not as a way of eliminating human injustice but as a way of transforming the world into a heaven on earth through nonviolent revolutionary change over time.[40]

Borg and Crossan agree that Jesus is best defined as a teacher of wisdom, based on his use of proverbs, aphorisms, parables, and beatitudes, but that the wisdom Jesus taught was not just about ethics or moral behavior. Instead, they point out, Jesus's wisdom was subversive rather than passive in the sense that it challenged the conventional wisdom of his day.[41] As we have seen, this nonviolent way of confronting social injustice and oppression served as the basis for the self-sacrificing actions of such modern-day spiritual leaders as Gandhi and Martin Luther King Jr.

Furthermore, other biblical studies conducted since the 1950s have revealed that the numerous future-oriented apocalyptic-sounding "Son of Man" sayings found in the synoptic Gospels actually came out of a post-canonical Christian tradition and are contradictory to Jesus's other claims that God's reign was already present,[42] as we find, for instance, in Luke 17:20-21: "Being asked by the Pharisees when the kingdom of God was coming, he answered them, 'The kingdom of God is not coming with signs to be observed; nor will they say, Lo, here it is! Or There! For behold, the kingdom of God is in the midst of you."

These same studies, mostly by twentieth century German scholar Philipp Vielhauer, suggest that some Christians in the years after the death of Jesus began to interpret the parables as a form of Jewish apocalyptic theology that predated Jesus.[43] This view is now shared by Stephen Patterson, professor of the New Testament at Eden Theological Seminary, in St. Louis. "The allegorization of the parables was the church's way of limiting this multiplicity of meaning by fixing it on a single imagined, unfolding apocalyptic scenario," he says.[44] "A good many of the parables, after all, begin in just this way: the reign of God is like ... When we remove from the parables the late, allegorical, apocalyptically charged editorial work of the evangelists, there is little in the tradition that would cause one to think that Jesus associated the reign of God with an apocalyptic event at all."[45]

Therefore, when it comes to the question of whether Jesus was an apocalyptic prophet as suggested in the Apostles' Creed, biblical scholars such as Patterson, Borg, and Crossan recognize that this description of Jesus's mission is inaccurate and insufficient. Rather than preach that God would intervene in the world on the side of justice in the midst of some future cataclysmic event, Jesus taught that God was already present. The evidence, as Jesus saw it, could be seen not only in the example of his own life but also in the lives of others who sought to overcome evil in the world through nonviolent resistance, compassion, and forgiveness.

However, in many of the more conservative Protestant churches today, the liturgy often refers to the Second Coming as an accepted fact. Along with this assumption is the conclusion that on that glorious day, all things will be "made right" and justice will be served. One must ask, what happens in the meantime? Must the world wait for ultimate justice, social or otherwise, until this uncertain point in time? This belief in an "end time" as a sudden solution to the problem of evil in the world amounts to a moral cop-out and a complete misunderstanding of Jesus's life and true intentions. Unfortunately, this portion of the creed has inspired an abdication of personal moral responsibility for the "least of these" among too many self-professed Christians when it comes to the issues of race, poverty, the economy, health care, the environment, and national self-interest.

Another popular assumption is that the living, risen Christ shall pass final judgment (either at some future date on Earth or in heaven) on each of us. Here again, the word *judgment* implies some sort of acceptance or rejection based on our past deeds. Despite all the other religions of the world and their revered leaders, Jesus is claimed to be the only one chosen by God to bring such final judgment. This is an arrogant religious statement that attempts to elevate Christianity above all other religions. Such exclusivist claims about the supposed supremacy of this or that religion continue to cause unnecessary division and bloodshed throughout the world. No evidence exists within the Bible or anywhere else that suggests God favors Christianity above all other religions. If Jesus was a master spiritual teacher sent by God, as many faithful Christians believe he was, then so were Buddha, Mohammed, Lao Tse, and others. There are many worthy religious paths to God besides Christianity.

In addition to the idea in the creedal statement now being examined—that Jesus shall come again to judge—is the proposition that his judgment will be passed on "the quick and the dead." This assumption seems to reflect the ancient, outdated belief that the dead remain dead until the Second Coming of Jesus. (The issue of the Second Coming will be examined at greater length in Chapter 3). However, the overwhelming evidence impressed on those throughout the ages who have seen visions and heard voices from departed loved ones and friends, along with the indisputable facts surrounding the millions of near-death experiences described within and without the modern worldwide medical community, suggests that life never ends but simply changes in substance and dimension.

"... the resurrection of the body ..."

Nevertheless, near the end of the Apostles' Creed, reference is made to a physical or bodily resurrection.

The resurrection of Jesus was the basis for considerable controversy among early Christians beginning soon after Jesus's death and continuing during the second, third, and fourth centuries, when the orthodox Christian creeds and doctrines were emerging. Considerations of the form and meaning of the Resurrection were major causes for the split between orthodox Christian theologians such as Tertullian and Irenaeus and Gnostic Christians such as Valentinus and Origen.

While both sides agreed that Jesus did appear to the apostles and others after his Crucifixion, early Christian interpretations differed considerably. Some insisted that Jesus's resurrection was spiritual in nature and that those who saw Jesus after his resurrection did not see him in physical form, whereas the orthodox theologian Tertullian emphatically declared, "Anyone who denies the resurrection of the flesh is a heretic, not a Christian."[46]

In this case, Tertullian was not suggesting that the soul separates from the body at death. Instead, he saw them as one and the same; immortality could occur only with a physical or bodily resurrection. From his point of view, shared by Irenaeus, every believing Christian could look forward to the future resurrection of his or her body because Jesus was resurrected. As Tertullian said, "It must be believed, because it is absurd!" Both of these theologians and their orthodox followers looked to the Gospels for their support. For instance, Jesus is described as being physically touched and having meals with the disciples in the Gospels of John and Luke as well as in the book of Acts (Luke 24:13–43, John 20:19–23, and Acts 1:3–5).

But those who objected to Tertullian's materialistic view also found support in the Gospels via the account of the Resurrection in John 20:17. Here, Mary recognizes the risen Jesus for the first time, and he says, "Do not hold on to me, because I have not yet ascended to the Father." This verse from John had special significance to Tertullian's critics insofar as it suggested that Jesus's resurrection involved some sort of powerful spiritual transformation beyond the mere resuscitation of a lifeless body. Likewise, the Gospel accounts of Jesus's sudden appearances and disappearances witnessed by the disciples in the Upper Room and at other locations such as on the road to Emmaus (as described in Mark 16:9-20, Matthew 28:9-10, Luke 24:13-43, and John 20:19-29 and 29:1-14) seemed to the Gnostics spiritual rather than physical in nature. Also referenced was the apparent failure of the disciples on the road to Emmaus to recognize Jesus immediately. The Gnostics could also cite Paul's supernatural encounter with Jesus on the road to Damascus in the form of a blinding light. In fact, Paul himself essentially described this encounter with the risen Christ as a spiritual, life-changing experience for him despite the lack of a physical Jesus at the scene.

The source of the controversies surrounding the nature and meaning of the Resurrection can be traced in large part to the differences between the early Greek and Jewish beliefs regarding eternal life. The Jewish culture had no concept of a soul distinct from the human body that could survive after death. Consequently, the Hebrew culture in the time of Jesus believed that eternal life could come only if the physical bodies of the dead and buried were to be restored to life at some future time through a miraculous act of God. Until then, it was believed that the soulless body remained earthbound, "at rest" in a grave or tomb. While the Jews did acknowledge the existence of a heaven, they thought of it only as a place where God and the angels (a nonhuman species) lived.[47]

By contrast, the Greek belief in immortal souls had existed for a very long time before the life of Jesus. Even though the Greeks believed in the existence of immortal souls with eternal spiritual bodies, separate from impermanent physical bodies, the concept of an eternal heavenly home as life's ultimate destination and reward actually originated with Persian Zoroastrianism. Zoroastrians referred to this heavenly "home" as the "realm of the God of Light."[48] As Christianity began to evolve after the death of Jesus, its early theologians were not immune to Greek philosophical concepts and Zoroastrianism, particularly as the concepts applied to immortal souls being released from physical bodies at death in order to ascend to an eternal heavenly existence.[49]

But since the Jewish community in these early centuries had no concept of an immortal soul or eternal life free and independent of a physical body, one can understand why many early Jewish converts to Christianity would have considered Jesus's resurrection to have been a resurrection of the *body*. As a result of the convergence of these contrasting Greek and Jewish views of death and resurrection within early Christian history, many Christians are left with a fundamental contradiction even today. As they recite the Apostles' Creed, they affirm the resurrection of the physical body as the only means of achieving eternal life at some unspecified time in the future.

At the same time, many of these same Christians will state their firm conviction that when people die, they go to heaven immediately, thereby affirming the existence of an immortal soul independent of the physical body. In doing so, modern Christians would seem to be engaging in doublethink or doubletalk when it comes to the Apostles' Creed and the subject of eternal life. The problem is that the Greek concept of immediate immortality and the Hebrew belief in some future restoration of the living physical body are irreconcilable.

Several illustrations from the New Testament, modern discoveries in quantum physics, the preponderance of near-death experiences now documented in modern medical literature, and the long-standing belief in the existence of eternal souls typical of the Hindu, Buddhist, and Tao religions all point to the reality of some sort of *spiritual transformation* in immediate terms, not only of Jesus but for every human life. Quite likely, Jesus's various post-resurrection appearances and disappearances were the result of his ability to manipulate energy and matter—a phenomenon the modern world is only beginning to fathom.

In his book *Jesus of Nazareth Holy Week: From the Entrance into Jerusalem to the Resurrection*, Pope Benedict XVII even says Jesus's resurrection was not simply a resuscitation of a corpse but a "new dimension of reality that is revealed."[50] Pope Benedict continues, "We are told that there is a further dimension, beyond what was previously known. Does that contradict science? Can there really only ever be what there has always been? Can there not be something unexpected, something unimaginable, something new?"[51]

Rather than being some sort of violation of the natural laws of nature, the Resurrection points to another dimension beyond conventional physical laws that, until recently, we did not know existed. Modern science, particularly as it relates to the field of quantum physics, is now beginning to reveal a world of spiritual interconnections and possibilities never before considered possible, including the conscious manipulation of matter and energy. With this in mind, perhaps it is possible that Jesus's various post-resurrection appearances and disappearances could have been the result of his spiritually advanced ability to affect nature directly. So a bodily resurrection in the sense of a mere resuscitation is not only improbable but also unnecessary. The spiritual dimensions and implications of Jesus's resurrection would seem to provide further proof of the existence of a soul that survives bodily death and continues to evolve through subsequent incarnations.

JESUS'S DEATH AS THE MEANS OF ATONEMENT FOR THE SINS OF HUMANITY

In addition to the popular images of Jesus we have already seen in the Apostles' Creed and in the orthodox concept of a Trinitarian God, there is the image of Jesus as "rescuer." In his role as rescuer, according to those church fathers who subscribed to the doctrine of atonement, Jesus is the one God sent to save humanity from its fallen, hopelessly sinful state and the divine punishment it deserved in the only way possible: through Jesus's sacrificial death. This idea of the need for God to seek some form of atonement for the collective sins of humanity was first suggested by Paul: "But God proves his love for us in that while we still were sinners Christ died for us. Much more surely, then, now that we have been justified by his blood, will we be saved through him from the wrath of God" (Romans 5:8,9).

It is also true that the Pauline idea of atonement for the collective sins of humanity was strengthened and given more weight in the fourth century by Augustine. Augustine's vision of atonement was of a cosmic struggle between good and evil. The basic idea that Jesus was the necessary means to atonement was then promoted in a variety of forms, especially during the medieval period of Christian history as critically examined by J. Denny Weaver in his recent book *The Nonviolent Atonement*. Even today, the belief enjoys support among the more conservative churches in America.

In the wake of Augustine's theology during the early centuries of Christian history, Jesus's death and resurrection were widely seen as a victory of good over the forces of evil led by Satan. This theory of atonement, known more recently as Christus Victor based on Gustav Aulen's 1930 book *Christus Victor: An Historical Study of the Three Main Types of the Idea of Atonement*, dominated Christendom from the fourth through the tenth centuries.[52] As Aulen points out, there were actually three versions of Christus Victor until the eleventh century. According to the first version, Satan supposedly defeated God when God's only son, Jesus, was killed. However, the resurrected Jesus turned defeat into victory, and humanity was saved from the power of sin (Satan), since God's control of the universe was then assured.

The second version of Christus Victor envisioned Christ's death as a ransom paid to Satan for freeing humanity from his power and control. A third version, which made the rounds in the sixth century, asserted that Satan was defeated through an act of deception on God's part. In other words, Satan supposedly failed to recognize that God was posing as Jesus and made this discovery only after Jesus's resurrection.[53] All three versions of Christus Victor assumed, of course, that a being known as Satan existed and had unique powers of evil that had to be acknowledged by God.

However, by the beginning of the eleventh century, the various forms of the Christus Victor theory of atonement had lost favor, since they required the faithful to believe that God would either pay a ransom to the Devil or engage in deception.[54] Likewise, there was little evidence of a victory of God's reign in the world, since it was perfectly obvious that sinful behavior continued to exist.

Another model of atonement emerged in the eleventh century, one that would later become a particularly important source of influence for Protestant reformer John Calvin in the sixteenth century. Its originator, Anselm of Canterbury (1033–1109),[55] identified it as "Cur Deus Homo." In contrast with Christus Victor, the idea behind Anselm's satisfaction atonement was that humanity, in its fallen state, had sinned against God, and some form of restitution was necessary to restore God's honor. Consequently, since God so loved the world, he sent his only son, Jesus, to "satisfy" God's offended honor by paying for the sins of humanity with his death.

Simply put, a debt payment was required, not only to restore God's honor but also to restore justice and peace in the universe. According to this idea, Jesus was the payment as required by God—a divine plan to save humanity and achieve reconciliation.[56] Since the Medieval practice of making payments to feudal lords for protection and bearing penalties for offenses against them was common in the eleventh century, the satisfaction-atonement theory can be seen as a reflection of this Medieval practice.[57] In any case, Anselmian theologians assigned the theory divine status.

In the sixteenth century, Martin Luther and John Calvin tended to place satisfaction atonement in a more legalistic and penal context. In their view, Jesus's death was a satisfaction of divine law and God was seen as the ultimate "trial judge." Since Jesus stood in the place of the condemned defendant (humanity), it meant that humanity could be "pardoned" without compromising the divine law. For this reason, the satisfaction-atonement model also came to be known as the "substitutionary theory" of atonement.[58] The common thread in these atonement theologies is the assumption that God ordained and orchestrated Jesus's death to achieve some sort of reconciliation between God and humanity. But progressive-minded Christians today are prone to asking, "What kind of God would orchestrate the murder of his own son as a means of achieving this reconciliation?"

Weaver basically argues that these early explanations of atonement are, for the most part, inconsistent with the stories of Jesus's ministry and death found in the New Testament Gospels. He offers his own theory of atonement, which he calls "narrative Christus Victor," as a more credible, nonviolent alternative to the earlier theologies. This idea of atonement does not interpret Jesus's death as a divinely arranged plan to provide some sort of ransom to satisfy the supposedly offended honor of God or to satisfy a requirement of divine law. Weaver also views sin not as disobedience or offense against God so much as self-imposed separation from God, whether from an individual or collective standpoint.

In the context of Jesus's time, sin was also viewed as bondage to the evils of imperial Roman rule, and in our own time as bondage to the various social structures that serve to dominate and oppress.[59] Conversely, Weaver sees salvation as freedom from bondage to the evil forces that separate and divide, and as individual or collective transformation (repentance) by the nonviolent spiritual presence of God.

Finally, Weaver maintains that God sent Jesus not to die a cruel death but to "witness to the rule of God."[60] Jesus's way was not to passively submit to the forces of evil as characterized by the earlier atonement models but to freely choose to resist them. He did so by means of nonviolent acts that those in positions of political and religious power saw as subversive and threatening to the established social system. In Weaver's own words:

> There is no need to play a sleight-of-hand language game concerning whether Jesus willed himself to die or whether God willed the death of Jesus. In either case, the answer is profoundly "No." Rather, in narrative Christus Victor the Son is carrying out the Father's will by making the reign of God visible in the world—and that mission is so threatening to the world that sinful human beings and the accumulation of evil

they represent conspire to kill Jesus. Jesus came not to die, but to live, to witness to the reign of God in human history.[61]

In the final analysis, Jesus was one of the most—if not *the* most—evolutionary individuals in history, one who, along with such people as the Buddha, Moses, and Mohammed, had directly experienced God. Besides being a spirit-filled healer and charismatic, Jesus was a social prophet within the tradition of the greatest prophets of the Old Testament. As such, he challenged the unjust social systems of his time and *every* time. He was also a teacher of unconventional wisdom based on his unique understanding of God's will and, as a devout Jew, strove to revitalize Judaism.[62] He was not the founder of a new religion known as Christianity; in fact, the words *Christian* and *Christianity* appear nowhere in the New Testament. Furthermore, James D. Tabor, chair of the department of religious studies at the University of North Carolina at Charlotte, makes the case that the Christian religion as something distinct from Judaism owes its beginnings to Paul rather than Jesus:

> The fundamental doctrinal tenets of Christianity, namely that Christ is God "born in the flesh," that his sacrificial death atones for the sins of humankind, and that his resurrection from the dead guarantees eternal life to all who believe, can be traced back to Paul, not Jesus. Indeed, the spiritual union with Christ through baptism, as well as the "communion" with his body and blood through the sacred meal of bread and wine, also traces back to Paul. This is the Christianity familiar to us, the Christianity of the creeds and confessions that separated it from Judaism and put it on the road to becoming a new religion.[63]

Be that as it may, I am convinced that Jesus was a highly evolved soul who had experienced many previous incarnations on Earth (and/or other locations in the universe) and was thereby extraordinarily enlightened. Having become so enlightened, he was passionately committed to awakening the world and helping to fulfill God's will.

While Christians do not widely endorse the concept of the reincarnation of souls today, that was not always so. During Jesus's lifetime, a belief in reincarnation was not uncommon, and this was apparently true of Jesus as well. We will return to this possibility again when we examine the subject of reincarnation in greater depth in Chapter 7. For now, it's enough to say that the issue of reincarnation as it applies to Jesus is legitimate and should no longer be avoided and rejected as it has been by the politics of orthodox Christianity since the fourth century CE.

If Jesus embodied the essential nature of God enough for us to see God through him, he also provided a Christ-like image of humanity that is attainable for every human being, subject to personal commitment and the time required for spiritual growth throughout each of our evolutionary journeys. That is the good news he brought to the world.

CHAPTER 3

Beyond Literalism: The Bible and the Roots of Fundamentalism

The Bible is not a book so much as a collection of books, or—to be more exact—two collections. Both collections contain texts written by different authors at different times. The first of the two collections is essentially the Hebrew Bible, whose books are generally understood by scholars to have been written between 950 and 150 BCE.[1] The books included in the second collection, which Christians know as the New Testament and Jews as the Christian Bible, were written approximately between 50 and 150 CE.

Overall, then, the Bible can be seen as a library containing a rich variety of works written mostly by Jewish men from decidedly patriarchal societies, with varying viewpoints and audiences, about the same subject: God. On the other hand, there are many conservative Christians who tend to believe that the Scriptures are the words of God communicated either directly or indirectly. This assumption is a major problem for many Christians today.

*

THE BIBLE AS THE WORD OF GOD

In many Protestant churches, the phrase "This is the Word of God" is often spoken from the pulpit after the reading of selected passages from the Bible. This has been a common practice in churches over the many centuries of Christian history—even while Christians, especially today, have been divided on what "the Word of God" really means. Marcus Borg maintains that this phrase—and much of the Bible—should be understood metaphorically rather than literally.[2] Seen in this way, *Word* refers to the revelation of God or a lens through which God can be seen and understood. Therefore, the Bible is assumed to be *about* God rather than *from* God.

Nevertheless, in the wake of the relatively recent fundamentalist and conservative evangelical movements of the late nineteenth and early twentieth centuries in America, referring to the Bible as "the Word of God" has contributed to a more literal understanding of the Bible on the part of many if not most Christians today. In my view, continuing to refer to the Bible as "the Word of God" has, at the very least, led to more confusion and conflict among Christians than clarity and consensus.

THE BIBLE AS A HUMAN PRODUCT SUBJECT TO HISTORICAL CRITICISM

Continually referring to the Bible as "the Word of God" seems counter-productive if the intention is to show that the Bible is, as Borg explains, "a human response to God" rather than a divine product.[3] Seeing the Bible as a human product rather than a divine one recognizes that the Scriptures address the relationship between God and humanity from a *human perspective*, which is to say the Scriptures tell us how the Biblical writers' beliefs about God, Jesus, and themselves were shaped by the times, places, and pre-scientific cultures in which they lived. However, this historically critical view of the Bible does not minimize the fact that the Scriptures often reveal universal truths about the human-divine connection that will always be relevant despite global evolutionary changes.

An important example of modern historical criticism is the ongoing search for the historical Jesus that actually began with the 1778 publication of the treatise *The Aims of Jesus and His Disciples*, by German theologian Hermann Samuel Reimarus. The treatise later came to the attention of Albert Schweitzer, who was also driven by the desire to separate myth from reality regarding Jesus. Schweitzer's 1901 book, *The Quest for the Historical Jesus*, led the way toward more comprehensive studies such as the Jesus Seminar, formed in 1985 by such scholars and theologians as Robert Funk, John Dominic Crossan, and Marcus Borg.[4]

The various books and articles produced by the Jesus Seminar scholars over the past three decades have greatly expanded our knowledge of Jesus and, for many modern Christians, made Jesus even more real and understandable than before.

This is not to say, however, that the Bible must be reduced to a collection of verifiable facts. Those associated with the Jesus Seminar and others who choose to reexamine the New Testament in an open and objective way are quick to recognize the importance of the metaphors and metaphorical narratives found throughout the Old Testament as well as the New. This is why Borg, in particular, favors what he calls a "historical-metaphorical" approach to the Bible.[5]

THE BIBLE SEEN METAPHORICALLY

The historical-metaphorical approach is a form of historical criticism that focuses on the broader meanings that can be discerned from the actual historical events depicted in the Bible. This approach essentially enables one to see and understand Jesus and the various biblical narratives in both the Old and New Testaments in multiple ways. One of the best examples comes from the Old Testament book of Exodus. Aside from the fact that the story is about an actual event in which the Jewish people escaped their long years of bondage in Egypt, the narrative has much more to tell us about the universal human conditions of bondage to various forms of oppression, addiction, and other unfortunate circumstances (slavery in Egypt), followed by the struggle to be free from such bondage (the Passover and the escape through the Red Sea), the resulting dislocation and insecurity (despair and doubt in the Sinai), and eventual freedom or transformation (arrival at the Promised Land).[6]

This metaphorical approach to the story of Exodus makes the event especially relevant and timeless, not only for Jews but for all people, everywhere. Other well-known Old Testament metaphorical narratives include the books of Job and Jonah. The fictional character of Job represents those innocent people among us who sometimes suffer while evil seemingly goes unpunished. In the story of Jonah and the Whale, the point is not that Jonah actually survived after being swallowed by the whale but that Jonah, as well as every human being, can never escape the presence of God.

Likewise, the stories about the birth of Jesus, as described in the Gospels of Matthew and Luke, are largely metaphorical. In addition to the fact that the Gospels of Mark and John make no mention of the birth of Jesus at all, the Nativity stories found in Matthew and Luke are quite inconsistent in terms of where Jesus was born (Nazareth, according to Matthew; Bethlehem, according to Luke) as well as what happened in conjunction with his birth (Matthew mentions "wise men" guided by a star but says nothing about a "heavenly host," shepherds, or an inn; the opposite is true for Luke). What seems more likely is that Matthew and Luke, along with directing their narrative to different audiences (a mainly Jewish audience for Matthew and a gentile audience for Luke), crafted the stories in dramatically creative ways meant to convey the overarching idea that Jesus's arrival on Earth was a turning point in history and a benevolent, loving act of God.[7]

The parables of Jesus are also decidedly metaphorical. He often used common objects and fictional characters as a means of pointing to certain universal truths beyond the objects and characters themselves. For instance, in Matthew 4:30-32, Jesus asks: "With what can we compare the kingdom of God, or what parable will we use for it? It is like a mustard seed, which, when sown upon the ground, is the smallest of all the seeds on earth; yet when it is sown it grows up and becomes the greatest of all shrubs, and puts forth large branches, so that the birds of the air can make nests in its shade."

To his listeners, the mustard plant would have been recognized as a plant that grew and spread outward, taking over much of the land—a dramatic example of the kingdom of God spreading far and wide, overcoming all earthly powers.

Jesus also used the parable of the prodigal son to illustrate the power of God's unconditional love and forgiveness even for those of us, like the prodigal son, who consider ourselves undeserving of such love and forgiveness:

Father, I have sinned against heaven and before you; I am no longer worthy to be called your son (Luke 15:18-19).

But while he was still far off, his father saw him and was filled with compassion; he ran and put his arms around him and kissed him (Luke 15:20).

The father said to his slaves, ... let us eat and celebrate; for this son of mine was dead and is alive again; he was lost and is found again (Luke 15: 22).

At the same time, Jesus uses this parable to expose the self-righteousness of the scribes and Pharisees in the audience. They are represented by the older son in the story, who considered himself to be more deserving of his father's favor than his brother: "For all these years I have been working like a slave for you, and I have never disobeyed your command; yet you have never given me even a young goat so that I might celebrate with my friends" (Luke 15:29). In other words, Jesus exposes the Pharisees' self-motivated obedience to the Jewish purity laws while ignoring the needs of others deemed to be less righteous and deserving of God's favor.

But among other metaphorical examples in the New Testament, the book of Revelation has been perhaps the greatest source of controversy among Christians in recent times. Many conservative Christians choose to interpret Revelation literally as a true and accurate picture of the future and accept the author's image of a violently punitive Jesus. (More will be said about this as it relates to modern fundamentalism later in this chapter.) In doing so, they overlook author John of Patmos's real purpose and the text's actual historical context, the Roman oppression of the Jews during the late first century.[8]

From a historical-metaphorical perspective, John's highly symbolic narrative can be recognized as his coded message of hope directed to the time's suffering Jewish people to assure them that God's power of love would ultimately overcome the power of their Roman oppressors. One can draw the broader metaphorical conclusion that the power of God's love inevitably overcomes imperial powers everywhere on Earth.

THE ENLIGHTENMENT AND BIBLICAL HISTORICAL CRITICISM

The inclination to see the Bible as a collection of human ideas and observations about the nature of God, the human condition, and the human-divine connection from historical and cultural perspectives is essentially an outgrowth of the Age of Enlightenment, which spanned the seventeenth and eighteenth centuries. This particular era in the evolution of human consciousness saw the emergence of revolutionary ideas in science, philosophy, politics, and religion.

Perhaps the most important idea behind all the changes that occurred in each of these areas of human thought can be found in Rene Descartes's rationalist system of philosophy.[9] Descartes was convinced that all established propositions that can be doubted *should* be doubted. In other words, he believed it was best to begin with the assumption that any conventional theory is false until it is proven otherwise through a process of severe skeptical questioning.

Largely as a result of this philosophical premise of Descartes's, the Enlightenment came to be shaped by a fundamental inclination toward skepticism and doubt rather than the earlier tendency to rely on sense experience as well as established institutions of authority and conventional ideas in general. Independent thinking was encouraged even when the Enlightenment challenged the dictates of religious authority, as reflected in Immanuel Kant's statement that "immaturity is the inability to use one's own understanding without the guidance of another."[10]

Given this philosophical undercurrent, the modern world emerged in the West at the expense of older hierarchical institutions and social systems. The best-known examples are the democratic revolutions against the monarchies of England and France that occurred in the latter half of the eighteenth century. But Enlightenment skepticism and individualism seriously challenged the authority of organized religion as well. In France, Voltaire spoke out against the Catholic Church as an institution that promoted paternalism, superstition, fanaticism, and supernaturalism.[11] The sixteenth century Protestant Reformation had already challenged the authority of the Catholic Church, and Protestantism continued to play an important role in the Enlightenment by promoting the principle of self-determination. Pierre Bayle, a French Protestant and one of the founding figures of the Enlightenment, lived in Holland during the seventeenth century in order to avoid censorship and imprisonment in his own country for openly challenging religious, metaphysical, and scientific dogmas. Like Descartes, he defended the individual's right to seek knowledge beyond the prescribed limits of established religious doctrines and beliefs.[12]

This persistent desire to search for truth and meaning beyond conventional beliefs also led Enlightenment thinkers such as Bayle and Descartes to challenge the authority of literally interpreted Biblical Scriptures. Ironically, the Enlightenment-era challenge to scriptural literalism marked at least a partial shift away from the Reformation's original goals, which had been to honor the Scriptures as the ultimate source of spiritual authority rather than the judgments of priests and bishops. In the light of emerging Newtonian physics, however, biblical literalism was recognized as being unsustainable and inconsistent with modernity.[13]

Largely as a result of the Enlightenment's dismissiveness regarding the various biblical miracles and myths on the grounds that they did not conform to the new materialistic Newtonian understanding of reality, a historical-critical method of interpreting the Bible known as Higher Criticism emerged at the early nineteenth century German Academy.[14] Higher Criticism made its way to America in 1876 when Charles Briggs, a former German Academy student, became professor of Hebrew at the Union Theological Seminary and a staunch advocate of this intellectually critical approach to the Bible.[15]

During his time at the German Academy before joining the Union Theological Seminary faculty, Briggs was a student of Isaac A. Dorner, who had much to do with shaping Briggs's own views regarding methods of biblical interpretation. Dorner had relied on a critical method of investigating the Scriptures that acknowledged the importance of their historical contexts even while denying that such intellectual criticism was a threat to Christianity. While at the academy, Briggs observed, "Dr. Dorner is exceedingly liberal and charitable, using all the results of critical study. He does not abuse the critics, whilst condemning their false tendencies and opinions."[16] This description of Dorner could very well have been used to describe Briggs himself in the years that followed his return to America in 1869.

HISTORICAL CRITICISM VERSUS BIBLICAL INERRANCY

During the 1880s, Briggs became known through some of his writings as an anti-conservative Presbyterian. In his 1889 book, *Whither? A Theological Question for the Times*, Briggs strongly criticized conservatives for promoting what he called "orthodoxism," which he defined as a perversion of church orthodoxy: "Orthodoxism assumes to know the truth and is unwilling to learn; it is haughty and arrogant, assuming the divine prerogatives of infallibility and inerrancy; it hates all truth that is unfamiliar to it, and persecutes it to the uttermost."[17]

Equally revealing were his views regarding orthodoxy: "Orthodoxy, so far as man is concerned, is relative and defective; it is measured by the knowledge that he has of the truth. Man's knowledge is not a constant quantity. It varies in different men, in different nations and societies, and still more in different epochs of history."[18]

Then, in 1891, after becoming professor of theology at Union, Briggs gave an inaugural address titled "The Authority of Holy Scripture" that generated a firestorm of criticism from the more conservative, literalist segments of the official Presbyterian community at large.[19] From this point on, the Princeton Theological Seminary, which had a long tradition of supporting scriptural inerrancy, became Briggs's principal antagonist. The seminary's objections to Briggs's address arose from his claims that Higher Criticism had proved that many of the Old Testament books were not actually authored by those whose names were associated with them and that the Old Testament was a historical record containing many errors.[20]

In a direct challenge to the seminary, Briggs referred to the school's doctrine of scriptural inerrancy as "a ghost of modern evangelism to frighten children."[21] In addition to calls from the seminary for Briggs to resign, the conservative New York Presbytery attempted, unsuccessfully, to bring heresy charges against him.

Despite his outspoken views in opposition to conservative orthodoxism, Briggs firmly believed that the Bible was the product of divine revelation or inspiration. The issue for him was not whether God communicated with the biblical authors but rather how that communication was perceived at the human level. Briggs insisted that divine revelation did not equate with absolute infallible truth, simply because of the finite limitations of the human mind to completely comprehend the infinite. In other words, the revelations received by the authors were inevitably filtered through their own historical and scientific understandings of the world.[22]

The dispute was essentially between two ways of understanding the divine inspiration process. While Briggs understood the process rather broadly to be one of "concept inspiration" in which the meaning is found beyond the scriptural words or language, his conservative Princetonian critics insisted that the minds of the biblical authors did fully comprehend divine revelations. Therefore, Briggs's conservative critics believed the Scriptures to be the inerrant words of God.

THE MODERN FUNDAMENTALIST MOVEMENT

The intense opposition to Briggs and to Higher Criticism in general from Presbyterian conservatives was symptomatic of a growing backlash against liberal challenges to biblical literalism and inerrancy in the light of an emerging modern scientific worldview. Consequently, to stem the tide of theological liberalism, the General Assembly of the Presbyterian Church (USA) agreed in New York in 1910 to produce a document that would be used to govern all future ministerial ordinations. Known as the Doctrinal Deliverance of 1910, it featured five doctrines deemed to be "necessary and essential" for those claiming to be Christians.[23] All those seeking Presbyterian ministerial ordinations were then required to affirm their belief in the following five "fundamental" doctrines in addition to the rather strict Calvinistic Westminster Confession of 1646:[24]

1. The inspiration and inerrancy of the Bible
2. The virgin birth of Christ
3. The substitutionary atonement of Christ
4. The bodily resurrection of Christ
5. The historicity of the biblical miracles

In the same year that these five fundamental doctrines were introduced, a wealthy Presbyterian layman named Lyman Stewart published a series of pamphlets called *The Fundamentals: A Testimony to the Truth*, severely critical of Higher Criticism. Henceforth, conservative Christians who supported and promoted these pamphlets and the five fundamentals came to be known as "fundamentalists."[25]

But in 1922, the liberal Baptist Harry Emerson Fosdick delivered a sermon at the First Presbyterian Church in New York titled, "Shall the Fundamentalists Win?" Fosdick's sermon essentially repudiated the five fundamentals and referred to the conservative fundamentalists as intolerant. It rejected what he considered to be a pessimistic Christianity preoccupied with sin and dark predictions about a second coming of Christ and earthly conflagration. By comparison, Fosdick's view was more positive and evolutionary: "I believe in the personal God revealed in Christ, in his omnipresent activity and endless resources to achieve his purposes for us and for all men."[26]

Along with his rejection of fundamentalist dogmas, he also refused to repeat the Apostles' Creed on the grounds that it was equally indefensible. What had begun during the nineteenth century as a split between conservative and liberal Presbyterians in America over the issue of biblical interpretation now spread beyond the Presbyterian community and intensified into a division between conservative and liberal Christians as a whole during the twentieth century and beyond.

THEOLOGICAL ROOTS OF FUNDAMENTALISM

Actually, the five fundamentals are little more than a restatement of the Apostles' Creed and point to the fact that twentieth century fundamentalism was just another manifestation of early orthodox Christianity. The legalistic and exclusive use of these fundamentals as a measure of one's identity as a Christian is reminiscent of the fourth and fifth century Christian polemicist bishops' charges of heresy against those who would question their orthodox views. The degree to which today's fundamentalists reduce Christianity to a system of rules and requirements is an indication of how much some segments of the Church have failed to grow and adapt to change through the various stages of Christian history.

Sola Scriptura and Sola Fide

Although the sixteenth century's Protestant Reformation seriously challenged the top-down structure of what was then the monolithic Roman Catholic Church, the ideas and actions of Martin Luther and his followers did not sweep away all aspects of fourth and fifth century Christian orthodoxy. Instead, the main thrust of the Reformation was its widespread anticlericalism resulting from deep-seated disillusionment with the pope and his corrupted, elitist clergy. The Protestant reformists no longer saw the clergy as a necessary means for their salvation. They claimed the Christian faithful could find salvation by directly experiencing and knowing God through reading and interpreting the Bible or hearing the Word preached or both.[27] They enshrined their claim in the phrase *sola scriptura* (by Scripture alone), meaning the Bible is the ultimate authority in matters of belief and moral behavior—essentially the Word of God and the only source of written divine revelation.

The second-most important principle stressed by the Reformation was encapsulated in the phrase *sola fide* (by faith alone). Here, "justification (salvation) is by grace alone through faith alone because of Christ alone."[28] The reformists essentially said that since the Roman Catholic Church opposed the idea of *sola fide*, it was no longer a legitimate institution.

Thanks to Johannes Gutenberg's invention of the printing press in 1439, printed copies of the Scriptures eventually became available to the masses (at least to those who were literate) for the first time outside the Church's interpretive control. However, even as the Reformation challenged the authority of the Roman Catholic Church, many of its long-standing doctrines and beliefs remained largely unchallenged. Such doctrines as humanity's fall from grace, original sin, hell as a place of eternal damnation, the Holy Trinity, the Second Coming of Jesus, and the Last Judgment were still widely accepted.

These foundational Christian concepts can mainly be traced to Paul's letters, which were the earliest writings in the New Testament, and to Augustine of Hippo, the venerated, fifth century pillar of Roman Catholicism.[29] These early Christian leaders had an inestimable impact in shaping the theology of the other great sixteenth century Protestant reformer, Jean Cauvin of France, also known as John Calvin.

The Teachings of John Calvin

In an article titled "Calvin's Reception of Paul," biblical scholar Barbara Pitkin says, "More than any other biblical writer or figure, Paul shaped

Calvin's work not only as a biblical scholar, but also as a reformer of the church and a theologian. Calvin gave priority to the Pauline epistles in his exegetical program and also viewed all of Scripture through a Pauline lens."[30] However, Calvin's "A Treatise on the Eternal Predestination of God" also indicates his great debt to Augustine, given the fact that he had been a faithful Roman Catholic like Luther long before endorsing Protestantism: "Augustine is so wholly with me, that if I wished to write a confession of my faith, I could do so with a fullness and satisfaction to myself out of his writings."[31]

In 1619, fifty years after Calvin's death, the Synod of Dordt was formed to defend his essential teachings from dissenting opinions. Calvin's teachings in particular, as outlined by the synod, can give one a sense of the connections among the Gospels, early orthodox Christianity, the Protestant Reformation, and modern fundamentalism.

The Synod of Dordt was a convention of Calvinist followers from various Protestant churches of western Europe who met for the purpose of countering the spreading growth of Arminianism, which threatened the legitimacy of some of Calvin's theology. The members of the synod mainly objected to Dutch theologian Jacob Arminius's rejection of Calvin's concept of predestination in favor of human free will. In response to Arminianism, the synod produced the "Canons of the Synod of Dordt," otherwise known as the five points of Calvinism.[32] What follows is an examination and critique of selected passages from the canons that best represent the five points of Calvinism and, more broadly, the historic precursors of Biblical literalism and modern fundamentalism.

Total Depravity

The first of the five points of Calvinism reveals Calvin's belief in the totally depraved state of humanity. Passages from the canons address this idea. For example: "Since all people have sinned in Adam and have come under the sentence of the curse and eternal death, God would have done no one an injustice if it had been his will to leave the entire human race in sin and under the curse, and to condemn them on account of their sin."[33] Here Calvin claims that every human being is conceived and born totally corrupt from a spiritual standpoint. Given this fallen state naturally inherited from Adam and Eve's original sin, no person is capable of seeking God or contributing anything to his or her own salvation.[34]

This characterization of the universal human condition as hopelessly sinful and undeserving of God's blessings is essentially a literal interpretation of the story of the Fall found in the third chapter of Genesis. It also reveals Calvin's faith in the concept of "original sin" first suggested by Paul in Romans 5:

> Therefore, just as sin came into the world through one man (Adam) and death came through sin, and so death spread to all because all have sinned (Verse 12).

> Therefore, just as one man's trespass led to the condemnation for all, so one man's [Jesus's] act of righteousness leads to justification and life for all (Verse 18).

> For just as by the one man's disobedience the many were made sinners (Verse 19).

One of the most interesting things about Genesis 3 is that the word *sin* is never used.[35] Before the fictional figures of Adam and Eve disobeyed God and ate the forbidden fruit that held the key to the knowledge of good and evil, we can assume they had no knowledge of good and evil. If we follow this line of reasoning, it could well be they were not aware that disobedience or false pride were wrong (sinful).[36] So it becomes difficult to defend the idea that they sinned when they had no knowledge of sin until after the fact.

Another way of looking at this issue is to assume that Adam and Eve were actually elevated intellectually and morally rather than being placed in some sort of permanently fallen state, since in Genesis 3:5 the author also says, "Behold, they've become like one of us, knowing good from evil."[37] In other words, Verse 5 suggests that Adam and Eve actually gained a likeness to God as a result of sampling the forbidden fruit.

In contrast with the traditional idea of a fall from God's favor caused by a sinful act on the part of Adam and Eve—a central belief among Christian fundamentalists—a very different interpretation of the Fall is presented in Neale Donald Walsch's 1997 book, *Conversations with God.* Here he gives more positive and hopeful meaning to the story, removing the whole idea of humanity's estrangement from God:

> What has been described as the fall of Adam was actually his upliftment—the greatest single event in the history of mankind. For without it, the world of relativity would not exist. The act of Adam and Eve was not original sin, but, in truth, first blessing. You should thank them from the bottom of your hearts—for in being the first to make a "wrong" choice, Adam and Eve produced the possibility of making any choice at all.[38]

Based on this interpretation, freedom of choice was God's greatest gift to humanity and to the world. But freedom of choice inevitably leaves open the possibility of making sinful as well as righteous choices. If we are truly God's children, it's more likely that the freedom of choice allows us to grow and evolve toward spiritual maturity by experiencing the natural consequences of our own moral choices. This would seem to be God's plan and purpose for human life.

Nevertheless, the more negative interpretations of the biblical stories of the Creation and the Fall still influence many Christians even today. As Laughlin says, "What suffers most as a result of the garden story, however, is not the nature or character of God (much less the well-being of all humankind), but the validity of the theological preconceptions that have commonly been misapplied to this ancient narrative."[39]

Curiously, the succeeding books of the Old Testament make almost no mention of the biblical story of the Fall, though they mention many sins. There is no indication that all the sinning that takes place in these later sections of the Old Testament resulted from Adam and Eve's original act of disobedience. In fact, no general theory of inherited sin was developed until well after the books of the Old Testament were written.[40]

The idea of Adam and Eve's banishment from the garden and fall from God's grace led to what the Catholic and Protestant traditions seem to agree was humanity's descent from its original state of perfection or innocence to a virtual imprisonment in sin and evil. Today, most biblical scholars agree that Augustine had much to do with crystallizing Paul's earlier views on the subject. In fact, Augustine was the first to fully articulate the concept of "original sin," or "*peccatum originale*," as he called it. He even referred to the entire human race as a "*massa perditionis*," or "mass of damnation," certain to be sent to hell.[41]

But Laughlin takes serious issue with Augustine's rather dark assessment of humanity. "On the basis of their [Paul and Augustine's] ideas about the radical nature and effects of sin, Christianity developed what appears to be the most negative view of human nature of any religion of which we are aware," he says. [42]

In addition, most Christians do not usually consider the fact that in many of the world's religions, the basic problem for humanity is ignorance rather than sin. This is especially true of the Eastern religions of China and India. While Judaism, Christianity, and Islam do acknowledge the reality of sin, Judaism and Islam tend to consider sin an act of going astray or a bad deed that contradicts the will of God but which can be overcome through repentance and personal reform.[43] In other words, these religions' followers tend to believe that we humans have the God-given capacity and freedom to atone for our sins directly to God without the requirement of some external divine means or intermediary.

On the other hand, largely as a result of the overarching influence of Paul, Augustine, and then Calvin, many Christians assume that humanity is inherently, even hopelessly, sinful and incapable of rising above this permanent state except through divine intervention in the person of Jesus. So, in deference to Paul and especially Augustine, orthodox Roman Catholics and Protestants have for a very long time considered sin a universal congenital condition stemming from Adam and Eve and their descendants. It would appear that in their opinion, sin is the rule, not the exception. The ancient Judaic practice of baptism as a symbolic act of purification or repentance was, in fact, transformed by Paul into a literal act of regeneration or unification with Christ for the remission of a person's congenital sinful condition.[44] It was Augustine in particular who went so far as to believe that infants who died before being baptized were damned.[45]

Today, this preoccupation with sin is also perpetuated by the inclusion of the Prayer of Confession in most Christian worship services. Every week, the faithful are reminded they are sinners by repeating, usually in unison, a litany of their failures and transgressions against God and their neighbors. Such prayers are offered for the sake of God's forgiveness, which is usually assured in the end by the pastor, minister, or priest leading the prayer. When such prayers are offered, perhaps many congregants wonder about the countless number of people, whether Christian or not, who suffer from circumstances beyond their control or who willingly give of themselves in service to others only to be told that they constantly—inevitably—fall short of God's expectations.

Perhaps those who attend church services would be better-served by being reminded of their essential goodness in being created for and by God. If a child or even an adult is constantly reminded that he or she is not good enough, or worse, that person's future potential will probably be negatively affected. If greater emphasis were placed on prayers of gratitude for the gifts of experiencing human life; prayers of assurance of God's love and sustaining presence; prayers of hope and healing for those who suffer physical and/or spiritual pain, and prayers of renewal and transformation for all of us as we evolve according to God's will and blessings, perhaps church services would be more uplifting and closer in spirit to Jesus's Sermon on the Mount.

Unconditional Predestination/Election

Following the rather negative characterization of humanity that we have already examined in the Canons of Dordt is Calvinism's second point, which refers to the beliefs in divine election (usually referred to as unconditional predestination) and reprobation. Both ideas are expressed this way in the canons:

> Before the foundation of the world, by sheer grace, according to the free good pleasure of his will, he chose in Christ to salvation a definite number of particular people out of the entire human race, which had fallen by its own fault from its original innocence into sin and ruin ...

> He predestined us whom he adopted as his children through Jesus Christ, in himself ...

> The election made by him can neither be suspended nor altered, revoked, or annulled; neither can his chosen ones be cast off, nor their number be reduced ...

... some have not been chosen or have been passed by in God's eternal election ... by their own fault, they have plunged themselves; not to grant them saving faith and the grace of conversion; but finally to condemn and eternally punish them (having been left in their own ways and under his just judgment), not only for their unbelief but also for all their other sins, in order to display his justice. And this is the decision of reprobation, which does not at all make God the author of sin (a blasphemous thought!) but rather its fearful, irreproachable, just judge and avenger.[46]

This concept of predestination's origin can actually be found in Paul's Letter to the Romans 8:28-30: "For those whom he foreknew, he also predestined to be conformed to the image of his Son, in order that he might be first-born within a large family. And those whom he predestined he also called; and those whom he called he also justified; and those whom he justified he also glorified."

What is quite apparent in Calvin's view of predestination, however, is the theme of divine judgment and separation whereby some are arbitrarily predestined (chosen) by God to be saved and others are not. This more legalistic approach to predestination on Calvin's part is actually more in line with Augustine, as seen in the latter's own words: "Even as he has appointed them to be regenerated ... whom he predestined to everlasting life, as the most merciful bestower of grace, whilst to those whom he has predestinated to death, he is also the most righteous awarder of punishment."[47]

Christ also appears to be a major factor in determining who is saved and who is not. Although many Christians today do not necessarily subscribe to the Calvinist concept of predestination, there is still a widespread belief among fundamentalists and other conservative Christians in a final day of divine judgment involving a second coming of Jesus, who will on God's behalf separate the damned from the saved. According to modern fundamentalists, those in danger of being rejected by God are non-Christians and others they consider to be insufficiently Christian. This is why many Baptists today, particularly those associated with the fundamentalist Southern Baptist Convention, tend to agree that "the Great Commission of each local church is to Evangelize everyone possible here and on each foreign field."[48] In short, saving souls is essentially the "Great Commission."

The other important theme found in these passages and still later, in modern Christian fundamentalism, is fear—that is, the ever-present fear of God's anger and retributive punishment for failure to believe in the Gospels and in Christ's sacrificial death. In recent years, fear of not being worthy of salvation and the possibility of divine punishment at the end of life has been exploited, especially by fundamentalist churches, for political as well as religious purposes.

Limited Atonement

The third point of Calvinism focuses on the redemptive, sacrificial purpose of Jesus's death, or, in short, the atonement. Calvin's model of the atonement is essentially the same as Anselm's "Cur Deus Homo" or the satisfaction model of atonement from the eleventh century mentioned in Chapter 2. The Synod of Dordt refers to it this way:

His justice requires (as he has revealed himself in the Word) that the sins we have committed against his infinite majesty be punished with both temporal and eternal punishments, of soul as well as body. We cannot escape these punishments unless satisfaction is given to God's justice.

> Since, however, we ourselves cannot give this satisfaction or deliver ourselves from God's anger, God in his boundless mercy has given us as a guarantee his only begotten Son, who was made to be sin and a curse for us, in our place, on the cross, in order that he might give satisfaction for us.[49]

As we have already seen, Jesus's perceived purpose as the necessary means of atoning for humanity's inherent sins was promoted in various forms well before Calvin. He simply perpetuates this long tradition, along with the image of Jesus as the "only begotten son" of God. But more important, the idea that God had Jesus die specifically to save the world from sin and remove the need for God's punitive justice still enjoys wide acceptance today among fundamentalists, evangelicals, mainline Protestants, and Catholics.

Irresistible Grace

The fourth teaching of Calvinism focuses on God's "irresistible grace" granted to the elect—those who God, from the beginning, has chosen to be saved. Even though God's chosen ones may resist the Gospel (the Word of God), such resistance will ultimately be overcome through God's initial bestowing of his grace on them. The following passages from the Canons of Dordt refer to this saving power of what Calvin considered to be God's undeserved grace:

> What, therefore, neither the light of nature nor the law can do, God accomplishes by the power of the Holy Spirit, through the Word or the ministry of reconciliation. This is the gospel about the Messiah, through which it has pleased God to save believers, in both the Old and the New Testament.

… Therefore, those who receive so much grace, beyond and in spite of all they deserve, ought to acknowledge it with humble and thankful hearts; on the other hand, with the apostle they ought to adore (but certainly not inquisitively search into) the severity and justice of God's judgments on the others, who do not receive this grace.[50]

Let's examine some especially noteworthy phrases in these passages—first, "it has pleased God to save believers," and second, "the severity and justice of God's judgments on the others." Just as in Calvin's notion of a divinely mandated separation between those elected and unelected by God, so Calvinism's fourth teaching seems to make a divine distinction between believers and those deemed to be unbelievers. According to Calvin, it is not enough for unbelievers predestined for damnation to seek redemption by becoming believers in the Gospel of the Messiah; God irreversibly predetermined their unelected status and ultimate damnation. On the other hand, if God's grace has been extended to the elect, they cannot resist or thwart such grace and their ultimate salvation. The Calvinist Loraine Boettner sums it up this way: "A man is not saved because he believes in Christ; he believes in Christ because he is saved."[51] In the end, it seems Calvin's idea of "irresistible grace" was largely formed on the basis of his own interpretations of certain passages from the New Testament:

For by grace you have been saved through faith, and this is not your own doing; it is the gift of God—not the result of works, so that no one may boast (Ephesians 2:8-9).

He saved us, not because of any works of righteousness that we had done, but according to his mercy, through the water of rebirth and renewal by the Holy Spirit (Titus 3:5).

Who [God] saved us and called us with a holy calling, not according to our works but according to his own purpose and grace. This grace was given to us in Christ Jesus before the ages began (II Timothy 1:9).

All that the Father gives me will come to me … And this is the will of Him who sent me, that I should lose nothing of all that He has given me, but raise it up on the last day (John 6:37, 39).

No one can come to me unless it is granted him by the Father (John 6:65).

However, the majority of New Testament Scriptures appear to say that belief must precede salvation rather than the reverse, as suggested by Calvin. The following are prime examples:

For God so loved the world that he gave his only Son, so that everyone who believes in him may not perish but may have eternal life (John 3:16).

They answered, "Believe on the Lord Jesus, and you will be saved, you and your household" (Acts 16:31).

The one who believes and is baptized will be saved; but the one who does not believe will be condemned (Mark 16:16).

Perseverance in Grace

The fifth and final point of Calvinism suggests it is impossible for believing Christians to be lost and beyond salvation because God enables them to "persevere in grace." From the Canon of Dordt we read:

Those who have been converted could not remain standing in this grace if left to their own resources. But God is faithful, mercifully strengthening them in the grace once conferred on them and powerfully preserving them in it to the end.

... So it is not by their own merits or strength but by God's undeserved mercy that they neither forfeit faith and grace totally nor remain in their downfalls to the end and are lost ... The sealing of the Holy Spirit can neither be invalidated nor wiped out.[52]

So it seems that for those fortunate ones predestined to be saved, salvation is assured, even if their belief in the Word weakens. However, this sense of inevitability seems to contradict Jesus's statement to the people of Jerusalem found in Matthew 23: "How often I have longed to gather your children together, as a hen gathers her chicks under her wings, but you were unwilling."

The source of Calvin's "perseverance in grace" idea can be traced in part to Paul, who said, "He will keep you strong to the end, so that you will be blameless on the day of our Lord, Jesus Christ" (1 Corinthians 1:8). Calvin also seems to have ignored the message found in the Letter to the Hebrews that suggests believing Christians can indeed become lost and be beyond salvation. Here the author of Hebrews (who scholars now believe may have been a later follower of Paul) intended to warn Christians not to waver in their belief for fear of falling from God's saving grace: "Therefore we must pay greater attention to what we have heard, so that we do not drift away from it. For if the message declared through angels was valid, and every transgression or disobedience received a just penalty, how can we escape if we neglect so great a salvation?" (Hebrews 2:1-3).

When taken as a whole, these five "indispensable" teachings of Calvin tend to emphasize humanity's spiritual inadequacy and inborn inability to follow God or avoid condemnation, except through his unpredictable and mostly unwarranted acts of grace. In other words, an inherently sinful humanity is entirely subject to the mercy of a sovereign and rather arbitrary God. The supernatural, mostly transcendent theism of early Christianity is clearly in evidence and is largely what motivates fundamentalist and evangelical Christians. So is continued preoccupation with sin, guilt, and the need to be saved from eternal damnation. Most of all, so is the underlying notion of a separation from God and one another when distinguishing the saved from the unsaved and "true" or elect Christians from all others, especially unbelieving non-Christians.

The Impact of Various Early Bibles

In addition to being heavily influenced by Paul and Augustine, Calvin's ideas were shaped in large measure by the Latin Vulgate translation of the Bible. In Calvin's time, this translation was the official Bible of the Roman Catholic Church, having been produced by Jerome on orders from Pope Damasus near the end of the fourth century.[53] As David Schaff mentions in his book *Our Father's Faith and Ours*: "For one thousand years the Vulgate was practically the only Bible known and read in Western Europe. All commentaries were based upon the Vulgate text ... Preachers based their sermons on it."[54]

Equally important is the fact that the Vulgate reflected many of Augustine's ideas, including predestination and the rejection of free will. Furthermore, since the Vulgate translation was still widely circulated during the sixteenth century, it had a major effect on Protestant churches not only in Europe but in England and America as well. In fact, Luther's 1523 German translation of the New Testament was largely based on the Vulgate, as was the case with the Geneva Bible, first produced in complete form in 1560.[55] Nevertheless, in England during the reigns of Henry VII and Henry VIII, Oxford Professor Thomas Linacre made it clear that the Latin Vulgate was filled with errors and bore little resemblance to the Gospels in their original Greek.[56]

The Geneva Bible came about when several Protestant scholars fled England and settled in Geneva, Switzerland, to escape the Catholic rule of Queen Mary I (1553-58). They produced the Geneva Bible, not only in response to Catholic oppression but as an alternative to what the Protestant reformers considered to be the pro-monarchical Anglican "Great Bible" (an English derivative of the Latin Vulgate) commissioned by Henry VIII and distributed by royal decree throughout England in 1539. Although its distribution was banned during the brief reign of Queen Mary, the "Great Bible" was officially reinstated soon after.[57]

Given that Calvin was the leading theological figure in Geneva during these years, it's no wonder that the most important feature of the Geneva Bible was its abundant and heavily Calvinist annotations. In fact, Calvin, along with the exiled English Protestant scholars, was directly involved in the creation of the Geneva Bible. In his book *The Bibles of England*, Andrew Edgar goes so far as to say, "At the time the Geneva Bible was first published, Calvin was the ruling spirit in Geneva. All the features of his theological, ecclesiastical, political, and social system are accordingly reflected in the marginal annotations ... The doctrine of predestination is proclaimed to be the head cornerstone of the gospel."[58]

Another individual who significantly contributed to the new revised Bible in Geneva was exiled Scottish firebrand John Knox. Because of Knox's involvement in the creation of the Geneva Bible, it was well-received in Scotland, where it appeared for the first time in 1579 and soon became the country's authorized Bible. Even though King James I of England objected to certain aspects of the Geneva Bible and subsequently authorized the well-known King James version of the Bible in 1611, it was still influenced significantly by the Geneva Bible. Biblical scholar H. Wheeler Robinson comments: "A large part of its [the Geneva Bible's] innovations are included in the Authorized Version [KJV] ...

Sometimes the Geneva text and the Geneva margin are taken over intact, sometimes the text becomes the margin and the margin the text. ... Very often the Genevan margin becomes the Authorized Version text with or without verbal change."[59] For the hundred years that followed its publication, the Geneva Bible remained popular among English-speaking Protestants in Scotland and England as well as in America. Since it was carried to the New World on the Mayflower, the Geneva Bible was a major factor in the spread of Calvinist theology within the early Pilgrim and Puritan communities.[60]

The Impact of the Westminster Confession

In addition to being influenced by the Geneva Bible, the early American colonists were guided in large part by the Westminster Confession, a systematic exposition of Calvinist theology instituted in England and Scotland in 1646 during the English Civil War against King Charles I of England (1642-49). The Westminster Confession, essentially a restatement of the five canons of the Synod of Dordt, was produced when the English Parliament entered into an alliance with the Scottish Covenanters for the two-fold purpose of overthrowing King Charles and initiating a reformation of the Anglican Church of England. Although the confession was nullified in 1660 when the British monarchy and the Anglican Church were restored under James II of England, it did not remain dead for long. When William of Orange replaced James II in 1690, it was reinstated by royal decree in Scotland, England, and Ireland.[61]

Along with endorsing the foundational doctrines of original sin, predestination, the Trinity, Jesus's sacrificial death, the atonement, and others so closely associated with Paul and later biblical interpretations, the Westminster Confession included specific Puritan statements of belief. For instance, the confession made it clear that the pope was the Antichrist, that the Catholic mass was a form of idolatry, that civil authorities had the divine prerogative to punish heresy, that a strict Sabbatarianism had to be maintained, and especially that the Protestant Reformation's bedrock principles of *sola scriptura* and *sola fide* would remain sacred.[62]

While the anti-Catholic statements about the pope and the Catholic mass were removed from the confession in later years, and while the American Constitution in 1789 removed the prerogative of civil authorities to intervene in matters of religion, and despite the eventual Presbyterian removal of the doctrine of predestination, the Westminster Confession has remained relatively intact since the seventeenth century.[63]

As we have seen, the confession was simply another manifestation of Pauline/Augustinian theology and, like so many similar theological documents before it, was largely a product of Biblical literalism. Furthermore, the Doctrinal Deliverance of 1910, which ushered in the modern fundamentalist movement in America, reflected much the same substance and tone to be found in the Westminster Confession—except that the fundamentalist emphasis on biblical infallibility represents a more extreme version of *sola scriptura*. In addition to their resistance to biblical historical criticism, Christian fundamentalists have tended to focus on four other contentious issues. These issues not only come from an endorsement of biblical literalism and inerrancy but also reflect Christian fundamentalism's strong reaction against the evolutionary changes affecting modern culture in general and modern science in particular.

FUNDAMENTALIST BIBLICAL INTERPRETATIONS AFFECTING SOCIETY AS A WHOLE

Creationism

The first literal interpretation of the Bible known as "Creationism" involves the effort to challenge the legitimacy of Darwin's 1859 theory of evolution.[64] Fundamentalist devotees of Creationism choose to consider the highly metaphorical stories of the Creation found in the first two chapters of Genesis as the most reliable source of scientific truth and authority relative to the creation of the world and human life. Even today, Creationists continue to insist that biblically based "Creation science" courses be offered in America's public schools as an alternative to the science of evolution.[65]

The unfortunate effect of the resulting controversy has been not only to cause divisions among American educators but to reinforce the idea that science and religion are mutually exclusive enterprises. Consequently, fundamentalist Creationists have raised objections to Darwin's theory as being anti-biblical. Furthermore, they have tended to view Darwin's ideas regarding the biological process of natural selection more broadly as an endorsement of "social Darwinism," or application of the "survival of the fittest" biological process to the future cultural and moral development of human societies in general. To mid-twentieth century Creationists especially, acceptance of Darwin's theory of evolution seemed to support Nazi Germany's concept of a "master race."

Dispensationalism

The second major issue raised by modern fundamentalism's biblical literalism concerns the eschatological theory known as "dispensationalism." As mentioned near the beginning of this chapter, the primary source of authority for fundamentalists regarding dispensationalism is the book of Revelation. Based on the literal interpretation of Revelation as a prophecy of a future "end time," fundamentalists are convinced that believing (chosen) Christians will suddenly be removed from the Earth in the near future due to a cosmic event known as the "Rapture" that will precede the "Great Tribulation." Those unfortunate souls considered by the returning Christ to be unbelievers or non-Christians will be left behind to suffer through this period of tribulation, a time of divine judgments and earthly conflagration. In addition, dispensational-ists contend that near the end of the Great Tribulation, the nation of Israel will finally embrace Jesus as their Messiah just before the Second Coming of Christ, who will then rule the world from Jerusalem for a millennium. For this reason, dispensationalists are mostly known as pre-millennialists; they look toward a near future when a thousand-year reign of Jesus Christ will begin.[66]

However, a dispensationalist worldview leaves no room for the concept of a participatory universe in which we freely engage with God as co-creators in an open-ended (not closed and predetermined) evolutionary process. Seeing ourselves as co-creators with God in an evolutionary process would seem to be more realistic, given the creative, compassionate, and nonviolent image of God presented to us in the person of Jesus. One of the negative consequences of a dispensationalist worldview is its assumption that efforts on the part of world leaders to seek a lasting peace among nations is fruitless and unnecessary, since the Second Coming of Christ will settle the matter once and for all. This, in effect, is the abdication of human responsibility and free will with the excuse that "God is in control."

Homophobia

The third fundamentalist issue stemming from biblical inerrancy concerns homosexuality. For many conservative fundamentalist and evangelical Christians, the Old Testament book of Leviticus appears to condemn homosexuality as a sin. Reference is often made to such passages as "You shall not lie with a man as with a woman; it is an abomination" (Leviticus 18:22) and "God will cast out those who defile themselves and the land will vomit out those who are thus defiled" (Leviticus 18:24). Likewise, fundamentalists often use Paul's comments to justify their anti-homosexual beliefs:

For this reason God gave them up to degrading passions. Their women exchanged natural intercourse for unnatural, and in the same way also the men, giving up natural intercourse with women, were consumed with passion for one another. Men committed shameless acts with men and received in their own persons the due penalty for their error. And since they did not see fit to acknowledge God, God gave them up to a debased mind and to things that should not be done (Romans 1:26-28).

Do you not know that wrongdoers will not inherit the kingdom of God? Do not be deceived! Fornicators, idolaters, adulterers, male prostitutes, sodomites, thieves, the greedy, drunkards, revilers, robbers—none of these will inherit the kingdom of God (I Corinthians 6:9-10).

Many Christians who believe that the Bible is the final authority in this matter continue to resist gay-marriage laws, clerical ordinations of gays and lesbians, and acceptance of homosexually oriented individuals in general. Unfortunately, more extreme fundamentalists have even used the Bible to justify violence against homosexuals—a direct contradiction of everything Jesus taught and died for. What anti-gay fundamentalists fail to recognize is that modern medical science has proved beyond a reasonable doubt that sexual orientation is determined by genetics, not behavioral choice.[67]

What is also overlooked is the fact that the book of Leviticus in particular endorsed slavery and the stoning of women for adultery and various other practices that are no longer considered to be serious crimes. By contrast, "The Way" of Jesus as revealed in the Sermon on the Mount and in various New Testament parables that emphasize forgiveness, nonviolence, and acceptance of every person as a child of God would seem to be a more legitimate and humane source of authority.

Anti-Abortion Beliefs

The fourth biblically related issue that has divided Christians, especially in America since the mid-twentieth century, is abortion. Those who define themselves as "pro-life" opponents of abortion tend to believe life begins at conception and see abortion as an act of murder against an innocent victim. In defense of their position, they most often turn to the Sixth Commandment of Moses, "Thou shalt not kill." Nevertheless, "pro-life" Christians are usually quite outspoken in support of the death penalty for criminals as well as lethal military action against foreign and domestic enemies. Conversely, "pro-choice" advocates who believe that abortions are justifiable in certain cases, based on medical advice and personal spiritual considerations, usually oppose the death penalty and favor diplomacy over military confrontation. In either case, strict adherence to the Mosaic Law has been compromised.

But if one turns to the Sermon on the Mount and to Jesus's life and teachings as a whole, the evidence suggests that Jesus did not advocate a rigid, mechanical observance of the law without exceptions. He was not above compromising the Mosaic Law when circumstances called for the higher priorities of compassion and self-sacrificing service to others in need. Examples include the parable of the Good Samaritan as described in Luke 10:25–37 and his various acts of healing on the Sabbath as told in Mark 3:2, Matthew 12:10, and John 5:5–18.

When applied to the current abortion issue, perhaps Jesus's willingness to err on the side of compassion and understanding is well-illustrated by the permitting of abortions for innocent victims of rape or incest; for women whose lives are at risk due to pregnancy; for poverty-stricken women who lack the means or circumstances to prevent pregnancy; for seriously compromised fetuses that have no chance of a meaningful life beyond the womb; or for any other reason that a women facing a pregnancy deems to be essential for her own well-being. Finally, today's evidence suggests the soul usually chooses to enter the fetus well after conception, but that's a subject that will be explored more completely in Chapter 6.

When viewed from a broader perspective, all these biblically related issues are defensive reactions against the rise of modern science and secularization that seem to suggest the abandonment of the Bible, or at least the weakening of its authority. Especially associated with the issues of Creationism, dispensationalism, homosexuality, and abortion is the need to judge and to separate unbelievers from Christian believers, or in Calvinist terms, the rejected from the divinely chosen. But as we have seen from Paul onward, the idea that salvation involves a divine separation process is not new.

THE BIBLE AS SEEN WITHIN THE CONTEXT OF A SPIRITUALLY EVOLVING WORLD

Contemporary biblical scholars and social visionaries such as Borg, Crossan, and Patterson recognize that reliance on biblical literalism and the Scriptures as inerrant sources of unquestionable authority is, by necessity, becoming a thing of the past as the world enters a new evolutionary phase. In other words, fundamentalism and the doctrinal- and creedal-based theology of orthodox Christianity are yielding to ever-expanding knowledge about the nature of God, the teachings of Jesus, and the evolution of human consciousness.

In the end, the Bible can be recognized as the foundation of a "building" still under construction. While the foundation is sound and solidly constructed, it is the beginning, not the end—it beckons further expansion, spiritually speaking. The biblical writers were not the last to be the recipients of divine inspiration and intervention. Furthermore, because of the mid-twentieth century discoveries of long-hidden Gnostic texts at Nag Hammadi and the Dead Sea scrolls at Qumran, we know more about the way in which the Scriptures came to be written than at any time during the previous sixteen hundred years. These discoveries have added greatly to our understanding of the biblical writers as individuals who were subject to disagreements, personal agendas, and differences in perception as well as divine inspiration—not to mention later editing by scribes and translators. In the next chapter we will examine the role these human elements played in the developmental struggles of early Christianity.

CHAPTER 4

Beyond "Sola Scriptura": Other Gospels and Writings

As a result of two extraordinary discoveries—the first occurring in the late nineteenth century and the second in the mid-twentieth century—the modern world now has a clearer, more complete picture of the earliest controversies that raged among Christians during the first three centuries after the death of Jesus. The Berlin Gnostic Codex, containing Coptic translations of three Christian Gnostic texts known as the Gospel of Mary, the Apocrypha of John, and the Sophia of Jesus, was discovered near Akhmim, Egypt, a few years before being purchased by the German scholar Dr. Carl Reinhardt in 1896.[1] Then, in 1945, a collection of thirteen ancient codices containing more than fifty Gnostic texts was discovered at Nag Hammadi, in northern Egypt.[2] Due to the interference of two world wars, the first group of texts from Akhmim, now known as the Berlin Gnostic Codex, was not translated until 1955. Then, in the 1970s, the second group of texts was translated, and they are now available to biblical scholars at the Gnostic Society Library in Nag Hammadi.

All the Gnostic writings from Nag Hammadi were fourth century copies of much earlier originals, mostly from the second and third centuries. They were hidden to avoid destruction by leading theologians of the emerging orthodox Christian church such as Justin Martyr and Irenaes of Lyons, from the second century; Tertullian of Carthage and Hippolytus of Rome, from the third century; and Alexander and Athanasius of Alexandria and Epiphanius of Salamis, from the fourth century.[3]

In her book *What Is Gnosticism?* Karen King refers to these early bishops as "ancient Christian polemicists" who tried to persuade other Christians, Jews, and pagans that the bishops alone were the legitimate voices of divine truth. She points out that until the Gnostic texts from Nag Hammadi were discovered, what was known about ancient Gnosticism came only through the filter of these bishops, who were on the winning side of the intense theological debates that divided Christians from the late first through the fourth centuries. The Gnostic writings of this early Christian period were claimed to be heretical, since they did not conform to the orthodox theological views of the polemicists.[4]

DEFINING GNOSTICISM

As biblical researchers examined the plethora of newly discovered Gospels, answers to the following questions were sought: Was Gnosticism an independent, non-Christian religion? Was it a pre-Christian phenomenon, or was it a contamination on the part of misguided Christians of a pure doctrine inherited from the apostles? The research has resulted in no clear agreement among scholars about how exactly to define Gnosticism.

Despite attempts on the part of the Nag Hammadi researchers to do so, the works included under the broad title of Gnosticism are too varied in terms of content and origin to be considered together as a related whole.[5] Accumulated evidence from researchers seems to rule out the possibility that Gnosticism could have been a pre-Christian religion that influenced and competed with Christianity in its formative stage of development. Likewise, the idea that Gnosticism was essentially a non-Christian tradition is no longer supported by most early Christian scholars.

Instead, the Nag Hammadi scholars tend to believe that the Gnostic texts represented various Christian ideas that arose after the death of Jesus at the same time as other, more orthodox Christian ideas.[6] In other words, Gnostic writings were not a later contamination of a previously established orthodox theology. What does seem clear is that during the first three centuries after the death of Jesus, as the early history of the Church unfolded, no single, dominant theology was in place. The period was marked instead by heated theological debates and relative instability.

EARLY CHRISTIAN THEOLOGICAL DISPUTES AND DIFFERENCES

Foremost among the Gnostic heresies, according to the polemicists, was the great importance the Gnostics placed on the possession of spiritual knowledge (gnosis) gained through personal revelations of the Divine. To the Gnostics, spiritual enlightenment was a personal matter not requiring priestly intermediaries or ecclesiastical requirements. They taught new Christian converts that every person has direct access to God through the spiritual search for self-knowledge.

As far as Irenaeus, Tertullian, and other orthodox bishops were concerned, this represented a direct challenge to the authority of priests and bishops. Irenaeus and Tertullian believed the Gnostic reliance on the inward pursuit of knowledge could lead to false interpretations of the Scriptures and seriously challenged the rule of faith as defined by the Orthodox Church and its priests, whom the polemicists considered to be the legitimate successors of the apostles.[7] Thus Tertullian commented: "In the last resort, however, it is better for you to remain ignorant, for fear that you come to what you should not know. For you do know what you should know. 'Your faith has saved thee,' it says, not your biblical learning. Faith is established in the Rule ... To know nothing against the Rule is to know everything."[8]

The heretics' refusal to accept the authority of orthodox bishops and priests as the true successors of the apostles was interpreted by the polemicists to mean the Gnostics had moved beyond the apostles' original teaching. On this point, Irenaeus said: "They consider themselves 'mature,' so that no one can be compared with them in the greatness of their gnosis, even if you mention Peter or Paul or any of the other apostles ... They imagine that they themselves have discovered more than the apostles."[9]

The polemicists also objected to the highly complicated and esoteric mythologies that formed the basis of many Gnostic writings. Such mythologies, according to the polemicists, denied that the God of the Hebrew Bible (the Old Testament) was the one and only God and creator of the universe. The Gnostic writers often presented the concept of a lower world inhabited by a fallen humanity who seek to be liberated and restored to the divine realm through the acquisition of secret spiritual knowledge. The polemicists were therefore convinced that the Gnostics denied the basic goodness of the Creation and hated the world as well as the body, since souls were supposedly imprisoned in physical bodies by a demiurgic creator.[10] This approach to cosmology, long believed to be typical of Gnosticism, has been referred to as "radical, anti-cosmic dualism" by Biblical scholars.[11]

In addition, the Gnostics were accused of misinterpreting the Scriptures by claiming that Jesus actually had no physical body, a school of thought also known as Docetism. To the polemicists, this meant that Christian believers would not and could not physically rise from the dead as Jesus did. Likewise, the Gnostics were charged with believing that only the spiritual elite having a unique heavenly origin would be saved. The implication was that faith in Christ was not the necessary path to salvation, which in turn raised serious ethical issues. For instance, if there was no need for a savior, then there would be no need for moral instruction and good works—still another rejection of priestly authority.[12]

THE OTHER SIDE HEARD FROM—FINALLY

Now, however, with the advantage of having actual Gnostic writings available for examination, we can judge both sides of these early controversies more fairly on their merits. The early polemicists' sweeping condemnation of all the Gnostic texts must now withstand the scrutiny of a more objective audience of modern scholars. As a result of the research done on the Nag Hammadi texts, scholars have discovered that some of the writings do not fit the polemicists' heretical mold and provide important new pieces to the puzzle of early Christianity.

Dr. Paterson Brown, a member of the Ecumenical Coptic Project, argues forcefully that three texts in particular—*The Gospel of Truth*, *The Gospel of Philip*, and *The Gospel of Thomas*—all speak to the reality and sacredness of human life instead of denying the basic goodness of the creation, as many of the other Gnostic works tend to do.[13] In addition, Karen King provides compelling evidence that the Gospel of Mary, discovered in the late nineteenth century, should also be included as one of the most relevant and insightful Christian works that have languished too long in obscurity. Given the unique nature of these four Gospels, I examine each of them in the light of the New Testament and our modern era.

UNIQUELY IMPORTANT GOSPELS

The Gospel of Truth

The Gospel of Truth is known to have been written by the Egyptian-born Valentinus, an important second century early Christian teacher and theologian. After first teaching in Alexandria, Valentinus went to Rome in 136 CE, where he founded a school later known as Valentinianism. This school of Gnostic ideas attracted many followers throughout the Roman Empire, including Bishop Clement of Alexandria, who was also influenced by Platonic philosophy, the culture of Hellenized Jews, and Theudas, a follower of Paul.[14] (The connections between Valentinian thought and Paul will be examined more closely later in this chapter.) Interestingly, the orthodox Bishop Marcellus of Ancyra noted in the fourth century that Valentinus introduced the idea of the Godhead existing as three hidden spiritual entities, eventually recognized as the Trinity:"For he was the first to invent three hypostases and three persons of the Father, Son and Holy Spirit and he is discovered to have filched this from Hermes and Plato."[15]

What's doubly ironic about Marcellus's claim is that, first, a person accused of being a Gnostic heretic introduced one of the most sacred orthodox Christian doctrines, and second, Valentinus's idea of the Trinity was derived from pagan polytheism. In the Gospel of Truth, Valentinus basically claims that human ignorance of God was the primary reason Jesus was sent into the world. Jesus's mission was to show the way to knowledge of the Father. As a consequence, Jesus was persecuted and crucified. Unlike some later works written by various Gnostic followers of Valentinus, the Gospel of Truth does not create the image of a weak and ignorant creator God who attempted to keep humanity from gaining the knowledge of good and evil.[16] Neither does the Gospel of Truth present the orthodox Christian image of a punitive angry God who is capable of initiating a Last Judgment resulting in the casting of some into everlasting hell while others are saved by virtue of their faith in Jesus. For example, the following excerpt from the Gospel of Truth paints a more positive picture of God: "For the Father is sweet and his will is good. He knows the things that are yours, so that you may rest yourselves in them. For by the fruits one knows the things that are yours, that they are the children of the Father, and one knows his aroma, that you originate from the grace of his countenance."[17] Valentinus also viewed Jesus as the divine Word of revelation:

"Moreover, while saying new things, speaking about what is in the heart of the Father, he [Jesus] proclaimed the faultless word. Light spoke through his mouth, and his voice brought forth life. He gave them thought and understanding and mercy and salvation and the Spirit of strength derived from the limitlessness of the Father and sweetness."

"He [Jesus] became a path for those who went astray and knowledge to those who were ignorant, a discovery for those who sought, and a support for those who tremble, a purity for those who were defiled."

"But this one (Jesus) because he is a righteous person, does his works among others. Do the will of the Father, then, for you are from him."[18]

Such statements as these are not at odds with the New Testament Gospels. Like the author of John's Gospel, Valentinus relies heavily on metaphor as a means of conveying the truth as he sees it. For instance, when referring to the Crucifixion, Valentinus interprets the event this way: "He was nailed to the cross. He became the fruit of the knowledge of the Father. He did not, however, destroy them because they ate of it. He rather caused those who ate of it to be joyful because of this discovery."[19]

In effect, Jesus becomes the fruit of the tree of knowledge (with the cross as tree). This not only reminds us of the metaphorical statement in John 6:35—"Jesus said to them, I am the bread of life. Whoever comes

to me will never be hungry"—but also provides a new metaphorical twist
to the tree of the knowledge of good and evil as found in Genesis 2:17.

But despite Valentinus's rather positive and hopeful images of God
the Father and of Jesus the savior who brings enlightenment to the
world, he was condemned as a heretic and an enemy of the Church. As
articulated by Tertullian: "He broke with the church of the true faith. Just
like those (restless) spirits which, when roused by ambition, are usually
inflamed with the desire of revenge, he applied himself with all his might
to exterminate the truth; and finding the clue of a certain old opinion, he
marked out a path for himself with the subtlety of a serpent."[20]

Perhaps in the end, what was most disturbing to Valentinus's orthodox detractors was that his Gospel, along with those of other Gnostic
writers, encouraged the inward pursuit of secret divine knowledge
beyond the orthodox requirements of priestly instruction and dependence. Beyond whatever faults the Gnostics still may be accused of having, they recognized that direct revelations of the Divine were a real and
legitimate means of obtaining such knowledge. Moreover, having direct
personal revelations of unearthly spiritual knowledge was considered
legitimate not only by Gnostic writers but by Paul as well.

In Romans 16:25 we read, "Now to God who is able to strengthen
you according to my gospel and the proclamation of Jesus Christ, according to the revelation of the mystery that was kept secret for long ages."
Likewise, in I Corinthians 2:7, Paul says, "But we speak God's wisdom,
secret and hidden, which God decreed before the ages for our glory."
And in II Corinthians 12:2-4 he says: "I know a person in Christ who
fourteen years ago was caught up to the third heaven—whether in the
body or out of the body I do not know; God knows. And I know that
such a person—whether in the body or out of the body I do not know;
God knows—was caught up into Paradise and heard things that are not
to be told, that no mortal is permitted to repeat." What's remarkable
is that Paul's references to "the mystery that was kept secret," "God's

wisdom, secret and hidden," "the third heaven," and "things that are not to be told, that no mortal is permitted to repeat" are also found in the writings of Valentinus and other Christians deemed to be heretics by the ancient orthodox polemicists.

The Gospel of Philip

While the Gospel of Truth largely consists of commentaries on various Gnostic themes such as the nature of reality, the soul, and the soul's relationship to the Father, the Son, and the world, the Gospel of Philip is a collection of references to a Christian Gnostic sacramental catechesis widely used from the second through the fourth centuries.[21] Since the Gospel of Philip also contains teachings based on Valentinian ideas, modern scholars believe that the author of the Gospel of Philip was one of Valentinus's many followers. Scholars also agree that Philip the apostle was not the author because he died in 80 CE, well before the original Gospel was written. What's more likely, according to Paterson Brown, is that Philip the Evangelist (mentioned in Acts 6:5) was the author. In any case, the existing copy is a Coptic translation of the Greek original, which was most likely produced in the late second century.[22]

In terms of content, the Gospel of Philip contains seventeen sayings of Jesus. Nine of these are citations as well as interpretations of Jesus's words as found in the New Testament Gospels. But the most unusual aspect of the Gospel of Philip is its frequent reference to the theme of marriage, particularly with regard to the relationship between Jesus and Mary Magdalene. Insofar as the original Greek manuscript refers to Jesus as Mary's "*koinonos*," or companion, this has led some such as Dan Brown, author of *The DaVinci Code*, to consider the possibility that Jesus and Mary Magdalene were actually married.

To further strengthen the notion that Jesus and Mary Magdalene may have been married, a fourth century papyrus copy of a second century original document identified as *The Gospel of Jesus's Wife* was presented by Karen King at the International Congress of Coptic Studies in Rome on September 18, 2012. Although firm conclusions about the authenticity and meaning of the document will have to wait for further study, no conclusive evidence exists that would rule out the possibility of a married relationship.[23]

Whether their marriage was fact or fiction is anyone's guess. What's more important is that Mary appears to have been a highly respected and well-loved companion of Jesus, as the following passage from the Gospel of Philip suggests: "There were three who always walked with the Lord: Mary his mother, and her sister, and Magdalene, the one who was called his companion. His sister and his mother and his companion were each a Mary."[24] It should be noted, however, that a translation problem leaves the reader wondering whether the sister was a sister to Jesus's mother or to him. We do know that in the following verse from the Gospel of Mark, Jesus is acknowledged to have had sisters: "Is not this the carpenter, the Son of Mary and brother of James and Joses and Judas and Simon, and are not his sisters here with us?" (Mark 6:3).

A second statement from the Gospel of Philip goes even further in describing a more intimate relationship between Jesus and Mary. Since there are words and letters missing from the ancient manuscript found at Nag Hammadi, translators have filled in the blanks based on the word clues that come before and after the missing parts. The following excerpt from the Gospel appears with the added words in parentheses:

> As for the Wisdom who is called "the barren," she is the mother of the angels. And the companion of (the savior was Mar)y Ma(gda)lene. (Christ loved) M(ary) more than (all) the disci(ples, and used to) kiss her (softly) on her (hand). The rest of (the disciples were offended by it and expressed disapproval). They said to him "Why do you love her more than

all of us?" The Saviour answered and said to them, "Why do I not love you like her? When a blind man and one who sees are both together in darkness, they are no different from one another. When the light comes, then he who sees will see the light, and he who is blind will remain in darkness."[25]

This passage not only suggests that an especially close relationship existed between Mary Magdalene and Jesus, but it also considerably elevates Mary Magdalene's status as an active participant in the Jesus movement—enough to generate jealousy among the twelve male apostles. In fact, according to Pamela Thimmes, a Franciscan sister and professor emeritus of religious studies at the University of Dayton, Mary Magdalene's participation was significant enough that she was called the "apostle to the apostles" by none other than the ardent orthodox critic of the Gnostics, Bishop Hippolytus of Rome![26]

Furthermore, Jeffrey Kripal, chair of Rice University's Department of Religious Studies, claims that the Gnostic texts in general seem to recognize Mary as an important visionary, spiritual guide, and interpreter of Jesus's teaching. In other words, she held a position of spiritual authority at least equal to that of the other twelve apostles.[27]

The legend that Mary Magdalene had been an adulteress and prostitute before Jesus "saved" her actually originated when Pope Gregory, in a homily given in 591, essentially linked her identity with that of the sinner Mary of Bethany.[28] Consequently, the image of Mary as a former prostitute persisted throughout most of the Church's long history despite the legend's lack of credibility and the fact that no references to this legend are found anywhere in the New Testament. While the New Testament canonical Gospels do acknowledge that Mary, along with a fairly sizable group of other women, supported and served Jesus throughout his ministry, they never present Mary as having the same kind of authority and spiritual knowledge as the twelve apostles.

A similar tradition of female diminishment is reflected today in the Catholic Church's firmly entrenched policy of apostolic succession that excludes women. In addition to what has already been said about the Gospel of Philip's commentary on the relationship between Jesus and Mary Magdalene, it is also known for its symbolic references to the "bridal chamber," as in the following passages (73 and 143, respectively): "The Lord did everything in a mystery, a baptism, and a chrism and a eucharist and a redemption and a bridal chamber"; "If anyone becomes a 'son of the bridechamber' he will receive the Light. If anyone does not receive it while he is in these places, he cannot receive it in the other place." Some scholars believe these passages refer symbolically to the joining of God (bridegroom) and humanity (bride) in a relationship of trust and devotion like that of a husband and wife in their bedchamber. This is a relationship based on unconditional love rather than fear, as is so often expressed in the orthodox need for atonement and salvation from sin.

Finally, the Gospel of Philip is unique in terms of its more inclusive interpretation of the Trinity. Rather than the orthodox Christian, all-male triad consisting of the Father, Son, and Holy Spirit, the author of Philip makes it clear in Passage 18 that the Holy Spirit is the feminine or maternal aspect of God: "Some say Mariam [Mary] was impregnated by the Sacred Spirit. They are confused, they know not what they say. Whenever was a female impregnated by a female?"

Here the author is referring to the fact that the word *spirit* in the ancient Semitic language that pre-dated the Old and New Testaments was of a feminine gender. What is so important about this interpretation of the "Holy Spirit" is that the Creator as a whole is both male and female: Father God and Mother Spirit. When it comes to the son in this particular Trinitarian arrangement, Jesus is seen as the product of a mystical union between the co-equal paternal and maternal aspects of the Divine. Although I am not one who believes in the existence of a triune God in the first place, I find the interpretation given by the author of the Gospel of Philip to be more inclusive and fair-minded than the comparatively more exclusive and narrow orthodox understanding of the Church's doctrine of the Trinity.

The Gospel of Mary

The third Gnostic text of special significance, according to Paterson Brown and Karen King, is the Gospel of Mary, written sometime during the early second century. As already mentioned, the existence of the Gospel of Mary came to light in the late nineteenth century in the form of a fragmentary fifth century copy written in Coptic. Two additional fragments in Greek were discovered in the twentieth century, though no complete copy has been found to date.[29] Despite the fact that very few fragments have been available for examination, they have yielded important information about the early Christian period in general and about Jesus and his relationship to the disciples in particular.

These fragments present a picture of Mary as the "apostle to the apostles" and close companion of Jesus in greater detail than that found in the Gospel of Philip. In addition, the Gospel of Mary recognizes the reality of God's spiritual presence within each of us and that it can be known and experienced directly and personally. In her book *The Gospel of Mary Magdala: Jesus and the First Woman Apostle*, King further elaborates on the enormous significance of this Gospel:

> This astonishingly brief narrative presents a radical interpretation of Jesus's teachings as a path to inner spiritual knowledge; it rejects his suffering and death as the path to eternal life; it exposes the erroneous view that Mary of Magdala was

a prostitute for what it is—a piece of theological fiction; it presents the most straightforward and convincing argument in any early Christian writing for the legitimacy of women's leadership; it offers a sharp critique of illegitimate power and a utopian vision of spiritual perfection; it challenges our rather romantic views about the harmony and unanimity of the first Christians; and it asks us to rethink the basis for church authority. All written in the name of a woman.[30]

Excerpts from King's translation of the Gospel of Mary are quite revealing in this and other respects. The following translation of a conversation—first between the risen Christ and the disciples and then among Mary, Peter, Andrew, and Levi—takes us well beyond the sixteen-hundred-year-old myth of a separation between Mary and the Twelve and between women and the Jesus movement, and beyond the idea of a doctrine-driven religion as a whole.[31] The risen Christ begins by addressing the assembled disciples and Mary: "Be on your guard that no one deceives you by saying, 'Look over here! or 'Look over there!' For the child of true Humanity exists within you. Follow it! Those who search for it will find it." And "Go then, preach the good news about the Realm. Do not lay down any rule beyond what I determined for you, nor promulgate law like the lawgiver, or else you might be dominated by it."

This statement, taken as a whole, seems prophetic in the sense that it warns against the great importance given to the various creeds and doctrines of orthodox Christianity since the fourth century. In many ways, Catholic and Protestant churches, as defined by their various "rules" of faith, sets of beliefs, denominational boundaries, and requirements for membership (and, in some cases, even for salvation), have seemed to "promulgate law like the lawgiver" over the centuries.

Returning to the Gospel of Mary narrative, we are told that after Jesus addresses the disciples he departs, causing them to feel great distress. After seeing Jesus crucified for preaching the "good news," the disciples rightly fear they could suffer the same fate. In the midst of their self-doubt, Mary attempts to reassure the Twelve: "Brothers and sisters, do not your hearts be irresolute. For his grace will be with you all and will shelter you." Peter then steps forward and makes a request: "Sister, we know that the Savior loved you more than all other women. Tell us the words of the Savior that you remember, the things which you know that we don't because we haven't heard them." Mary Magdalene then reveals to the disciples in great detail what Jesus taught her about the "ascent of the soul." Nevertheless, her lengthy explanation is not met with approval, and the disciple Andrew steps forward to challenge Mary's integrity: "Say what you will about the things she has said, but I do not believe that the Savior said these things, for indeed these teachings are strange ideas."

Despite Peter's initial interest in hearing what Mary has to say, he also reacts negatively by questioning whether she is worthy of being so favored by Jesus: "Did he then speak with a woman in private without our knowing about it? Are we to turn around and listen to her? Did he choose her over us?" Then Levi quickly comes forward in defense of Mary and challenges Peter: "Peter, you have always been a wrathful person … For if the Savior made her worthy, who are you then for your part to reject her?"

Whether this account is historically accurate or not, the underlying message is clear and important, both in this Gospel and in the Gospel of Philip: Mary Magdalene seems to have had the same authority and wisdom as any of the twelve apostles, granted to her by Jesus. What a hard pill to swallow for those early patriarchs of the Orthodox Church! Also, since the canonical gospels point to the fact that numerous women—such as Mary, mother of Jesus; Suzanna; Martha, sister of Lazarus; and Miriamne, sister of Philip—were important participants in Jesus's ministry, there is nothing to suggest that Jesus did not embrace gender equality overall. If true, that poses a serious challenge to the orthodox Christian and Jewish order of things as reflected in 1 Corinthians 14:33b–35: "The women should keep silence in the churches; for they are not permitted to speak, but should be subordinate, even as the law says." (While there is serious doubt among scholars that these were actually the words of Paul, it still reflects a general mind-set typical of that period, no matter who wrote them.) Unfortunately, this attitude toward women, as reflected in the Gospel of Mary and in the culture of Jesus's time, still lingers today within the more conservative Protestant churches in general and within the Catholic Church's priesthood in particular.

The Gospel of Thomas

In addition to the three Gospels already discussed, the Gospel of Thomas is perhaps the most important one in historical terms. It predates not only the Gospel of Truth, the Gospel of Philip, and the Gospel of Mary but also all four canonical Gospels of Mark, Matthew, Luke, and John. The text discovered at Nag Hammadi is a fourth century Coptic copy of the original Gospel of Thomas written in Greek before the death of the apostle James in 62 CE and before Mark, the earliest canonical Gospel, written around 70 CE. (The Nag Hammadi copy of Thomas is far more complete than the spare fragment written in Greek that was discovered in the late nineteenth century at the Egyptian site known as Oxyrhynchus.) Support for this conclusion is found in Thomas, Saying 12, which refers to Jesus's brother James in the present tense: "His disciples said to Jesus: 'We know you will leave us. Who will be our leader then?' Jesus responded: 'Wherever you are, turn to Jacob (James) the Just, for whose sake the sky and the earth came into being.'"[32]

In terms of format, Thomas contains about 150 sayings presumed to have been spoken by Jesus. About half of these are found in the Gospels of Mark, Matthew, and Luke, but not in John's Gospel. However, the sayings in Thomas are not contained within a larger narrative like the stories found in the synoptic Gospels. The Gospel of Thomas is actually a haphazard list of Jesus's sayings presented in no particular order, seemingly derived from oral rather than written sources. Although some of the sayings from Thomas do appear in the Synoptic Gospels, they do not appear in the same order as found in Thomas. Consequently, Harvard Divinity School Professor Helmut Koester believes that the Gospel of Thomas was one of the sources for the Synoptic Gospels rather than the other way around.[33]

In addition, none of the major Christian ideas associated with the Crucifixion and the Resurrection or even references to Jesus as the Messiah or Christ or the son of a virgin are found in the Gospel of Thomas.[34] Such omissions most likely point to the fact that the major Christian themes later found in the canonical gospels were still not fully developed.

But the Gospel of Thomas was not the only source available to the later writers of the canonical Gospels. Most New Testament scholars have, within the last thirty years, come to acknowledge that another collection of sayings, apparently more systematically organized than the Thomas collection, was written during the years before the emergence of the canonical Gospels. This second source, now lost, is known as Q or the Q Gospel. (Q comes from *quelle*, the German word for *source*.)

Biblical scholar John Kloppenberg's extensive research into the influential nature of the Q Gospel indicates that that there was an important difference between the Q Gospel and the Gospel of Thomas in terms of how Jesus is understood. For instance, the sayings of Q seem to claim that Jesus was an apocalyptic prophet who preached that the Kingdom of God would come in the near future and that one must repent before being allowed into the kingdom, while Thomas claims that the Kingdom of God exists on earth and in every person even though most people do not see or understand this truth.[35] Saying 3 illustrates this point when Jesus says:

If your leaders say to you, "Look! The Kingdom is in the sky!" then the birds will be there before you are. If they say the Kingdom is in the sea, then the fish will be there before you are. Rather, the Kingdom is within you and it is outside of you. When you understand yourselves you will be understood. And you will realize that you are Sons of the living Father. If you do not know yourselves, then you exist in poverty and you are that poverty.[36]

In his annotations for the book *The Gospel of Thomas: Annotated & Explained*, Stevan Davies makes the following crucial point with respect to Saying 3: "Being Sons of the Father is to be like Jesus himself, a status one does not attain anew but that one realizes one has always had."[37] The Gospel of Thomas asserts, therefore, that each person is capable of finding the divine truth within himself or herself and in the world at large. It is a message of hope that claims that God is within every human being, that we are all within God, and that no God-ordained separation exists. In other words, Thomas presents a panentheistic image of God in contrast with orthodox theism. To further emphasize this point, the message "seek and ye shall find" appears frequently throughout Thomas, as in Saying 2: "Jesus said: The seeker should not stop until he finds. When he does find, he will be disturbed. After having been disturbed, he will be astonished. Then he will reign over everything."[38]

This message contrasts with the Gospel of Q, which suggests perfection can be found only in heaven at some future time. Thomas implies the positive prospect of the growth and transformation of all things through active engagement with the world in loving service to others and through a continuous process of seeking and finding, since we have the God-given capacity to do so. In other words, it affirms the reality of an ongoing cosmic evolutionary process, in terms of both the world and each individual life.

This is not to say that suffering and loss can always be avoided in the process. In fact, among the many sayings of Jesus found in the Gospel of Thomas is the especially sobering Saying 16: "People think, perhaps, that I have come to throw peace upon the world. They don't know that I have come to throw disagreement upon the world, and fire, and sword, and struggle."[39] This saying indicates that Jesus understood the world enough to know that those who dare to change the status quo in search of truth and a more compassionate, just world are likely to suffer the hardships of resentment, alienation, or worse. The Jesus found in the Gospel of Thomas is not the passive victim or suffering servant often portrayed in some of today's church hymns and sermons. Instead, we meet the proactive revolutionary willing to stand up for truth against power.

The two visions represented by Thomas and Q largely led to the emergence of two contrasting streams of Christian thought that are expressed in varying degrees throughout the New Testament Gospels. One of these streams, emanating from Q, understood Jesus to be an apocalyptic prophet who pointed to the imminent coming of the kingdom of God. This train of thought is particularly evident in the Gospel of Mark, in the writings of Paul, and at various points in the Gospels of Matthew and Luke.[40]

The second stream is especially evident in the Gospel of John, where the apocalyptic image of Jesus is also noticeably absent. Here, the message is that the kingdom of God is already here and Jesus is understood to be a savior sent by God to enlighten the world, not unlike the way Jesus is presented in the Gospel of Thomas.[41] For instance, in John 1:3, we read, "All things were made through the word (logos, or the light)," and in Thomas, Saying 13, we read, "Jesus said to Thomas: I am not your teacher; you have drunk from and become intoxicated from the bubbling water that I poured out."[42] In both Gospels, Jesus is considered to be the divine light of wisdom that came into existence with the Creation and spiritually connects all things.[43]

The gospels of Thomas and John are also similar in the sense that both authors focus on what Jesus taught his disciples privately rather than dwelling on the various stories about Jesus, as the synoptic Gospel authors did. For example, the so-called farewell discourses of Jesus found in John 13-18 resemble the various secret sayings of Jesus found throughout Thomas.[44] In both cases, Jesus seems to reveal privileged information of a mystical nature to his closest associates.

However, despite these important connections between the authors of Thomas and John, there are also important differences between the two. While Thomas repeatedly teaches that every person has the divine capacity to seek and to know God, John insists that one must first believe that "Jesus is the Messiah, the Son of God, and that through believing, you may have life in his name" (John 20:31).

Although Thomas and John agree that the divine light is found in Jesus, John asserts that it resided *only in Jesus* rather than in every person since the Creation.[45] John holds that believing in Jesus is the key to salvation, whereas Thomas urges us in Saying 24 to seek beyond belief: "There is light within a man of light, and he lights up all of the world. If he is not alight there is darkness."[46] And in a recent translation of Saying 70, we read, "If you bring forth what is in you, what you bring forth will save you. If you do not bring forth what is in you, what you do not bring forth will destroy you."[47] What this saying implies is that discovering the divine light within one's self will illuminate the world, since, like Jesus, we are spiritual beings first and foremost.

This particular disagreement between the two Gospel writers appears to explain why John is the only New Testament Gospel in which the disciple Thomas is portrayed as the "doubter" (John 20:24-27). Unlike the other disciples in the story, Thomas refuses to believe in the Resurrection until confronted by the risen Christ. The attempt by the author of the

Gospel of John to discredit Thomas appears to have been a part of the overall bias against the Gospel of Thomas by the Orthodox Church and helps to explain why Thomas was relegated to obscurity along with the other Christian voices previously mentioned.[48]

In addition to what has already been said about the various differences and similarities among the Gospel of Thomas, the Gospel of Q, and the canonical gospels, Thomas provides a unique explanation of the transformational consequences to be expected by everyone who follows Jesus's urging to seek and to find. For instance, in the Gospel of Thomas, Saying 22, Jesus explains the nature of "Kingdom consciousness"—or what could also be called cosmic consciousness—to his disciples:

> Jesus saw infants being suckled. He said to his disciples: "These infants taking milk are like those who enter the Kingdom." His disciples asked him: "If we are infants will we enter the Kingdom?" Jesus responded: "When you make the two into one, and when you make the inside like the outside and the outside like the inside, and the upper like the lower and the lower like the upper, and thus make the male and the female the same, so that the male isn't male and the female isn't female. When you make an eye to replace an eye, and a hand to replace a hand, and a foot to replace a foot, and an image to replace an image, then you will enter the Kingdom."[49]

Here we find at least three important messages of a universal nature. First, Jesus uses the image of infants suckling at their mothers' breasts to illustrate the feminine and mothering aspects of God. Just as in the Gospel of Philip, Thomas here shows God not to be limited by one gender or the other and shows God's love for humanity to be as deep and abiding as the love between a mother and her child. This feminine characteristic is missing in the predominantly male image of God promoted by orthodox theism.

Second, Jesus describes the various revelations that come as a consequence of seeking and acquiring cosmic consciousness. Making the two into one, the inside like the outside, the upper like the lower, and the male like the female—all refer to the disappearance of these worldly dualistic concepts at the level of cosmic consciousness, the experience of oneness.

Third, when Jesus talks about the replacement of eyes, hands, feet, and so on, he refers to the physical transformation that takes place after having been immersed in the light of cosmic consciousness. Those who have had an otherworldly spiritual experience, such as the disciples in the midst of Pentecost, Paul on the road to Damascus, or the many individuals who have returned from near-death experiences, are often recognized as having been changed physically as well as spiritually—even to the point of acquiring miraculous healing powers and insights.[50]

In the final analysis, the significance of the Gospel of Thomas as an authentic revelation of the mystical nature of Jesus and the Gospel's important contribution to the overall history of Christianity, long obscured by the Orthodox Church, is finally being recognized. Perhaps Andrew Harvey, in his foreword to *The Gospel of Thomas: Annotated & Explained*, says it best: "In Jesus's astonishing, incandescent vision of the Kingdom in the Gospel of Thomas, humanity was shown what it could still achieve if only it woke up and realized the splendor of its divine secret identity." And:

> The Gospel of Thomas makes clear that Jesus discovered the alchemical secret of transformation that could have permanently altered world history, had it been implemented with the passion and on the scale that Jesus knew was possible. Its betrayal by the churches erected in Jesus's name has been an unmitigated disaster, one major reason for our contemporary catastrophe.[51]

THE CONDEMNED WRITINGS OF BISHOP ORIGEN

The story of the suppression of many dissident Christian voices during the formative years of the Orthodox Church, including the four we have already examined, would not be complete without also mentioning another early Christian scholar whose writings were not among those found at Nag Hammadi. He was the prominent third century theologian and church father Bishop Origen of Alexandria, Egypt. Origen was known as the first systematic theologian and philosopher of the Christian Church and one of the greatest biblical scholars of the early Christian period.[52]

According to the fourth century bishop Epiphanius, Origen wrote over a thousand highly influential works that included textural criticisms, scriptural explanations, and various theological commentaries.[53] Unlike many Gnostic Christians, he was a strict advocate of orthodox Christianity, particularly in his beliefs that the Church provided the only means of salvation and that the Bible was divinely inspired by God. Consequently, his theological positions always had a scriptural basis.

Nevertheless, some of Origen's views eventually proved to be too liberal for the more conservative church fathers during the last years of his life and in the years that followed his death in 254 CE, when the Church's orthodox dogmas became increasingly more rigid and entrenched. Origen's views, which eventually led him to be condemned as a heretic by the Fifth Ecumenical Council in 553 CE, do not seem so extreme today, at least not to those who consider themselves to be progressive Christians.[54] Among the many theological positions Origen held, there were four in particular that invited the wrath of the early polemicists. The first of these controversies arose over Origen's view regarding the relationship between Jesus and God the Father. In one of his best-known treatises, *On First Principles*, Origen stated his firm belief in the existence of a divine triad consisting of the Father, a purely spiritual mind without body; Christ the Son (Wisdom), the first emanation of the Father; and the Holy Spirit, which "proceeds from the Son and is related to Him as the Son is related to the Father."[55]

This hierarchical version of the Holy Trinity clearly differs from the co-equal Trinity of orthodox Christianity, since Origen considered the Son to be less than the Father and the Holy Spirit to be less than the Son. Nevertheless, he still accepted the idea that the power of each of the three divine entities exceeded that of all other beings created by God.[56] Even though he supported the idea of a Holy Trinity in general, he did not regard Jesus to be God incarnate. In other words, his position differed significantly from the decision eventually taken by the bishops who instituted the Church's early canon law at the Council of Nicea in 325. The official ruling from the council was that "the Son was True God, co-eternal with the Father and begotten from His same substance."[57]

The second disagreement centered on the issue of the resurrection of Jesus. Although Origen believed that Jesus did rise bodily from the tomb, he maintained that God transformed Jesus's body into an ethereal or spiritual body. Furthermore, he rejected the notion of a physical resurrection for any earthly bodies—that is, for human beings in general. Instead, Origen insisted that material bodies eventually die and are cast off in favor of an immaterial or spiritual form of existence.[58] So while accepting the pivotal importance of the resurrection of Jesus, Origen seemed to be saying that a physical rather than spiritual resurrection was not necessary to justify one's faith in the risen Christ. The Orthodox Church fathers, on the other hand, insisted on nothing less than the complete physical restoration of Jesus's body and that every believer in Jesus could look forward to a bodily resurrection.[59]

The third point of contention stemmed from Origen's belief in the Greek concept of *apocatastasis*, or the ultimate restoration and redemption of all beings through a divinely guided educational process that ultimately leads to reunion with God. He saw this as the culmination of a cooperative human/divine process wherein all souls would be "saved" over time, even the most evil, including the Devil himself.[60] Origen found support for this view in Paul's words in I Corinthians 15:28: "When all things are subject to him, then the Son himself will also be subjected to the one who put all things in subjection under him, so that God may be all in all." As a result of Origen's firm belief in the principle of apocatastasis, he rejected the orthodox notion of an ultimate separation of the "saved" from the eternally "damned." Instead, he interpreted salvation to mean enlightenment rather than a release from divine punishment.[61]

Furthermore, Origen strongly believed that ignorance is the cause of irrational and sinful acts, or the absence of the good, whereas the cultivation of reason embraces the good, which Origen considered to be God. In Origen's opinion, true freedom comes through the pursuit of reason, while evil brings only enslavement.[62] For this reason, he believed that punishment is not the way to overcome sinful behavior and evil. However, the more punitive, theistically minded leaders of the emerging Orthodox Church could not bring themselves to accept this more idealistic approach regarding the issue of sin. Origen's position on this subject is, in my view, strikingly similar to the more modern idea of an ongoing cosmic evolutionary process that governs the world and expands human consciousness over time. (More will be said about the whole issue of evolution in Chapters 9 and 10.)

The fourth issue that helped lead to Origen's eventual denouncement was his belief in the preexistence of souls. In his view, God's initial creation before the beginning of material existence was a collection of souls or "rational beings" that were given the freedom in the spiritual realm to endlessly contemplate God's divine wisdom and mysteries. Origen maintained that these souls grew weary of such contemplation and began to "fall away" from God. These preexistent souls then "fell" into three categories based on the level of their love for God.

According to Origen, the souls who came to love God the least became demons, whereas those whose love was diminished less became human souls clothed in physical bodies. The third category of souls, whose love for God remained stronger than the others', became angels. However, one soul in particular, whose love for God remained pure, became the Word (Logos) of God and became Jesus in human form.[63]

While Origen's theory of fallen preexistent souls could be questioned today for its rather rigid stratification, the basic idea of preexisting souls having eternal life before and after inhabiting human bodies not only has merit but has been confirmed by modern investigation into the phenomenon of reincarnation. (The whole subject of reincarnation will be examined later in Chapter 7.) As an otherwise orthodox Christian, Origen seems to have supported the concept of reincarnation even while opposing the idea of transmigration, which maintains that the soul may migrate from a human body to that of an animal.[64] Origen considered transmigration to be pointless if the purpose of the soul was to ascend to higher states of consciousness. He seems to leave no doubt about his belief in the reality of reincarnation in this excerpt from his *Against Celsus*—which he wrote in defense of Christianity:

> But we know that the soul, which is immaterial and invisible in its nature, exists in no material place. Accordingly, it at one time puts off one body which was necessary before, but which is no longer adequate in its changed state, and it exchanges it for a second; and at another time it assumes another in addition to the former, which is needed as a better covering, suited to the purer ethereal regions of heaven. When it comes into the world at birth, it casts off the integuments which it needed in the womb; and before doing this, it puts on another body suited for its life upon earth.[65]

Unfortunately, Origen's apparent endorsement of reincarnation was officially condemned and essentially removed from serious consideration by the Orthodox Church after the fourth century. The more conservative bishops would have seen the concept of the soul's progressing toward greater spiritual maturity through a series of multiple reincarnations as a diminishment of the Orthodox Church's power and authority over matters of salvation. Today, official Christendom still gives no serious consideration to reincarnation, despite its profound spiritual implications and mounting scientific evidence of its universal existence.

Despite all the stringent measures the early Orthodox Church leaders took to permanently ban the teachings and writings of the early Christians featured in this chapter, their efforts never completely succeeded. Perhaps Bishop Origen and the authors of the Gospel of Truth, the Gospel of Philip, the Gospel of Mary, and the Gospel of Thomas would be gratified to know their more inclusive recognitions of the feminine nature of God, the transcendent spiritual power of Jesus, the inseparable human/divine connection, the apostolic role of Mary Magdalene, the preexistence of souls, and the freedom of souls to reincarnate are at last being open-mindedly reexamined in the light of a new day. The forward vision of these early Christian mystics and teachers seems all the more prophetic when considering how the world has evolved scientifically as well as spiritually over the last sixteen hundred years. The nature of this evolution in human consciousness, or spiritual awakening, will now become the focus in Part 2.

PART 2

*Evidence for an Interconnected,
Evolving World*

CHAPTER 5

Our Divine Interconnection:
The Spiritual Dimensions of Quantum Physics

S ince the beginning of the twentieth century, discoveries in the field of quantum physics have increased our knowledge not only of the material aspects of the world and the universe but of the spiritual nature of our existence as well. Because of these discoveries and continuing research, we are beginning to see a growing confluence of science and spirituality. This increasing realization of the interconnection between science and spirituality signals a change from the rather materialistic and mechanistic ideas about the universe that scientists have generally held since at least the eighteenth century's Age of Enlightenment.

SCIENCE VERSUS RELIGION

The disciples of the Enlightenment attacked religion in general by claiming it promoted blind belief and superstition. They held "reason" in higher esteem than faith and even placed a "Goddess of Reason" in Paris's Notre Dame Cathedral.[1] On the other hand, before the Enlightenment, Catholic inquisitors waged a war of sorts against science when they charged Galileo with heresy for having agreed with Copernicus that the Earth revolves around the sun.

Even today, many Christian fundamentalists dismiss evolutionary theories and look to the Book of Genesis as the ultimate source of geological and zoological truths. Consequently, fundamentalists tend to divide the world into "believers" (themselves) and "unbelievers."[2] The bias against religion and spirituality continues within the scientific community as well. For instance, evolutionary biologist Richard Dawkins makes it clear in his recent book *The God Delusion* that science and religion are mutually exclusive and incompatible. His attacks on traditional religious assertions have been defended by scientists such as molecular biologist and geneticist James Watson and psychologist Steven Pinker.[3] Likewise, the late Carl Sagan seemed to rely heavily on the primary legitimacy of science in saying, "The Cosmos is all that is or ever was or ever will be."[4]

But as Albert Einstein famously said in 1940, "Science without religion is lame, religion without science is blind."[5] The truth is, science and religion are two sides of the same coin. They represent two ways of attempting to comprehend the mystery of God. Scientists attempt to describe the structure and operation of God's universe by objectively observing, measuring, and testing, whereas the various religions attempt to understand what it all *means*. Both contribute to the growth of human consciousness and a deeper understanding of life.

Our task in this chapter, then, is to examine the ways that some of the world's more progressive-minded physicists have been leading us to a better understanding of the spiritual dimensions of our physical existence and to consider some of the social and spiritual implications of this development. Perhaps the best way to understand the true revolutionary nature of modern quantum physics is to begin by considering the early history of physics as a distinct field of science.

THE ADVENT OF 'CLASSICAL PHYSICS' AND ITS MATERIALISTIC VIEW OF REALITY

From 1687, when Isaac Newton's mathematic observations of the natural world and universe appeared in his book *Mathematic Principles of Natural Philosophy*, until the early 1900s, his explanations of how large-scale things move in relation to each other were largely accepted as truth and formed the field of science known as "classical physics."[6] According to Newton and his followers, the universe was composed of separate, independent elements.

Even before Newton had fully developed his theories regarding motion, the influential French philosopher Rene Descartes claimed that the human mind was separate from the physical body. He regarded the body as a marvelously complex machine operating within a strictly mechanical, material universe. In his opinion, the human mind was only capable of observing the mechanical workings of a universe already created. Both Newton and Descartes essentially separated God and life itself from the world of matter.[7]

This objective and rather soulless interpretation of the universe was eventually buttressed by Darwin's theory of evolution. From a materialistic perspective, Darwin essentially viewed the universe as an accidental happening in which life is random, predatory, and solitary. Darwin's idea that life on Earth has evolved from a series of random genetic mutations in the midst of an ongoing struggle for survival contributed further to the acceptance of scientific materialism as the conventional wisdom.[8] When applied beyond the parameters of biology, scientific materialism has led to the widespread assumption that our purpose as human beings is to survive by being the fittest in a competitive eat-or-be-eaten world. In such a world there is a tendency to exclude or minimize the need to share and to place little or no value on interdependence and cooperation.

For instance, in today's corporate and political worlds, competition most often trumps human compassion and a moral obligation to the "least of these." Furthermore, if being the best is thought to enhance one's chances of survival, it becomes more likely that one will decide to diminish—if not eliminate—those people and things deemed to be obstacles in the quest for superiority. While the prime example was Nazi Germany's attempt to produce a "super race" by "cleansing" the world of those it considered to be inferior, ethnic cleansing has occurred more recently in places such as East Africa and the Middle East. So while the theories of Descartes, Newton, and Darwin were instructive on some levels, they did not lead to a better understanding of the spiritual nature of who we really are and how we are all spiritually interconnected with one another and the universe at large.

CHALLENGES TO SCIENTIFIC MATERIALISM AND THE DISCOVERY OF A LIVING, INTERCONNECTED UNIVERSE

The materialistic assumption that the universe and the world are composed of separate entities such as humans and animals, matter and space, space and time, and so on actually met with challenges as early as the late nineteenth century. Experiments that James Clerk Maxwell and Michael Faraday conducted in 1867 led them to believe that some forces could not be explained by Newton's approach to physics.[9] They found that the universe consists of fields of energy that affect one another, posing the first challenge to Newton's concept of the universe as a massive mechanical system in which space and time are absolute.

Then in 1905, when Albert Einstein discovered that time is relative and cannot be separated from space as proposed by Newton, our whole understanding of the universe changed. In fact, Einstein considered time to be the fourth dimension—a central feature of his theory of relativity. His new view of the world led to the establishment of the field of physics now known as relativity physics.[10]

Five years earlier, however, physicist Max Planck had introduced another theory that has had even more radical long-term ramifications. Planck became convinced that the world, at its most basic subatomic level, consists of countless emissions of energy called "quanta" and that they appear as "particles" of light called photons.[11] He came to conclude, in 1944, that matter does not exist as an absolute and independent thing, but only as a probability:

> As a man who has devoted his whole life to the most clear-headed science, to the study of matter, I can tell you as a result of my research about atoms this much: There is no matter as such. All matter originates and exists only by virtue of a force which brings the particle of an atom to vibration and holds this most minute solar system of the atom together. We must assume behind this force the existence of a conscious and intelligent mind. This mind is the matrix of all matter.[12]

As a result of Planck's revolutionary findings, a new approach to physics known as quantum physics was introduced. Subsequent quantum research revealed that subatomic light particles can also, at times, become "waves" of light energy. This led quantum physicist Werner Heisenberg to introduce what he called the "uncertainty principle" in 1927. He recognized that since the energy level of any particular particle constantly changes, it is impossible to establish a specific reliable level of energy. He also found that no subatomic particle is completely stationary, since it is always in motion to some degree. So, like Planck, Heisenberg discovered that solid objects actually consist of the same constantly moving subatomic light particles (or waves) that exist in space.[13] Investigative journalist, Lynne McTaggart, who is one of the most important spokespersons on the subjects of consciousness, quantum physics, and modern medicine, describes it in spiritual terms: "To the religious or the mystic, it is science proving the miraculous. What quantum calculations show is that we and our universe live and breathe in what amounts to a sea of motion—a quantum sea of light."[14]

THE COMMONALITY OF MATTER, SPACE, AND THE UNIVERSE

Since the entire physical universe exists in the form of different vibrations of energy and what is normally considered to be solid matter is not solid at all at the quantum (subatomic) level, space is actually not empty. Space is something rather than nothing. We now know that space and matter are both composed of electromagnetic energy known as photons or light energy. With this in mind, it is possible to conclude that at the subatomic level, space and matter (including all human life) are simply frequency variations of the same electromagnetic energy.

A more recent generation of physicists in the 1960s offered still another explanation of how the universe operates called string theory physics. String theory served to connect all the previous theories concerning space, time, and electromagnetic energy. Proponents of the theory understood the universe to be a system of tiny vibrating strings of quantum energy, all connected and interwoven as in an infinitely expansive cosmic fabric. String theory could be seen as a further refinement and expansion of quantum physics, but the density and rate of vibration of light-energy particles remained as the common determining factor. The existence of such energy in every aspect of the universe, including life itself, has been described by quantum physicists as a "field" or "web" that connects everything.[15] Former aerospace computer-system designer Greg Braden puts it this way: "The key is that the energy connecting everything in the universe is also part of what it connects!"[16]

At our most fundamental level, we are all packets of quantum energy that constantly communicate with other quanta within the energy field known as the universe. Human perception essentially happens as a result of the exchange of energy between the subatomic particles of our brains and the universal sea of quantum energy. However, McTaggart again presents from a spiritual perspective what is especially important about discoveries made by modern quantum physicists in recent years:

> Through scientific experiment they'd demonstrated that there may be such a thing as a life force flowing through the universe—what has variously been called collective consciousness or, as theologians have termed it, the Holy Spirit. They provided a plausible explanation of all those areas that over the centuries mankind has had faith in but no solid evidence of or adequate accounting for, from the effectiveness of alternative medicine and even prayer to life after death. They offered us, in a sense, a science of religion. Unlike the worldview of Newton and Darwin, theirs was a vision that was life-enhancing. These were ideas that could empower us, with their implication of order and control. We were not simply accidents of nature. There was purpose and unity to our world and our place within it, and we had an important say in it. What we did and thought mattered—indeed was critical in creating our world.[17]

EXPERIMENTS WITH SUBATOMIC PARTICLES AND THEIR SPIRITUAL IMPLICATIONS

At the University of Geneva in Switzerland in 1997, an experiment was conducted on the particles of light known as photons. Using sophisticated equipment designed especially for this experiment, the scientists were able to split a single photon into separate but identical particles of light. They then fired both particles in opposite directions using fiber-optic pathways that reached out from the laboratory for a distance of seven miles each way for a total separation distance of fourteen miles.

When the particles reached the end of their respective pathways, they were forced to choose between two possible routes that were identical in each case. Interestingly enough, both particles made the same exact choices at the same time. What is even more fascinating is that the same thing occurred in each of several succeeding experiments. In other words, no variations occurred in the photons' behavior even though the photons were separated and presumably could not communicate with one another. Since they acted as if they were still connected as one, the scientists called it "quantum entanglement." Equally interesting was the discovery that when twin photons are spatially separated and one is changed in a certain way, the other photon changes in the same way instantaneously.

What these experiments clearly demonstrated was that physical objects in the visible world are not separate and independent as previously thought, at least not at the subatomic level. Likewise, in subsequent experiments, it became clear that this "quantum entanglement" exists throughout the universe. Braden refers to this apparent universal quantum entanglement as a "Divine Matrix," meaning that its web-like structure is governed by intelligence and purpose.[18]

Today most mainstream scientists believe this universal web of intelligent energy originated between thirteen and twenty billion years ago in a gigantic explosion that astronomer Fred Hoyle called "the big bang" in 1951. According to this theory, just before the big bang occurred, the entire universe was compressed into a pea-size ball that was several times hotter than our sun is today. It is estimated that the universe, in this minutely compressed state, would have had a temperature of about eighteen billion million million million degrees Fahrenheit. Shortly after the greatest explosion ever known occurred, scientists believe that the temperature may have cooled to a mere eighteen billion degrees.

Scientists generally agree that the force of the big bang spread in all directions, establishing an eternal pattern or interconnected web that continues to expand out across the cosmos today as the true substance of the universe.[19]

The relationship between this theory of the origin of the universe and the behavior of the two parts of a photon split apart in the Geneva experiment is especially important if we are to understand the true nature of the Divine Matrix and life itself. Originally, everything in the universe was physically joined, and then all its particles seemingly became separated by increasing amounts of space. Nevertheless, as we are discovering, all particles of the universe remain connected regardless of the amount of space they occupy. The reality of quantum entanglement points to the inevitable conclusion that everything is joined even though things may appear to be physically separated. Not only is everything connected by energy, but *everything is energy*.

In addition to the revolutionary ramifications of quantum entanglement that have come about as a result of the Geneva split-photon experiments, there are other equally amazing things that we have learned about the nature of the Divine Matrix. Various experiments that were conducted from 1993 to 2000 have further expanded our understanding of human consciousness as a crucial element in God's eternal creative process.

RESEARCHING THE POWER OF HUMAN CONSCIOUSNESS

The 'DNA Phantom Effect'

The first was a report on the research completed in 1995 by quantum biologist Vladimir Poponin and his colleague Peter Gariaev from the Russian Academy of Sciences. Their findings seemed to show that because of quantum entanglement, the energy field (the Divine Matrix) enables human DNA to have a direct effect on the physical world. They referred to this phenomenon as the "DNA Phantom Effect."[20]

The purpose of their experiment was to test the behavior of DNA on the photons that are found everywhere at the subatomic level. This was done by first removing all the air from a specially prepared tube to create a vacuum. Conventional wisdom would have assumed that the tube was truly empty, but the sophisticated equipment they were using clearly indicated the presence of photons within the vacuum. In addition to being located within the tube, the photons appeared to be distributed everywhere within the tube's space in a haphazard, random way.

The next step involved placing samples of DNA inside the tightly sealed tube. As a consequence, the particles of light energy suddenly arranged themselves in a different way. Conventional physics provided no answers for this remarkable phenomenon. Even more amazing was the fact that when the DNA samples were removed from the tube, the light particles remained in their newly ordered state, as if the DNA were still present in the tube.

The scientists were left wondering what had actually affected the photons and whether the DNA and light particles were actually connected even when they were no longer together in the vacuum tube. After getting the same results in further testing, the researchers had to conclude that the DNA and light particles were, in fact, connected by a new energetically responsive field.[21] The implications of these findings are profound and far-reaching: The experiments essentially proved that each of us directly affects the world we live in since we are all a part of a universal, intelligently responsive universal energy field that Braden refers to as the Divine Matrix. If, at the subatomic level of pure energy, there is no such thing as a separation of entities, then human intention—what we think, say, and do—is energy that affects and influences everything else in existence, either directly or indirectly depending on the focus of the intention.

Effect of Human Emotion on Human Cells

In another experiment conducted in the 1990s, scientists working with the U.S. Army decided to find out whether human emotions can continue to have an effect on living human cells even when those cells are removed from the body. The second goal was to determine how different types of emotions expressed by the donor might affect the same cells.

The first step in the experiment was to collect DNA from a volunteer's mouth before taking it to another room in the same building. The DNA was then prepared in such a way that it could be measured electrically if and when it responded to the emotions of the donor, who was situated in another location. The final step involved showing the volunteer a variety of video images intended to stimulate different emotional responses within the body.

What amazed the experimenters was that the donor's cells and the DNA registered simultaneous electrical responses to the donor's emotional changes and to the same degree. In effect, the DNA acted as if it were still joined to the donor's body. Later studies of this type involved much greater distances, up to 350 miles. In such cases, an atomic clock gauged the cell's responses. In every case, no time elapsed between the emotion and the cell's response—the responses were instantaneous despite the great distances. According to one of the investigators, "There is no place where one's body actually ends and no place where it begins."[22]

In Braden's view, the most revolutionary implication of this experiment is that the whole issue of having energy travel from one point (donor) to another (donor's DNA) would seem to be irrelevant. It was apparent that the donor's emotions were already present in the DNA, so distance was of no consequence. In addition, one of the most basic questions raised by the experiments centers on the issue of organ donations. If a living organ is placed in another person's body, do the organ donor and recipient remain connected to each other? If so, in what ways and to what degree? In this case, researchers seem to agree that the quality of that connection depends on how conscious one or both of the individuals are of its existence. An energy field links not only human tissues but human beings with all other living things, so emotional influences are limitless.[23]

The Effect of Human Thought on Other Living Things

In 1966, before the Army experiment revealed the human emotion/ DNA connection, an event occurred that proved other living forms, such as plants, respond to human emotions as well. Dr. Cleve Backster, a pioneer in the field of biocommunication, made a discovery that shaped his subsequent career as a biocommunication scientist.[24]

On a day when Backster was in his office, he chose to water his dracaena plant and then decided, on the spur of the moment, to try to measure the rate of moisture as it worked its way up through the plant stems and leaves. He did this by attaching the end of a leaf to a polygraph machine he had been using to test human subjects. He knew that an upward movement of the ink tracing on the polygraph chart would indicate an increase in the leaf's electrical conductivity caused by a change in the leaf's moisture content.

He was surprised to find that the plant leaf tracing trended downward, which, in the case of human subjects, would indicate some element of resistance. Soon thereafter, the tracing showed movement similar to those of human subjects, possibly revealing some fear of detection. Since the plant was showing human-like reactions, he decided to see if the plant was capable of responding to other, more aggressive human emotions and thoughts. He thought about getting a match so that he could burn the leaf.

At the time, no one else was in his office and the plant was about fifteen feet away. Precisely at the moment Backster had an image of a burning leaf in his mind, the polygraph recording pen jumped almost to the top of the chart. At that particular instant, no match had been lighted and no match was in Backster's hand. Likewise, no words had been spoken and no part of the plant leaf had been touched. Nevertheless, the leaf with the attached electrode showed a dramatic, even wild reaction to nothing more than a person's intention to do something to it![25]

After this initial event, he decided to design his experiments in ways that would prevent human intervention as a possible influencing factor. He devised a copper-screen cage to shield the plants from electromagnetic interference and even used grounded, lead-lined boxes for this purpose. As an added precaution, he avoided overplanning the subject-response arrangement in order to ensure spontaneous biocommunication. To this end, he decided to see if certain plants would respond to the natural deaths of brine shrimp because of their unusually short life span and placed them in a separate room far away from the plants.[26] Most of the twenty-one charts produced by virtue of the experiment proved that the plants actually registered a stress reaction to the death of brine shrimp. These findings were subsequently published in the *International Journal of Parapsychology* (Volume 10, winter 1968) in an article titled "Evidence of a Primary Perception in Plant Life."[27]

The Human Heart as a Source of Human Feeling and Emotion

Another experiment of great importance was conducted by researchers at the Institute of HeartMath, an internationally recognized research and education organization whose mission is "to help establish heart-based living and global coherence by inspiring people to connect with the intelligence and guidance of their own hearts."[28] Toward this end, research conducted by the IHM has led to a greater understanding of heart-brain interactions. From 1992 to 1995, the institute focused its research on the heart as the possible source of human emotion, in contrast with modern science's long-standing assumption that the heart is not "intelligent" in this way.[29] As a result of their extensive research, the IHM determined that the heart actually does communicate with the body and the brain in at least the following four ways:

It sends neurological information to the brain and other parts of the body.

It sends energy in the form of blood-pressure waves as indicated by pulse.

It communicates on a biochemical level through the release of a hormone known as atrial peptide that inhibits the release of other stress hormones.

It communicates electromagnetically, as indicated by the standard EKG. What is especially important here is that the heart's electromagnetic signals are not only noticeable within the body but can be measured in the space surrounding the body in a doughnut-shaped field of energy. This measurable field surrounds the heart and radiates in all directions beyond the body up to a maximum distance of about ten feet.[30]

The IHM experiments involved the isolation of human DNA in a glass beaker before exposing the DNA to a particular form of human feeling known as "coherent emotion." This type of emotion is created through special self-management practices that calm the mind while focusing one's attention in a positive way on the heart area. After performing a series of tests in this way, scientists analyzed the DNA samples both visually and chemically in order to determine what changes, if any, occurred as a direct result of the projected coherent emotions. The researchers discovered that human emotions actually caused the DNA samples to physically change their shape by winding up or unwinding. According to Braden, the implications of these experiments were truly revolutionary:

> We've been conditioned to believe that the state of the DNA in our body is a given. Contemporary thinking suggests that it's a fixed quantity—we "get what we get" when we're born—and with the exception of drugs, chemicals, and electrical fields, our DNA doesn't change in response to anything that we can do in our lives. But this experiment shows us that nothing could be further from the truth.[31]

THE BROADER IMPLICATIONS OF UNIVERSAL BIOCOMMUNICATION

As we have seen, the experiments conducted by Poponin and Gariaev, the U.S. Army, Dr. Cleve Backster, and scientists at the Institute of HeartMath all prove that our thoughts and emotions significantly affect the DNA within our bodies as well as everything around us and throughout the universe. In other words, universal biocommunication exists 1) because of a so-called matrix, or energy field, that connects any one thing with all things, and 2) because our DNA gives us access to this connective field of energy.[32] The conclusion that this seemingly unlimited connective field of energy is divinely intelligent simply confirms Max Planck's views mentioned earlier.

If, as these experiments show us, we are able to affect our world in tangible terms, both individually and collectively through conscious intention, we are not the wretched, hopeless souls that the orthodox Christian doctrines of original sin and the atonement have led us to believe we are. Unless, of course, we choose to be. Far from being detached observers of a divine universal creative process, we are central participants in it. In fact, it has been said that we are "co-creators" with God. All human beings, connected as we are, have the capacity to make God's peace on Earth a reality. When we will reach a level of spiritual maturity that will make that possible is still an open question, but it will occur—that is why we are here.

THE POSSIBLE HOLOGRAPHIC NATURE OF THE DIVINE MATRIX

Along with what we have learned from quantum physicists and bio-communication researchers about the existence of a universal energy field over the last one hundred years, a new, even more revolutionary model of the universe has emerged. A number of leading scientists are now convinced that the Divine Matrix is actually holographic. But before getting into the specifics of how this is possible and what it means from a spiritual standpoint, we will look at what a hologram is, how it functions, and how this remarkable technology began.

In basic terms, a hologram is produced with the aid of a laser beam that produces coherent light. Unlike the normal white light we're accustomed to from standard lighting, which contains light waves of varying sizes that bend differently when projected through a prism, a laser beam contains light waves that are equal in size and bend the same way. To produce a hologram, a laser beam must be split into two separate beams with the help of a plate known as a beam splitter. If the beam-splitter plate is placed at the correct angle in reference to the laser, it accomplishes two things.

The first of the two split laser beams is directed to the object that is to be photographed, where the image of the object is then "bounced" toward a holographic emulsion plate. Before the laser beam reaches the object, it passes through a diffusing lens, which spreads the beam into waves much like the ripples one sees after dropping a pebble into water.

In the meantime, the second split laser beam passes straight through the beam splitter, where it is then deflected by the first of two mirrors.

After striking the second mirror, it is directed to the same holographic emulsion plate that received the image of the object. Before arriving at the holographic plate, however, the second beam also passes through a diffusing lens.

The net effect is that the two split laser beams (after being diffused) collide with one another as they arrive at the holographic plate. This creates an "interference pattern" that is recorded on the holographic plate.

Again, the pebble-in-the-water analogy is useful. For instance, when two pebbles are dropped into a pond, ripples radiate outward from both spots where the pebbles enter the water. The two ripples cross through each other, thereby causing an "interference pattern"—much like the interference pattern created on the holographic plate by the two diffused split laser beams as they cross through each other. Once the interference pattern is recorded on film, a three-dimensional image of the original object will appear if a laser beam or other bright light source is directed through the film.[33] But one of the most important aspects of holography is that any part of the total image field captured on the holographic emulsion plate contains everything in the field. In other words, the entire image of the object is found at any and every point on the holographic emulsion plate.[34]

The science of holography actually began in 1947, when Dennis Gabor, a Hungarian electrical engineer, developed the basic operating procedures to produce a holographic image. Eventually, in 1971, Gabor was awarded a Nobel Prize for his invention. However, holography as a light-optical technique did not come into its own as a tool with wide applications until 1960, when the laser was developed at Hughes Research Laboratories in California. Soon after, the first practical hologram to record 3D objects was produced.[35] But the hologram, with all its potential for practical uses, was also soon recognized as having far greater implications. It held the key to achieving a greater understanding of the relationship between the physical and spiritual realms and to the nature of the universe as a whole—that is, the concept of a holographic universe.

Perhaps the two most important individuals responsible for presenting the case for a holographic universe were Karl Pribram, a neurophysiologist at Stanford University, and David Bohm, one of the world's most highly respected quantum physicists, from the University of London. Interestingly enough, both researchers independently arrived at the same conclusion in the mid-1960s while working in two different fields with different goals. Both men had been dissatisfied with the inadequate explanations offered by the standard theories of their respective fields as they applied to certain paranormal and mystical experiences.[36]

KARL PRIBRAM'S HOLOGRAPHIC THEORY OF THE BRAIN

As a neurophysiologist, Pribram came to doubt the widespread scientific assumption that memories are localized in the brain. In the mid-1940s, most scientists believed that every memory a person has is stored at a specific site in the brain cells. This assumption resulted from experiments conducted in the 1920s by neurosurgeon Wilder Penfield. Penfield had discovered that when he electrically stimulated the temporal lobes of a fully conscious patient's brain, his patient was immediately able to re-experience a variety of episodes from his past in great detail. Based on these experiments and subsequent scientific papers, Penfield convinced the scientific community that specific memory traces called "engrams" are located within the brain and that it would be only a matter of time before certain neurons or molecules were identified as the engrams in question.[37]

However, Pribram's doubts about Penfield's theory were confirmed when he began working with the famed neuropsychologist Karl Lashley at the Yerkes Laboratory of Primate Biology in Orange Park, Florida, in the 1940s. Lashley had been searching for the particular parts of the brain that are responsible for memory, but his experiments with rats led him, as well as Pribram, to conclude that memories are not located at particular sites in the brain. Instead, they both became convinced that memories are somehow distributed throughout the electromagnetic fields of the brain.[38]

Nevertheless, Pribram remained at a loss as to how and why this occurred—that is, until he came across an article in *Scientific American* in the mid-1960s that described the development of the first hologram. In Pribram's opinion, the hologram provided the best explanation for the phenomenon of memory distribution throughout the brain. The key fact, as said earlier, was that the complete image of the recorded object is contained within any fragment of the holographic film. Given this reality, Pribram thought it was reasonable to assume that "every part of the brain contains all the information necessary to recall a whole memory."[39]

The Brain's Holographic Memory

Since that time, it has become even more evident that Pribram's theory of a holographic brain has merit. While researchers generally agreed that the human brain must store about 280 quintillion bits of information over the course of an average lifetime, they were unable to explain how the brain could do this—that is, until the theory of a holographic brain was applied.[40] As we have seen, a hologram is capable of storing immense amounts of information at any particular location on an exposed piece of holographic film. Ordinarily when a laser beam strikes the holographic film, an image of the originally recorded object is revealed. However, it is possible to record different images on the same film by adjusting the angle of the laser beam each time. As a consequence, these different images can be retrieved by redirecting the laser beam on the exposed film at the various angles originally used to record the images. Furthermore, it has been determined that the amount of information contained in as many as fifty Bibles could be stored in just a one-inch-square piece of holographic film![41] Since directing a laser beam at a certain angle on a section of holographic film is much the same as our act of seeing certain objects in the world around us, Pribram's early work has convinced many in the scientific community that our abilities to recall (or forget), associate certain sensations with past events, and recognize familiar things all stem from directing our sight at a particular angle on our holographic brain.[42]

Vision as a Holographic Process

In Pribram's opinion, vision itself can be considered to be a holographic process. Once again, Lashley's experiments with rats seemed to point to this possibility. He found that the removal of the visual centers of the rats' brains—even as much as 90 percent of the visual cortex—did not result in blindness. The surgically altered rats continued to perform tasks that called for complex visual skills. This would be comparable to a theater audience's being able to successfully view a movie even with 90 percent of the screen missing.[43]

This flies in the face of the long-standing assumption within the scientific community that there is a one-to-one relationship between what the eye sees and the way the image is comprehended in the brain. The common assumption among scientists was that when we see an object, our visual cortex forms a photographic image of the object on its surface and that damaging the visual cortex in the manner of these early experiments would make this impossible. But after seven more years of experimenting with monkeys, Pribram was able to document that this was not true. He also knew that under normal circumstances, when an electrical message reaches the end of any of the neuron branches of the brain, it radiates outward like the ripples on the surface of water.[44]

Given the fact that millions of neurons form a dense network in the brain, the expanding ripples of electricity radiating from many neuron branches at once will crisscross one another and produce an endless variety of interference patterns such as those that create holographic images.[45] In short, Pribram provided a plausible explanation of the holographic nature of the human brain.

The Brain as a Frequency Analyzer

In the late 1970s, further evidence suggested that our visual system operates much like a frequency analyzer used in a television set. For instance, a TV camera typically converts the image of an object into electromagnetic frequencies before delivering them to a TV set. The TV set's frequency analyzer then converts the frequencies back into the original image. Experiments aimed at determining how human brain cells in the visual cortex respond to simple wave forms (comparable to the electromagnetic frequencies of a TV camera) proved that these brain cells do, in fact, convert such wave forms into recognizable images.[46] Once again, this is essentially the same process associated with holography.

The similarity between the activity of a TV frequency analyzer and the ability of human brain cells to convert wave forms into recognizable images opened up an even more radical possibility, according to Pribram. If the objects we recognize and touch in the world around us are, in reality, a virtual "soup" of wave forms converted by the frequency-analyzing function of our brains into objective reality, then is the real world what we see, or is what we see actually an illusion? Does consciousness originate in the brain, or is consciousness instead the result of the brain's ability to convert the wave forms of a nonlocal "collective consciousness" (Divine Matrix) existing everywhere into meaningful thoughts and images? In the midst of considering these possibilities,

Pribram became aware of the quantum physicist David Bohm's claims that the entire universe is a hologram.

DAVID BOHM'S THEORY OF A HOLOGRAPHIC UNIVERSE

As a quantum physicist, Bohm already knew that the basic ingredients or "building blocks" of the entire universe are quanta (countless electrons) and that quanta appear to exist only when they are observed, as mentioned earlier. He was also aware that when an electron is not being observed it is a wave, hence the scientific term *wave particle*. Danish physicist Niels Bohr was also aware of the mysterious behavior of quanta, but while Bohr tended to believe that quantum theory was the final explanation and that there was no deeper reality beyond the subatomic world, Bohm was not convinced this was true.[47] Instead, he remained satisfied that electrons actually do exist when not being observed. The problem was that he could not demonstrate how this could be so.

While working on his doctorate in the 1940s, Bohm experimented with gases containing heavy concentrations of electrons and positive ions known as plasmas. He was surprised to find that despite the seemingly random movements of each of the electrons, the effects that all the electrons produced collectively were organized, rather than random in nature. It seemed that all the electrons were working in concert and that each individual electron knew what all the others were doing.

These initial experiments strengthened Bohm's belief that there was, in fact, a level of reality beyond the subatomic level. In the 1950s he pushed for the existence of a new field of physics he called "quantum potential" for the purpose of exploring this deeper sub-quantum level of reality.[48] While most physicists remained convinced that Bohr's theories were unassailable, Bohm remained convinced that particles do not randomly interact but that their activity is based on information about the entire environment provided by an intelligently guided, quantum interconnectedness that exists throughout the cosmos.

In 1959, Bohm and fellow researcher Yakir Aharonov found that in some instances, electrons seem to be aware of nearby magnetic fields despite the fact that the electrons are moving in some areas of space where the field strength is zero.[49] Then in 1982, a research team in Paris organized by French physicist Alain Aspect conducted an experiment aimed at proving quantum interconnectedness. The results showed that widely separated subatomic particles can communicate instantaneously in ways not governed by the speed of light.[50] Buttressed by Aspect's experiments, Bohm couldn't help but conclude that reality, in the final analysis, cannot be reduced simply to particles and waves.

The 'Implicate' and 'Explicate' Orders of a Holographic Universe

As a consequence of Aspect's experiments, Bohm promoted a more holistic concept of the universe that amounted to a state of complete universal wholeness he called the "implicate order."[51] Bohm considered the physical world, by contrast, to be the "explicate order" that is derived from the implicate, or nonphysical, order. He considered the explicate order to be an "unfolding" of the implicate order, and the implicate order to be an "enfoldment" (folding into) of the explicate order.[52]

He became confident that his theory about the interconnection between the two orders had merit after seeing what he considered to be a simple demonstration of this fundamental interconnection on a television program in the 1960s. The demonstration involved the use of two concentric glass cylinders with a space between them that was filled with glycerin. After a drop of ink was placed in the glycerin and the outer cylinder was turned clockwise, the droplet became a thin line before disappearing altogether as the cylinder continued to turn. When the outside cylinder was turned back in the opposite direction, however, the thread-like line of ink reappeared and reformed as a droplet once again. Essentially, what happened was that the drop of ink was enfolded into the glycerin to start with and then unfolded from the glycerin after the direction of the outer cylinder was reversed.[53]

This provided the evidence Bohm needed to prove his claim that the whole organizes the parts, as opposed to the conventional scientific notion that a whole results from the interaction of its parts. As far as Bohm was concerned, wholeness was what governed reality. As an extension of this idea of the supremacy of wholeness, Bohm could claim that reality cannot be reduced simply to the states of either order or disorder. Instead, he considered order to be a relative term, which is to say that reality consists of different degrees of order. To further illustrate this point, he suggested that all the objects and events that are thought to be separated from one another in the visible, or explicate, world we live in are actually "subtotalities" unfolded from a "deeper, implicate order of unbroken wholeness."[54]

The analogy he used was that of a stream or narrow river in which one often sees swirls, ripples, and waves as distinct-but-temporary events and structures that cannot, in the end, be separated from each other or the body of water from which they emerged. If the ripples could be thought of as the explicate unfoldments of the implicate wholeness of the river, the river could be considered the implicate order into which the surface disturbances will inevitably enfold. In effect, the constant flow of enfoldments and unfoldments constitute an undivided wholeness.[55]

Bohm settled on the hologram as the ultimate metaphor to explain how the implicate and explicate orders relate to the world, the universe, and ourselves. Just as with the earlier example of the glycerin, the interference pattern recorded on holographic film contains a hidden, enfolded order that unfolds as a three-dimensional image of an object when illuminated. Bohm further suggested that the entire universe is essentially a limitless hologram, or "holomovement," as he called it.[56] He viewed our physical world of seemingly solid objects as an unfoldment of the implicate order that Braden refers to as the Divine Matrix, or Holy Spirit.

To put it another way, our world and everything in it is a living organism consisting of subatomic particles that continually unfold from and enfold back into the implicate order. It is the rate of vibration of subatomic particles and waves that determines the degree of solidity and stability of physical objects. Solid matter forms (unfolds) as the vibration of subatomic particles slows and congeals.

But Bohm's theory of a holographic universe with its implicate and explicate orders did not concern just the nature of matter. He also saw the implicate order as the source of all life and consciousness. Like Pribram, Bohm thought an individual's consciousness is expressed in words that are an unfolding of meaning initially enfolded in thought.[57] Bohm went on to conclude that the entire holographic cosmic process amounts to a "movement of meaning" and that inanimate as well as animate matter ultimately consists of particles and waves that are affected by the same intelligent force or responsive field.[58] From his perspective, there is no such thing as unintelligent matter. He believed instead that there is a "protointelligence" in matter that enables a continuous, universal evolutionary process to occur.[59] Bohm essentially confirmed Planck's earlier proposition that there is a conscious and intelligent mind that is the "matrix of all matter."

The Possible Coexistence of the Past, Present, and Future

Bohm pointed as well to the equally important possibility of a holographic universe. Since every part of a hologram contains the image of the whole and, in a holographic universe, every part of the universe contains (enfolds) the whole, then the past, present, and future could very well coexist.[60] Assuming this to be true, then, it is possible that countless futures already exist for each of us, subject to change based on our thoughts and actions freely chosen at any moment.

Here I'm reminded of words allegedly spoken by God in Neale Donald Walsch's book *Home With God: In a Life That Never Ends*: "Time is not going anywhere. Time is 'in place' right now. It is static, stable, stationary. It is always there, right where it is. Wherever you are in time, it is always Now. It is you who are on a journey. You are moving through Time."[61]

It is difficult for us to conceive of time in this way from our earthly perspective, but as science and spirituality come together, we will have to adjust our thinking not only about time but about reality as a whole. We do not live in a static, unchanging universe. Creation continues to evolve—it is a "journey" that involves the participation of every human being through time.

A PRE-TWENTIETH CENTURY VISION OF A HOLOGRAPHIC UNIVERSE

Having examined Pribram's and Bohm's scientific cases for the existence of a holographic universe, it's surprising to realize that their experiments actually served to strengthen the authenticity of information given much earlier to the eighteenth century Swedish mystic and teacher Emanuel Swedenborg. On several occasions, Swedenborg reportedly left his body while in a meditative, trance-like state and entered a heavenly realm where he conversed with angelic beings of light. After each of his otherworldly visits, Swedenborg faithfully recorded in writing what he saw and what his spiritual guides told him. His reports closely resemble those of many other individuals who have had what modern medical professionals now call the near-death experience.

The information Swedenborg shared with the world is particularly fascinating in that it anticipates much of what Pribram and Bohm discovered centuries later. In essence, Swedenborg provided a holographic explanation for the relationship between material and spiritual existence despite the absence of modern holographic technology and a working knowledge of quantum physics.[62]

Among the many things Swedenborg learned from his angelic guides was that each human being is a microcosm of the divine, which is similar to saying that each of us is a given point on the cosmic "holographic plate" that replicates the whole of spiritual and material existence. Dr. George F. Dole, a professor of theology at the Swedenborg School of Religion and an expert on Swedenborg's extensive writings, relates what else Swedenborg learned from his spiritual journeys: "We are constituted by the intersection of two flows—one direct from the divine, and one indirect, from the divine via our environment. We can view ourselves as interference patterns, because the inflow is a 2 wave phenomenon, and we are where the waves meet."[63]

The close relationship between the information given to Swedenborg by spiritual means and more recent evidence of a holographic universe gained through modern scientific research strongly suggests that the time has come for us to adjust our thinking about the world and our place in it. The revelations from both forms of investigation seem to confirm the codependence of the spiritual and material realms of existence.

THE HUMAN ENERGY FIELD AND HOLISTIC MEDICINE

The information we have gained so far about the world of subatomic particles and its holographic activity has important practical as well as spiritual ramifications. For instance, the existence of a visible human energy field known as the "aura" dramatically demonstrates the intelligent behavior of subatomic particles or waves and the possibility that we are all holographic manifestations of a divinely orchestrated impli-cate order. The aura can be seen as a luminous body that surrounds and interpenetrates every person's physical body. The various colors, textures, and intensities of visual sensation that can be distinguished within this luminous body are the result of electromagnetic radiation emitted by an individual's psyche or spiritual being. In essence, the aura is a person's own energy, or psychic "fingerprint," that can effectively telegraph the psychological and physical condition of that person.[64]

While most people do not see or recognize auras, there are some who are naturally inclined to distinguish the various colors of human auras quite clearly. Still others have learned to do so through proper training and effort. Today we know enough about the physics of the human energy field that it is possible to reduce or eliminate psycho-logical and physical suffering; by "reading" the colors of a particular person's aura well enough, one might diagnose a patient's various ail-ments and heal them by manipulating the patient's visible energy.[65] Among those who have an innate ability to "read" auras and accu-rately diagnose physical or psychological problems is renowned healer and teacher Barbara Brennan. Before becoming a full-time therapist and healer, Brennan worked as an atmospheric physicist at NASA's Goddard Space Flight Center. Her interest in physics largely stemmed from her childhood ability to see auras and to sense energy fields with her hands without realizing how or why. In 1982, after leaving NASA, Brennan founded the Barbara Brennan School of Healing in Boca Raton, Florida, which has trained students from the United States and many other parts of the world to become licensed practitioners of energy healing. Graduates of the school's intensive four-year pro-gram of study stress a holistic approach to medicine and often work in coordination with conventional medical doctors and hospitals. As a physicist, Brennan agrees with Pribram's idea that the human body and the brain are holographic in nature. "From the point of view of the holographic universe, these events (the aura and the healing forces required to manipulate its energies) emerge from frequencies that transcend time and space; they don't have to be transmitted," she says. "They are potentially simultaneous and everywhere."[66]

As a form of holistic medicine, the art of recognizing and utilizing the human energy field to diagnose and heal human ailments is gaining greater acceptance by the traditional medical community. This acceptance appears to have come particularly as a result of the research done by Shafica Karagulla, an experienced neurologist and psychiatrist. In the process of writing her book *Breakthrough to Creativity*, she became aware that several highly respected doctors and teachers in the medical profession had what she calls "higher sense perception" (HSP), or the natural ability to see and sense human energy fields. "I was continually surprised to find how many members of the medical profession had HSP abilities," she writes. "Most of them felt a little uneasy about their gifts, but finding them useful in diagnosis, they used them. They came from many parts of the country, and although they were unknown to each other, they all reported similar types of experiences."[67]

Nonlocal Energy Healing Through Prayer and the Power of Intention

Healing energy can be directed not only through the hands but from a distance as well. Evidence suggests that since the human energy field is part of the universal energy unfolded from the implicate order, and since human intention is directed energy, then prayers generated for the benefit of others can have tangible, measurable effects. Practicing physician Dr. Larry Dossey has devoted much of his professional life to the study of this phenomenon and the evidence that such prayers affect their recipients. He maintains that loving and compassionate communication with the "Absolute" on behalf of others can and does make a difference. In an interview for the *Chicago Tribune* in 1994, Dossey said, "There are more than 130 studies showing that if someone adopts a loving, caring attitude toward another living organism, human or not, that organism becomes healthier."[68]

In the interview, he also referred to a 1988 study in which four hundred heart patients were divided into two groups. The first names of one group of heart patients were given to groups of individuals who agreed to pray for them. Neither the patients nor their physicians were informed that this was happening. Meanwhile, no organized prayers were offered for the second group of heart patients. Ten months later, it was discovered that there were fewer deaths among those patients who had been prayed for and no one continued to need a mechanical ventilator, whereas twelve patients in the non-prayed-for group still needed such assistance.[69]

If the visible human energy field is a manifestation of the implicate order as suggested by Barbara Brennan and others familiar with the concept of a holographic universe, it also seems to offer at least a partial explanation for Jesus's ability to heal simply through the power of intention and human touch. This is not to say that modern practitioners of energy healing possess the same spiritual power as Jesus, but modern recognition and use of the human energy field to achieve tangible, documented healing results does suggest a meaningful relationship with those long-ago healings by Jesus. In other words, the power that Jesus knew he had and used to alleviate the suffering of others is the same God-given power we all possess. The difference is in the degree to which we are aware of such power and the level of our spiritual maturity. We may not be as spiritually enlightened as Jesus, but the potential for our being so is there. This, it seems, is another purpose of our evolutionary journey.

Furthermore, the concept of a universal energy field involving the continual unfolding and enfolding of the explicate and implicate orders as defined by Pribram and Bohm seems quite consistent with a panentheistic understanding of God—that is, the revelation that everything is *in* God and God is *in* everything. Paul's statement from Acts 17:28 seems to reflect this understanding that in God "we live, move and have our being." As did Jesus when he said: "If your leaders say to you 'Look! The Kingdom is in the sky!' then the birds will be there before you are. If they say that the Kingdom is in the sea, then the fish will be there before you are. Rather, the Kingdom is within you and it is outside of you" (Thomas: Saying 3). Or consider this story about Jesus found in Luke 17:20-21 (KJV): "And when he was demanded of the Pharisees, when the kingdom of God should come, he answered them and said, The kingdom of God cometh not with observation: Neither shall they say, Lo here! Or, lo there! for behold, the kingdom of God is within you."

Overall, the various ideas and developments that have come from the work of quantum physicists strongly suggest that the world is at the threshold of a new spiritual awakening. If Newtonian physics and Darwinian theories of natural selection tended to focus on a mechanical and physical explanation of the way things are divinely engineered, quantum physics is leading us to a very different worldview.

Rather than looking mainly at material causes for how and why the universe exists, quantum physics is shifting the focus toward the immaterial realm. Energy in the form of electromagnetic frequency vibrations is gaining recognition not only as the foundation of our material existence but also as a manifestation of the divine consciousness.

As we have seen, scientists such as Einstein, Planck, and a more recent generation of physicists have been willing to recognize this truth. Not since the pre-Enlightenment era has there been such a willingness to consider the spiritual basis of our material existence. In this sense, we seem to be going "back to the future," but our present spiritual awakening is not simply a return to the past. The shift among quantum physicists toward spirituality is based not on religious beliefs so much as on scientific evidence.

Furthermore, since we have come to realize through quantum

research that human consciousness, emanating from the divine consciousness, is energy that can move and affect all aspects of the physical world, we have the God-given capacity and responsibility to protect, heal, and sustain all that God has created and is creating. The energy of human consciousness is now known to have more to do with directing and controlling our own health and the health of the planet than genetic or chemical manipulation. In fact, according to developmental biologist Bruce Lipton, the new science of epigenetics is showing that "our perceptions, emotions, beliefs, and attitudes actually rewrite our genetic code."[70] We are imperfect, evolving participants in the Creation. And if the Creation is a divine evolutionary process, change is necessarily an unsettling part of the process.

Despite the relatively recent confluence of quantum physics, holistic medicine, and spirituality, there seems to be little or no acknowledgment or understanding of the spiritual implications of this development within more rigidly traditional Christian churches today. (The exception is perhaps at the grass roots, where a new emphasis on spirituality is beginning to challenge traditional beliefs and practices.) Reluctance on the part of many Christians to move beyond the theistic, exclusivist, and literalist dogmas of the past toward a more universal cosmology will not long withstand the evolutionary nature of God's creation.

CHAPTER 6

Near-Death Experiences: Transformative Messages of Oneness and Purpose

ANCIENT TRAVELS TO THE SPIRIT WORLD

In a letter Paul wrote to his newly established church in Corinth in the first century, he described being transported to paradise during an episode that occurred sometime after his initial encounter with the risen Christ on the road to Damascus:

> I know of a man in Christ [Paul] who fourteen years ago was caught up to the third heaven—whether in the body or out of the body I do not know, God knows. And I know that this man was caught up into Paradise—whether in the body or out of the body I do not know, God knows—and he heard things that can not be told, which man may not utter (II Corinthians 12:2-4).

However, in an earlier letter to the Corinthians, Paul had been more explicit about the existence of an eternal, spiritual body that is capable of leaving the physical body:

> There are celestial bodies and there are terrestrial bodies; but the glory of the celestial is one, and the terrestrial is another ... So it is with the resurrection of the dead ... It is sown a physical body, it is raised a spiritual body. If there is a physical body, there is also a spiritual body ... I tell you this, brethren; flesh and blood can not inherit the Kingdom of God, nor does the perishable inherit the imperishable (I Corinthians 15:32-50).

These otherworldly descriptions by Paul were not unique to him. Similar accounts were recorded well before Paul in the Hindu Rig-Veda scriptures, Buddhism's Tibetan Book of the Dead, various Zoroastrian sacred texts, and the ancient Jewish Talmud. The Rig-Veda refers to the deceased entering a world of perpetual light: "Place me in that deathless, undecaying world / Wherein the light of heaven is set."[1] Also mentioned in the *Rig-Veda* are reunions with departed forefathers and a life review during which heavenly beings read a record of the deceased's earthly life.[2] Likewise, the Tibetan Book of the Dead refers to death as a time when the disembodied soul meets "the Buddha of Infinite Light" in a beautiful landscape before having the soul's good and evil deeds weighed and judged.[3] Zoroastrian scriptures also mention the soul's seeing and experiencing God as pure light, but while the Zoroastrian scriptures refer to life reviews, they are intended only for souls deemed to be unrighteous. However, those judged to be righteous are greeted by deceased friends.[4] Although the ancient Hebrew Torah only refers to a shadowy afterlife deep within the earth, these scriptures also contain passages that refer to images of Divine light,[5] as in "The Lord is my light and salvation; whom shall I fear?" (Psalms 27:1) and "The Lord will be your everlasting light" (Isaiah 60:20).

But what is significant about Paul's descriptions of the afterlife along with those from more ancient texts is that they all resemble more recent reports coming from those who have experienced what the International Association for Near-Death Studies (IANDS) defines as a near-death experience, or NDE:

> The near-death experience is an intense awareness, sense, or experience of otherworldliness, whether pleasant or unpleasant, that happens to people who are at the edge of death. It is of such magnitude that most experiencers are deeply affected, many to the point of making significant changes in their lives because of what happened to them. Aftereffects often last lifelong and can intensify over time.[6]

MODERN STUDIES OF NEAR-DEATH EXPERIENCES

Since 1980, a whole new field of near-death studies has emerged and is experiencing rapid growth and development for two major reasons. In the first place, modern medicine's more advanced resuscitation techniques and machines have made it possible for an increasing number of people who are clinically dead for a brief period to be brought back to life. Second, the near-death experience has become more widely known as a result of the pioneering work on this phenomenon by Dr. Raymond Moody, author of the 1975 book *Life after Life*, and Elisabeth Kubler-Ross, who produced the pivotal 1979 book *On Death and Dying*. In their roles as medical doctors within hospital settings, they saw and heard firsthand reports from patients who survived clinical death. They were so impressed by the sincerity of these patients—and by the corroboration of their reports by medical staff members caring for them—that they felt compelled to share this information with other doctors and the public at large while continuing to investigate NDEs in greater detail.

A comprehensive study carried out by the Gallup Poll in the mid-1980s found that from 35 percent to 40 percent of America's adults who came close to death reported having near-death experiences.[7] This figure did not include the number of children who had had NDEs at the time of that survey, and far more cases of NDEs among children have been documented since that time. In fact, the growing number of research studies of children since the 1980s has yielded especially credible evidence showing that the NDE is real and profoundly transformative. Furthermore, it has been determined by similar studies in other countries around the world that the number of people who have had near-death experiences is still growing exponentially. In her recent book *Near-Death Experiences: The Rest of the Story*, P.M.H. Atwater points out that about 5 percent of the world's population of more than seven billion people have had some form of near-death experience.[8] This would mean that more than three hundred million people around the world have had such experiences.

CONDITIONS AND EVENTS GENERALLY ASSOCIATED WITH NEAR-DEATH EXPERIENCES

As we begin to consider the various events associated with NDEs, it is important to know that in the majority of near-death experience cases, none of the physical vital signs—such as brain waves, breathing, and heart rate—are detected for ten to fifteen minutes. There are actually a few recorded cases in which individuals have remained in this clinically lifeless state for as long as an hour or more before being successfully resuscitated,[9] although experienced medical professionals have found that the brain can sustain permanent damage if it is deprived of sufficient oxygen for a period of only five to ten minutes.[10]

However, many of those who have had comprehensive near-death experiences after the cessation of vital signs are not only free of brain damage but can often show remarkable brain enhancements.[11] Then there are other instances, mostly involving children, in which near-death experiences can occur inexplicably even without loss of vital signs.

In recent years, the subject of near-death experiences has been popularized in books and films and on TV to the point where most people are familiar with at least some of the basic aspects of the phenomenon. But all too often, the true nature of NDEs has been trivialized and taken out of context enough to cause confusion, uncertainty, and skepticism in the minds of many.

According to the so-called "classical" model of an NDE, which has been popularized since publication of Moody's book in 1975, NDEs include some or all of the following events, not necessarily in the order presented:[12]

Becoming aware of unusual sounds

Leaving one's physical body and witnessing it from a distance

Hearing one's self being pronounced dead

Having feelings of peace and quiet

Traveling rapidly and effortlessly through a dark but non-threatening tunnel

Meeting deceased family members, friends, or other spiritual beings

Being immersed in a very bright light that communicates as a being of light

Undergoing a panoramic life review

Being prevented from proceeding beyond a certain point

Returning to one's physical body

Feeling frustration when attempting to describe the whole experience in words

Adjusting to various psychological, physiological, and spiritual after-effects

Completely losing the fear of death

Receiving independent verification of events one witnessed while out of his or her body

In the years since this general model of a near-death experience first became known, subsequent research has shown that NDEs do not always conform exactly to this format. NDEs can vary somewhat in terms of the number of events and their content. There are certain core elements common to all NDEs that generally account for at least a third of the events listed.[13] However, the similarities and consistencies among near-death experience cases as a whole are what make these events so significant and credible. In addition, researchers now have a much greater understanding of the true dimensions of near-death experiences, including the profound long-term effects they have on individuals who have had such life-changing episodes.

CATEGORIES OF NEAR-DEATH EXPERIENCES

Based on her forty years of research involving interviews with children and adult NDErs, Atwater has determined that there are four major categories of near-death experiences that contain some if not all of the "classical" events listed above.[14]

'The Initial Experience'

Atwater refers to the first of these major types of NDEs as "the initial experience." Those who have this type of NDE usually have a brief out-of-body experience involving a state of darkness that projects a sense of intense love or "wombishness" and, in some cases, hear a comforting voice. The experience tends to be vivid and memorable enough to open the NDEr to new ways of viewing and understanding reality. In such instances, the near-death experience does not develop beyond this rather brief but powerful episode.

A typical example of an initial experience comes from an interview conducted by Atwater with a person who, at the age of four, remembered jumping into the deep end of a swimming pool despite her mother's warnings:

> So I jumped. Part of me was down below, splashing around, not able to see much. The other part was floating up, way up higher than the lifeguards. I heard something behind me, all around me, "speak" an unspoken question: "Do you want to live?" I thought about that. Dying seemed somehow good, nice. Dying feels normal. And then I thought about my parents and how sad they would be. Even though it seemed nice to go, I said, "I'll stay." I slowly went back down in the water to the other half of me. The next thing I knew I was being held by a fat lady in a polka-dot bathing suit. I thanked her for helping me.[15]

In this case, the young NDEr did not experience several of the other stages associated with the "classical" near-death experience, including the cessation of all physical vital signs, but did separate from her physical body enough to experience the presence of an otherworldly "guide." In the process, she lost her fear of dying, which is what most NDErs report, no matter what category of near-death experience they encountered.

The 'Unpleasant or Hell-Like Experience'

According to Atwater, this category of NDEs is less prevalent than any of the other types, but those who do go through this type of experience are strongly impacted. They generally report being in a "threatening void" or "hellish purgatory" in which startling and disorienting images appear and disappear.[16]

One such experience is described by medical doctor Eben Alexander in his book *Proof of Heaven: A Neurosurgeon's Journey into the Afterlife.* At the beginning of his rather lengthy NDE, Alexander found himself out of his physical body in the midst of a disturbing environment: "Darkness, but a visible darkness—like being submerged in mud yet also being able to see through it. Or maybe dirty Jell-O describes it better. Transparent, but in a bleary, blurry, claustrophobic, suffocating kind of way."[17] He continues:

> Grotesque animal faces bubbled out of the muck, groaned or screeched, and then were gone again. I heard an occasional dull roar. Sometimes these roars changed to dim, rhythmic chants, chants that were both terrifying and weirdly familiar—as if at some point I'd known and uttered them all myself …[18]

I edged ever closer to panic. Whoever or whatever I was, I did not belong here. I needed to get out. But where would I go?

Even as I asked that question, something new emerged from the darkness above: something that wasn't cold, or dead, or dark, but the exact opposite of all those things. If I tried for the rest of my life I would never be able to do justice to this entity that now approached me ... to come anywhere close to describing how beautiful it was.[19]

Another example of an unpleasant or hell-like experience is described in the book *Return from Tomorrow*, by George G. Ritchie, a medical doctor who, many years before at the age of twenty, had an extraordinary transcendent NDE after being pronounced dead from pneumonia. He vividly recalls that during the early stages of his NDE, he witnessed a hellish scene while in the presence of a being of light he said was Jesus:

If I suspected before that I was seeing hell, now I was sure of it. Up to this moment the misery I had watched consisted in being chained to a physical world of which we were no longer a part. Now I saw that there were other kinds of chains. Here were no solid objects or people to enthrall the soul. These creatures seemed locked into habits of mind and emotion, into hatred, lust, destructive thought patterns ...[20]

In a realm where space and time no longer followed any rules I knew, could He [Jesus] be standing with each of them as He was with me?

I didn't know. All I clearly saw was that not one of these bicker-
ing beings on the plain had been abandoned. They were being
attended, watched over, ministered to [by angelic beings]. And
the observable fact was that not one of them knew it.[21]

During the early years of NDE research, particularly before the 1980s,
there was virtually no common acknowledgment of a distressing form of
near-death experience. For instance, references to this type of NDE are
not found in Moody's *Life after Life* or in Kenneth Ring's well-known
1980 publication *Life at Death*. Then, in 1981, an interdisciplinary study
conducted at Evergreen State College, Washington, found that among
the fifty-five NDE subjects who were interviewed for the study, eleven
had had negative experiences involving fear, anger, and even visions of
"threatening or taunting demonic creatures."[22] However, they also found
that these same experiences usually evolved into "a positive experience in
which all negativity vanishes … and peacefulness is achieved."[23]

Since that time, other NDE studies have acknowledged that out
of the total number of documented NDE cases, a relatively small percentage tend to be unpleasant or distressing. In 1992, Atwater claimed
that 105 of the more than 700 NDE subjects she had interviewed at
that point actually reported having had very stressful, disturbing experiences.[24] Likewise, studies by Nancy Evans Bush, NDE researcher and
president emerita of IANDS, showed that 17 percent of the NDErs
interviewed reported having unpleasant experiences.[25]

There are those whose religious orientation would lead them to believe
that this type of NDE proves that hell is a tangible reality as described in
the literature of the Middle Ages and fundamentalist Christian teachings.
Others who approach the issue more from a psychological perspective
tend to believe, as Atwater does, that it has more to do with the NDErs'
state of mind before and during the experiences. However, both these
explanations seem inadequate and have been challenged.

Studies have shown that many NDErs who fully expected some sort of divine judgment or had deep preliminary feelings of guilt, fear, or anger—or even attempted suicide—actually experienced pleasant, even radiant near-death experiences.[26] These facts would seem to question the validity of an inevitable correlation between a person's state of mind or religious beliefs and a negative NDE. Perhaps the most important fact to remember is that distressing NDEs most often progress from darkness to the light—from the illusion of being isolated and trapped to the reality of a reunion with the source of all love—all in the same NDE, as in the experiences of George Ritchie and Eben Alexander.

Christopher M. Bache, a professor of philosophy and religious studies at Youngstown State University, Ohio, helps to bring greater understanding to the issue. In his opinion, "a frightening NDE is not an alternative NDE but an incomplete NDE."[27] In the same vein, meditation teacher Shenzen Young provides this additional perspective: "Two traditions describe these [frightening NDEs or visions] in great detail as stages associated with spiritual growth, Shamanism and Buddhism … Such phenomena are best interpreted as part of a natural process of release from the deep archetypal levels of the mind."[28]

In the final analysis, what is now known about unpleasant hell-like NDEs from research conducted over at least the last twenty years is that 1) the experience is not permanent and seems to have no relationship to a person's basic good or bad qualities, 2) some of these experiences evolve into peaceful and heaven-like encounters, and 3) frightening NDEs are not forms of divine punishments so much as contacts with the darker side of the human psyche on the path toward spiritual growth.

THE 'PLEASANT OR HEAVEN-LIKE EXPERIENCE'

As indicated by Atwater, this type of NDE occurs more often than any of the others and involves most if not all of the "classical" events mentioned earlier. It is this type of NDE that has been featured most often in films and books and on TV. Although this has been a good thing insofar as it has led to an increased awareness that life continues after death, such exposure in the popular media has often resulted in sensationalized interpretations lacking depth and true meaning.

In an attempt to provide greater depth and more accurate information, I have chosen to present portions of personal accounts of this type of near-death experience as they relate to the various stages of the "classical model." These reports come from investigative studies conducted over the last forty years by Atwater and other leading NDE researchers. Not all the stages described below occur in every heaven-like NDE, nor do they necessarily occur in the same order as presented here. Nevertheless, there are enough similarities among reports from independent individuals of all ages, religious faiths, cultures, and locations that they can be considered reliable, credible, and deeply meaningful.

The Out-of-the-Body Experience (OBE):

An out-of-body experience tends to be the beginning stage not just for pleasant NDEs but for all types of NDEs. This next episode was reported by a person with heart problems who was hospitalized with severe chest pain when she suddenly suffered a cardiac arrest:

> I was quite uncomfortable lying on my back so I turned over, and as I did I quit breathing and my heart stopped beating. Just then, I heard the nurses shout, "Code pink! Code pink!" As they were saying this, I could feel myself moving out of my body and sliding down between the mattress and the rail on the side of the bed—actually it seemed as if I went *through* the rail—on down to the floor. Then, I started rising upward, slowly.

At that point the patient could see and hear everything from a point near the ceiling of the room. "As I saw them below beating on my chest, and rubbing my arms and legs, I thought, 'Why are they going to so much trouble? I'm just fine now,'" she recalled.[29]

When those who are having a near-death experience realize they are out of their physical bodies, they soon recognize that they still have a "body," but it is hard to describe and functions differently. A person who experienced having a "spiritual body" put it this way: "During that time, I kept getting in and out of my physical body, and I could see it from directly above. But, while I did, I was still in a body—not a physical body, but something I can best describe as an energy pattern. If I had to put it into words, I would say that it was transparent, a spiritual as opposed to a material being. Yet, it definitely had different parts."[30]

An individual who had "died" in an automobile accident described the experience of being in spiritual form outside his physical body: "People were walking up from all directions to get to the wreck. I could see them, and I was in the middle of a very narrow walkway. Anyway, as they came by they wouldn't seem to notice me. They would just keep walking with their eyes straight ahead. As they came real close, I would try to turn around, to get out of their way, but they would just walk *through* me."[31]

In other cases, this out-of-body experience includes the ability of a person's "spiritual body" to travel effortlessly to other locations. People who experienced this state recounted their ability to pass through walls and closed doors, down hallways, and to other, more distant locations that they could describe later in minute detail. Not only were they able to accurately describe these locations far from where their lifeless physical bodies were at the time, but they also were able to recall words spoken by people in these distant locations—much to the shock and surprise of those people, who later confirmed the facts.

One such example from among many that have been verified and corroborated is the case of a woman who suffered a cardiac arrest while in an unfamiliar hospital far from her home. The next day after her resuscitation, she told her nurse that she had left her body and then watched her medical team from a spot near the ceiling before moving outside the hospital altogether. Her nurse explained what happened next: "Specifically she said, having been distracted by an object on the ledge of the third floor on the north wing of the building, she 'thought herself up there.' And when she 'arrived,' she found herself ... 'eyeball to shoelace' with—of all things—a tennis shoe on the ledge of the building!" The nurse then told how the patient described the shoe to her in great detail, including the fact "that the little toe had a worn place in the shoe and that one of its laces was tucked underneath the heel."[32]

The woman proceeded to plead with the nurse to have someone locate the shoe in order to prove that her experience was real. With some misgivings and considerable doubt, the nurse decided to see for herself. As she inspected the five windows on the third floor, she found the tennis shoe on the ledge outside the middle window exactly as it had been described to her.

Perhaps even more extraordinary are the documented accounts of people, blind since birth, who were able to see clearly during their near-death experiences. In 1994, Kenneth Ring and co-researcher Sharon Cooper interviewed thirty-one blind people, including fourteen who had been totally blind since birth. Twenty-one of these people had had at least one NDE. Ring and Cooper found, to their amazement, that the near-death experiences of these blind individuals were virtually the same as those of sighted people.[33]

The following account comes from a blind woman who had left her body while being treated at a hospital after a seemingly fatal car crash. From a vantage point near the ceiling, she saw a body lying on the ER examining table and did not recognize it until she noticed that the hair looked like hers and the body was wearing her customized wedding ring. "I went up through the roof then," she said. "And that was astounding! ... Whew! It's like the roof didn't ... it just melted." She soon found herself above the roof of the hospital and became aware of exterior details. "Lights, and the streets down below, and everything. I was very confused about that." As Ring said, "This was happening very fast for her, and she found seeing to be disorienting and distracting. At one point, she even says that seeing was 'frightening' to her."[34] The woman also told of having an incredible sense of freedom from any bodily limitations.

This individual, like many others who were blind before their NDEs, resumed her blind state when she rejoined her physical body after resuscitation. The reasons are unknown, but perhaps such outcomes involve divine purposes beyond our immediate understandings.

Moving through a Tunnel before Being Immersed in the Light

Soon after leaving their physical bodies, many individuals have described being drawn into a dark void or tunnel in which they moved effortlessly and peacefully in a rapid manner toward what they perceived to be a bright white light. While there are certain variations in how NDErs experience this stage, there are also important common elements.

The first description is from an individual who was particularly impressed by the speed at which he traveled through a loosely described tunnel and by the nature of the light at the end:

> You do realize that you're going just so fast and you're covering vast distances in just hundredths of a second ... and then gradually you realize that way, way off in the distance—again, unmeasurable distance—it appears that it might be the end of the tunnel. And all you can see is a white light ...

And then, before you is this—excuse me [he pauses here]—is this most magnificent, just gorgeous, beautiful bright white or blue-white light [another pause]. It is so bright, it is brighter than a light that would immediately blind you, but this absolutely does not hurt your eyes at all …

The next sensation is this wonderful, wonderful feeling of this light … It's almost like a person. It is not a person, but it is a being of some kind. It is a mass of energy. It doesn't have a character like you would describe another person, but it has a character in that it is more than just a thing. It is something to communicate to and acknowledge.[35]

In this next example, the NDEr experienced the tunnel in a slightly different way with broader implications:

Everything around me was dark, with the exception of several stars that hurtled toward me and I noticed their different colors. I had no time to look at anything because I was moving so fast. Things slowed down when I saw that I'd ended up in a kind of hourglass and that I was being "sucked" toward the opening. Then I realized that I wasn't alone because a flow of translucent beings was heading the same way as me and another flow was moving in the opposite direction. When I thought about reincarnation, it later dawned on me that it could well be this flow.[36]

This particular reference to reincarnation is not the only one to have been reported by NDErs. In the course of his NDE research, Ring found that many NDErs became more accepting of reincarnation after their experiences despite previous doubts or non-belief. For this reason, and because of its profound spiritual importance, reincarnation will be explored in greater depth in Chapter 7.

Meeting a Being of Light and Deceased Friends and Family

After moving through a tunnel and entering the light, a person having a heaven-like experience often meets and communicates with a being of light. Depending on their particular religious orientation, NDErs often identify such beings as guardian angels, guides, or a religious figure such as Jesus. Either before or after this occurs, the NDEr may also meet deceased family members or friends. Excerpts from descriptions of three such encounters follow. The first came from a man who had an NDE in the midst of a surgical crisis:

> She wasn't a nurse. She was clothed in light, extraordinarily beautiful and loving. She was the most beautiful woman I had ever seen, and I almost cry when I think about it. She wore a loose-fitting white gown, and it gave off light of its own … The light around her was flooding into me, and seemed to pour into everything…
>
> I could literally feel her love and care … I had the impression that she knew me very well, and that I was very familiar to her, but she didn't say.[37]

The next NDE account was reported by a person who had left his body after a cardiac arrest:

> I saw both my dead grandmother and a man who looked at me lovingly but whom I didn't know. Over ten years later, my

mother confided on her deathbed that I'd been born from an extramarital affair; my biological father was a Jewish man who'd been deported and killed in World War II. My mother showed me a photograph. The unfamiliar man I'd seen more than ten years earlier during my NDE turned out to be my biological father.[38]

The third example is particularly interesting because it reveals that life continues "on the other side" without the usual deteriorating physical effects associated with aging on Earth: "Suddenly I recognized all these relatives. They were all around thirty-five years old, including the little brother I'd never known, because he had died during the war when he was two years old, before I was born. He had grown up a lot. My parents were there, too, and they smiled at me, just like the others."[39]

Experiencing a Life Review

In the majority of near-death experiences, people report having a panoramic life review presented to them soon after encountering one or more beings of light. It immediately becomes obvious to the person having the NDE that this being of light, or spiritual guide, already knows every detail about the person's life and that the purpose of the review is to give the person a chance to reflect and learn from all of his or her life experiences rather than to pass judgment or find fault. Every thought, word, and deed from a person's life is included in rapid sequence, from birth to the time of the review.

In addition to the NDEr observing all the events of his or her own life in great detail, all the emotions and feelings associated with these events are experienced. In fact, many report that they vividly experienced the feelings of others whose lives they touched, for better or for worse. The message that is always communicated is that the two most important things in life are to learn to love others and to acquire knowledge. The following selections from three personal stories illustrate this message:

> My whole life so far appeared to be placed before me in a kind of panoramic, three-dimensional review, and each event seemed to be accompanied by an awareness of good and evil or by an insight into its cause and effect. Throughout, I not only saw everything from my own point of view but also knew the thoughts of everybody who'd been involved in these events, as if their thoughts were lodged inside of me. It meant that I saw not only what I had done or thought but even how this had affected others, as if I was seeing with all-knowing eyes. And so even your thoughts are apparently not wiped out. And throughout, the review stressed the importance of love. I can't say how long this life review and insight into life lasted; it may have been quite long because it covered every single subject, but at the same time it felt like a split-second because I saw everything at once. It seemed as if time and distance didn't exist. I was everywhere at once, and sometimes my attention was focused on something and then I was there, too.[40]

> Instantly my entire life was laid bare and open to this wonderful presence, "GOD." I felt inside my being his forgiveness for the things in my life I was ashamed of, as though they were not of great importance. I was asked—but there were no words. It was a straight mental instantaneous communication: What had I done to benefit or advance the human race?[41]

> He seemed very interested in things concerning knowledge, too. He kept on pointing out things that had to do with

learning, and he did say that I was going to continue learning, and he said that even when he comes back for me (because by this time he had told me that I was going back) that there will always be a quest for knowledge. He said that it is a continuous process, so I got the feeling that it goes on after death.[42]

Clearly, one of the most significant points about the life review is the fact that every aspect of our lives, no matter how insignificant it may seem to be at the time, is permanently recorded in what might be called the cosmic consciousness. Equally significant is the fact that we will experience others' emotional reactions to our thoughts and actions, or, in other words, we will ultimately see ourselves through the eyes and hearts of others. As said earlier by one of the NDE respondents, "I not only saw everything from my own point of view but also knew the thoughts of everybody who'd been involved in these events, as if their thoughts were lodged inside of me. It meant that I saw not only what I had done or thought but even how this had affected others."

Having this new perspective on one's life often leads to personal transformation. In fact, this is what happens to most if not all of those who have had near-death experiences, as discovered not only by NDErs themselves, but also by others who know them.

Returning to Physical Life

Most NDErs relate that their experiences in the light were so overwhelmingly beautiful, peaceful, and filled with love that they had an intense desire to not return to their physical bodies and resume their earthly lives. They often report being given the choice to remain or return. Sometimes the NDErs chose to return for the sake of relatives or others who they know would suffer greatly from grief, loneliness, or the need for some form of physical or emotional support. In other cases,

NDErs were told they must return despite their pleas to remain. In such cases, they were usually informed that their life's mission on Earth was not complete or, at times, were even given a glimpse into the future they were destined to experience. The following example is key to an account cited earlier, given by a woman who met her deceased brother-in-law during her NDE:

> I remember thinking, "Okay, I'll go back, but I know how I can get back up here." At that same instant, his thoughts were mine, saying, "You can't take your own life (suicide). That isn't the answer, that won't do it. You have to live your life's purpose." I understood, but I still remember thinking, "I don't want to go back," and his thought came to me, saying, "It's okay, we're not going anywhere. We'll be here for you again." The last thought of his was, "Tell your sister I'm fine."
>
> With those final thoughts, I felt myself going back, dropping downward instantly through darkness. I didn't feel that I had a choice. I didn't feel afraid, but rather calm. Then, instantly, I felt myself slam into my body.[43]

The second example comes from the man quoted earlier who found himself in the presence of a beautiful angel of light:

> I never wanted to leave her. It may be that she felt the circumstances provided an unfair comparison to my wife. She showed me some details about my children (who were not yet born) and revealed a view of another woman even more lovely and desirable—the wife I was married to. She then said it was time to return, that my breathing had stabilized, and that my nervous system was able to work on its own ... I saw her light

begin to withdraw from me as she retreated from my view. This light persisted for two or three seconds as I awakened, while my wife was holding my face in her hands.[44]

Difficulty in Sharing NDEs

Given the extraordinary breadth and depth of NDEs and how transformative they are—especially the radiant, heaven-like type—it's no wonder they're difficult to describe and process when attempting to resume earthly life. All too often, when NDErs attempt to tell family members, friends, and even some clerics what happened to them, their stories are met with disbelief and rejected or dismissed.

A study conducted in 1992 by Dr. Cherie Sutherland, a leading Australian expert on the study of near-death experiences, showed that the stories told by NDErs were rejected by as many as 50 percent of family members, 25 percent of friends, 30 percent of nurses, 85 percent of doctors, and 50 percent of psychiatrists.[45] When they experienced these acts of rejection, both children and adult NDErs usually suppressed their secrets for years before finding others who were more understanding and willing to listen. The result was often a sense of loneliness or isolation. Suffice it to say the physical, psychological, and spiritual transformations that almost always occur to people as the result of their NDEs often require serious life adjustments in terms of their relationships with others and the world in general. This is particularly true of marriages.

Independent studies conducted by Atwater in the mid-1980s, Nancy Evans Bush in 1991, and professional counselor Dr. Rozan Christian in 2005 showed the divorce rate among NDErs to be as high as 75 percent.[46] Since NDErs tend to see others and the world from a different perspective after their experiences, they are often unable to bridge the new gap in understanding between themselves and others, including their marriage partners. Much depends on the responses NDErs receive from family members, friends, and associates after their NDEs. If their stories are taken seriously and they are met with understanding and acceptance, they are more apt to maintain lasting relationships, continue to grow spiritually, and foster the same kind of growth in others. If not, what NDErs have learned and demonstrate as spiritually transformed human beings will be stifled and restricted. Facing serious life adjustments is especially true for individuals whose heaven-like NDEs were more extensive and penetrating. That brings us to the fourth major category of near-death experiences.

The Deeper Transcendent Experience

People who have gone through more prolonged and deeper NDEs than most seem to have greater intellectual and visual access to the environment of the "other side." Some have told of entering the light and then moving into and through indescribably beautiful landscapes or cities with buildings of light. That's what happened to the following two NDErs:

> I suddenly found myself on a green plain. I had a body again. I was aware of a body. And this was a beautiful green meadow, with beautiful flowers, lit again with this glorious light, like no light we've ever seen, but there was a sky, grass, flowers that had colors that I'd never seen before. ... Just utter glory in color. And I walked along and saw that there were other people up on a little rise in front of me. So I started walking toward that rise to talk with these people and when I had just gotten up there, I could see a city.[47]

> I moved closer to the lights and realized they were cities—the cities were built of light. At the moment I realized what it was

... we were there ... I stood in the square of a brilliant, beautiful city ... The building I went in was a cathedral. It was built like St. Mark's or the Sistine Chapel, but the bricks or blocks appeared to be made of Plexiglas. They were square, they had dimension to 'em, except you could see through 'em and in the center of each of these was this gold and silver light. And you could see the building—and yet could not for the radiance ... Now this cathedral was literally built of knowledge. This was a place of learning I had come to.[48]

But perhaps the most incredible reports come from those who not only had views of buildings and other landmarks from an elevated position soon after leaving their physical bodies but went on to travel effortlessly and rapidly into outer space, where they saw views of the Earth, other planets, and vast regions of the universe while absorbing incredible knowledge and understanding. One such case is that of a man who was "dead" for what was estimated to be an hour and a half while suffering from a serious brain condition in 1982:

At the time, it seemed like I was being propelled somewhere. I don't know if I was moving anywhere in space, but suddenly I could see the world fly away. I could see the solar system fly away. I could then see galaxies and—it went on. Eventually I got the feeling that I was going through everything that had ever been. I was seeing it all—galaxies became little stars, and super clusters of galaxies, and the worlds upon worlds, and energy realms. It was just an amazing sight to behold. And it felt like I was zooming somewhere, but I really think it was my consciousness just expanding at such a rapid rate. And it happened so quickly but it was in such detail that there came another light right at me, and when I hit this light, it was like [pause] I dissolved or something. And I understood at that moment that I passed the big bang. That was the first light ever and I went through the big bang. That's what happened. I went through that membrane into this—what I guess the ancients have called the void. Suddenly I was in this void and I was aware of everything that had ever been created. It was like I was looking out of God's eyes.[49]

Finally, well-known psychologist Carl Jung told of the out-of-body experience he had during his heart attack in 1944. What is especially significant about this report is that his description of outer space is totally consistent with the views astronauts have had only since the late 1960s! This is how Jung described his experience:

It seemed to me that I was high up in space. Far below I saw the globe of the earth, bathed in a gloriously blue light. I saw the deep blue sea and the continents. Far below my feet lay Ceylon, and in the distance ahead of me the subcontinent of India. My field of vision did not include the whole earth, but its global shape was plainly distinguishable and its outlines shone with a silvery gleam through that wonderful blue light. In many places the globe seemed colored, or spotted dark green like oxidized silver. Far away to the left lay a broad expanse— the reddish-yellow desert of Arabia; it was as though the silver of the earth had there assumed a reddish-gold hue. Then came the Red Sea, and far, far back—as if in the upper left of a map—I could just make out a bit of the Mediterranean. My gaze was directed chiefly toward that. Everything else appeared indistinct. I could also see the snow-covered Himalayas, but in that direction it was foggy or cloudy. I did not look to the right at all. I knew that I was on the point of departing from the earth. Later I discovered how high in space one would have to be to have so extensive a view—approximately a thousand miles! The sight of the earth from this height was the most glorious thing I had ever seen.[50]

THE NEAR-DEATH EXPERIENCES OF CHILDREN

While the majority of the stories presented so far have been those of adult NDErs, it is important to recognize that the NDEs of children are equally significant and verifiable according to researchers. What's more, the stories told by these children, especially those of a very young age, are far less influenced by the sorts of biases and beliefs accrued by most adults. Their accounts reflect little to no chance of contrivance or preconceived notions.

Probably the best-known and most experienced researcher of child NDEs is Dr. Melvin Morse, who has studied NDEs, specifically among children, since the mid-1980s. As part of his research, he studied the cases of twenty-six children who nearly died and compared them with 131 very ill children who, while in intensive care, were mechanically ventilated, received drugs such as morphine, valium, and anesthetics, and had a lack of oxygen to the brain—but were not near death.

Morse discovered that twenty-three of the twenty-six children who had come close to death had NDEs, while none of the other 131 children had such experiences. The results of this and other studies Morse conducted have convinced him that NDEs are not caused by a lack of oxygen to the brain, various drugs, hallucinations related to coma, or stress brought on by the fear of dying. Instead, he and other NDE researchers are convinced that those who have had NDEs have had actual death experiences.[51]

Later, Morse completed a long-term follow-up study of children who had had NDEs, called "the Seattle Study," to determine what if any long-term effects the NDEs had on their lives.[52] He found that their NDEs were profoundly transforming and vividly remembered into adulthood.

RESPONSES TO NDEs BY THE SCIENTIFIC, MEDICAL, AND RELIGIOUS COMMUNITIES

Despite these compelling reports and the extensive studies undertaken by a variety of professionally recognized researchers for the past thirty years, the whole concept of the NDE continues to be challenged by some in the scientific and medical communities. Similar challenges have come from Christian traditionalists who, in certain cases, have even gone so far as to characterize these experiences as "the work of the Devil."[53] Such Christians tend to believe that Satan may appear as an angel of light to deceive people into thinking that their visions are from God.

In addition, I have personally seen how some Christian church communities respond with denial, disbelief, or indifference to the subject. The underlying reason is usually the fear of death and the resulting reluctance to explore the whole subject. In our modern scientifically oriented world, people also have a tendency to reject those things that conventional scientific or medical theories cannot explain. But attempts on the part of skeptics to explain away near-death experiences on the basis of traditional scientific assumptions are being challenged in the light of new scientific research.

The various explanations offered by NDE skeptics tend to focus on certain pharmacological, physiological, or psychological effects on the brain. In other words, it's assumed that NDEs are ultimately caused by the brain's and central nervous system's reactions to medically administered drugs, a lack of oxygen, or certain neurological diseases. Likewise, many believe NDEs are more psychologically rooted in that they are simply imaginary and the product of dreams or neurosis. However, those who have had near-death experiences as well as the members of the scientific and medical communities who have studied this phenomenon over the past thirty years can provide evidence to the contrary.

Problems with the Pharmacological Explanation

To begin with, when it comes to the pharmacological explanation for NDEs, it is important to realize that many individuals who have had near-death experiences were given no drugs before or during the event. This would seem to suggest that there is not necessarily a cause-and-effect relationship between NDEs and the use of therapeutic drugs.[54] Likewise, even though drugs given to patients during a medical crisis have been known to cause them to experience visions or have hallucinations, this type of hallucinatory experience differs from a typical NDE in a number of important ways. For instance, drug-induced patients do not tell of seeing their physical bodies from a vantage point outside their bodies or of seeing and hearing what happened around them when their brains showed no signs of activity. It is also true that patients can describe their hallucinations only in a vague way without remembering much in the way of details. NDErs, on the other hand, remember many intricate details, even many years later.

Problems with the Physiological Explanation

Another common assumption among skeptics is that a near-death experience is a "compensatory gasp" of the brain as it dies from a lack of oxygen. However, NDE reports have shown that consciousness, involving memory and perception, occurs even after the brain stops functioning entirely and respiration has ended. As cardiologist Pim van Lommel points out, there is "compelling evidence that the NDE occurs during the period of clinical death and not shortly before or after the cardiac arrest."[55]

So how can a patient whose brain has ceased to function, with no electrical activity in the cerebral cortex, as indicated by a "flat" electroencephalogram (EEG), be fully cognizant of everything from a vantage point outside his or her body? As we read in Chapter 5, Karl Pribram considered the possibility that the functioning brain serves as a kind of frequency analyzer that converts the wave forms of a collective consciousness outside the brain into meaningful thoughts and images. In short, Pribram was pointing to the possibility that consciousness is nonlocal in origin.

Van Lommel's research and professional experience as a cardiac specialist has led him to agree. Like Pribram, van Lommel believes that while the brain can be said to function as a transmitter, receiver, and processor, it does not necessarily produce and store our thoughts and memories.

To further prove this point, computer expert Simon Berkovich has determined that the brain's capacity for storing the memories of a person's entire life is insufficient despite the brain's enormous number of synapses. For instance, his calculations show that at any single moment of a day during which a person is fully awake, there are approximately 10^{24} actions per second in the brain. If one adds "the required capacity for long-term memory storage," he says, "the total data storage capacity would have to be 3.10^{17} bits/cm^3, which, based on our current understanding of neuronal processes in the brain, is inconceivable."[56]

Even more compelling evidence in favor of the existence of nonlocal consciousness was featured in a 1980 *Science* magazine article titled "Is Your Brain Really Necessary?" The article reported the case of a person with a university degree in mathematics and an IQ of 126 whose brain scan showed that 95 percent of his skull was filled with cerebrospinal fluid and his cerebral cortex was only two millimeters thick. His total brain mass was determined to weigh only one hundred grams, while a normal weight compares at fifteen hundred grams. Despite this startling fact, his brain functioned quite well with regard to memory and information recall.[57] Again, this case strongly suggests that the brain does not produce consciousness but can adapt and evolve in relation to it through our mental, intellectual, and physical activities throughout life.

Our individual consciousness essentially evolves and grows in relation to a nonlocal or higher consciousness that exists everywhere. To further demonstrate this point, meditation is known to produce physical changes in the brain. The study of this process is known as "spiritual neuroscience."[58] Such studies of meditating Buddhist monks have revealed that their brains show much higher-than-normal gamma-wave activity, particularly in the forehead and sides of the head, which remained at least to some degree after meditation ended. Also significant is that the parts of the brain relating to empathy and compassion showed a marked increase in activity.[59] Furthermore, extensive scientific studies of the NDE and of lucid consciousness during a period when all brain activities cease to exist strongly suggest the existence of a spiritual or higher, cosmic consciousness.

While it is also true that diseases of the brain, spinal cord, and nervous system can cause experiences similar in some ways to NDEs, the differences are significant. Even though some people who have had neurologically caused seizures reported having out-of-body experiences and so-called life reviews, the remembered images in these cases usually occurred in random fashion rather than in the order typical of NDEs. By the same token, the images in the review are usually not connected to important life events and do not necessarily have any spiritually educational value. Instead, the images tend to be more superficial and less apt to be remembered later than those of typical NDEs, which are deeply meaningful and vividly remembered. [60]

Problems with the Psychological Explanation

The assumption among those who claim near-death experiences are purely psychological in nature is that NDEs are pure wish-fulfilling fantasies arising from dreams or delusions. I have heard this said by intelligent people I know and by various "experts" appearing on TV and in the popular media. However, consider that NDE reports of what happens at death go well beyond what is commonly imagined and that these reports come from a variety of NDErs in both Western and non-Western cultures. It then seems highly unlikely that NDEs are caused merely by dreams, delusions, or wishful thinking.[61] Furthermore, as Moody points out, NDE reports are for the most part quite similar to descriptions of death found in various ancient writings unknown to most if not all modern NDErs.[62]

Even if near-death experiences are not the result of dreams, delusions, or wishful thinking, there is another psychological phenomenon that can cause one to experience something remarkably similar to an NDE. It is true that prolonged isolation can lead to authentic otherworldly experiences that are real and long-lasting. Individuals who have been in isolation for long periods of time, whether by choice or not, have told of being in the presence of spiritual guides or deceased loved ones and of being at least partly separated from their bodies. Such individuals have also reported that in the midst of their periods of isolation, they saw past events from their lives and described feeling "at one" with the universe.[63]

History also provides plenty of examples of these kinds of events as experienced by various mystics and shamans from Native American, South American, and Asian cultures. Nevertheless, as similar as these phenomena are to those associated with NDEs, these isolation-induced experiences are more limited in terms of the number of events and after-effects than more comprehensive NDEs typically are.[64]

From all the evidence presented so far, then, it is fair to contend that NDEs 1) are real and not the product of dreams, hallucinations, delusions, or fantasies, 2) are not directly related to the use of mind-altering drugs or medications, and 3) are frequently but not always induced by life-threatening medical crises. Furthermore, detailed observations reported by many patients while in a state of clinical death have been corroborated and verified.

LIFE-CHANGING EFFECTS OF NEAR-DEATH EXPERIENCES

Perhaps even more important than the extraordinary nature of the near-death experience and its assumed causes are the long-term, transformative effects that result, especially in regard to the radiant, heaven-like type of NDE. Imagine having an intense experience in an unearthly dimension beyond space and time, where you are accepted with unconditional love and infused with incredible knowledge. It's no wonder that upon "reentry," NDErs approach every aspect of life and the world with a changed outlook.

With a new broader and deeper understanding of the real purposes of life on Earth, some adjust to their restored physical life in positive ways, while others have a more difficult time. In either case, it's perfectly clear that most NDErs undergo profound psychological, physiological, and spiritual changes that result in a radically different approach to death as well as to life. This appears to be true of child and adult NDErs alike. It's only natural, then, that researchers have conducted extensive follow-up studies on such people over a period of many years. What is emerging from the many continuing studies by researchers such as Ring, Atwater, Sutherland, and Morse is their agreement that the transformative effects of near-death experiences are real and have evolutionary implications.

Psychological Changes

Among the important psychological effects or personality shifts that occur as a result of heaven-like NDEs is complete loss of the fear of death. People who have had near-death experiences realize that after leaving their bodies, life continues without interruption in a dimension filled with unconditional love. The only uncertainty they have is about the process and manner in which death will eventually occur. Eight years after one NDEr's encounter, he was able to say emphatically, "I'm no longer afraid of death, because I'll never forget what happened to me there. Now I'm certain that life goes on."[65]

As a result of being able to review and experience their entire lives in the presence of one or more spiritual guides, NDErs also gain a clearer sense of their lives' true purpose: that they are on Earth at this particular time to help make life better for others and the world in general. The majority tend to see this as their new mission in life and often seek service-oriented careers. Despite what may well have been, for some, a self-focused life before their experience, NDErs usually become more generous with their time and money, lose their previous desire for possessions, recognition, and rewards, and tend to be more accepting of others.[66]

NDErs also come away from their experience in the light with an increased sense of life's sacredness and tend to live more fully in the moment without worrying about the future. For this reason, they often pay less attention to the passage of time and may even refuse to adhere to schedules. This nonconformist type of behavior can be exasperating at times for loved ones and others with whom they interact on a daily basis.[67]

Another oft-noted change in an NDEr's behavior is a newly acquired thirst for knowledge and an openness to new and more inventive ways of thinking. This often leads NDErs to feel frustrated with friends, family members, and others who lack the NDErs' spiritually expanded perspective on life and greater understanding of the "big picture."[68]

Physiological Changes

As significant as all these psychological changes are, the physical changes that commonly happen to NDErs are especially remarkable. In his "Omega Project" study conducted in the early 1990s, Kenneth Ring found that many of his subjects claimed their nervous systems were functioning differently from how they did before their NDEs. By the same token, others were certain their brains had been physically altered during and after their NDEs.[69] These changes seemingly resulted from what NDErs refer to as the phenomenon of being immersed in a powerfully bright field of light, one that radiates not only total unconditional love but also an extraordinary amount of electromagnetic energy.

Whatever the cause, there is ample evidence to show that NDErs acquire new abilities and physical sensitivities once they return to their physical bodies. More specifically, researchers have found that more than 75 percent of individuals who have near-death experiences are left with some or all of the physical effects researchers such as Van Lommel and Atwater describe as hyperesthesia, synesthesia, acquisition of psychic abilities, and heightened electrical sensitivity.[70] Because so many NDErs are affected by some if not all of these physiological changes, we'll further examine each of them here.

Hyperesthesia can result in heightened sensitivity to bright lights in general and often leaves NDErs with acute sensitivity to sunlight in particular. The effect can also be painful enough to force NDErs to wear sunglasses or other protective eye coverings, even in lighting conditions considered tolerable by most people.[71] NDErs may also experience other types of hyperesthesia, such as hypersensitivity to sound, touch, smell, and even taste. While such sensitivities may not be highly debilitating, they can prompt affected NDErs to avoid large public gatherings and certain kinds of food that never bothered them before their NDEs. Furthermore, metabolic changes are a factor in more than 50 percent of these hyperesthesia cases, and they can cause experiencers to absorb substances such as medicines and vitamins more quickly than before their NDEs. This means doses must be reduced from pre-NDE levels to avoid negative reactions and in some cases avoided altogether due to new allergic reactions.[72]

Another type of physical effect, known as synesthesia, is one in which the brain appears to have been "rewired" in such a way that sensory impressions overlap and affect one another. Again, in more than half of NDE cases, the parts of the brain that normally process information become more closely connected and can often cross-communicate. This means the NDEr may hear or smell colors or see smells and sounds.[73]

Enhanced intuitive sensitivities or psychic abilities also result from a large percentage of NDE cases, according to Sutherland and Bruce Greyson, professor of psychiatric medicine at the University of Virginia. Among the various sensitivities and abilities gained by NDErs are clairvoyance, telepathy, precognition, occasional contact with deceased spirits, perception of auras, and even paranormal healing abilities.[74]

These types of psychic awakenings characteristic of many NDErs can be a blessing or a curse, depending on circumstances. For instance, the ability to hear and understand the thoughts of others can be disconcerting and embarrassing for NDErs as well as for those whose thoughts are intercepted. On the other hand, some who become psychically sensitive in this way have been able to help those whom they know are suffering inwardly from anxiety or fear due to life issues the NDEr clearly perceives.

Dannion Brinkley, two-time NDEr and author of the book *Saved by the Light*, recalls when he first discovered that he had new psychic capabilities after his near-death experience: "Right after being struck by lightning, as I lay in my hospital bed and people took my hand, I found that I was suddenly them in a certain situation. For example, I would see this person fighting with someone in his family. I didn't necessarily know what the fight was about, but I could feel the pain or anger that the person felt."[75] Like Brinkley, other NDErs have reported a radical life change in that they feel closer to other human beings than they did before. As one NDEr put it, "I feel an empathy with everyone and everything and am aware of the interconnectedness and oneness of all"[76]

Another psychic change experienced by a significant number of NDErs is a newfound ability to positively affect the health of others through the transfer of energy. In such cases, NDErs may discover that their hands discharge an unusually high level of energy in the form of heat. In her research on NDE after-effects, Sutherland found that while only about 8 percent of the subjects she surveyed had any healing abilities before their NDE, as many as 70 percent of them had exceptionally high-energy "healing hands" after their experiences.[77] Energy emitted from the hands of these transformed individuals is capable of reducing or eliminating pain and other physical disturbances in others, especially when applied in a loving and compassionate way.

One individual who discovered she had this ability after two NDEs is Barbara Harris, whose psychic gifts have been observed and studied by IANDS researchers. In her book, *Full Circle: The Near-Death Experience and Beyond*, she tells of an incident that occurred while she massaged the shoulders of a man suffering from fatigue. He asked Harris if she was aware of the energy radiating from her hands. She replied, "I know that my patients feel better after I massage them … There is heat that comes from my palms when I do it, but I never thought of it as energy."[78] Harris went on to describe what usually preceded her healing activity: "I'd feel pressure building up inside my head, but it always went away when I put my hands on the patients … I couldn't explain it then, but helping them somehow always helped me, too. Even when the headaches stopped, I'd come home after being on my feet for eight hours and I was supercharged. I knew it was because I was touching these people."[79]

This ability to perform hands-on healing is quite similar to the energy-healing practices taught by Barbara Brennan as mentioned in Chapter 5, except that in Harris's case she acquired her healing ability spontaneously as a result of her NDE. According to Kenneth Ring, "There is indeed something about an NDE that tends to unleash what is probably a latent potential in us all—the ability to mediate healing energies to others."[80] This seems to give further credence to the idea that the spiritual energy that we all possess and that constitutes our spiritual essence represents a potential power for good that is greater than most of us imagine.

Furthermore, the relationship between this type of healing ability and the biblical stories of Jesus's miraculous healings, along with those later performed by his disciples after Pentecost, seems to be more than a coincidence. In Acts we read, "Awe came upon everyone, because many wonders and signs were being done by the Apostles" (Acts 2:43). And the story of Pentecost relates an event in which "divided tongues, as of fire, appeared among them, and a tongue rested on each of them. All of them were filled with the Holy Spirit and began to speak in other languages, as the Spirit gave them the ability" (Acts 2:4). The common cause of the spontaneous acquisition of psychic gifts by Jesus's disciples and by some NDErs appears to be the transformative power of high levels of energy in the form of light, despite differences in where and how this transformation took place. Unlike NDErs, the disciples at Pentecost were not at the point of death or in a lifeless state. Nevertheless, in both cases the lasting effect seems to have been the capacity to transfer some degree of this divinely initiated energy to others in a healing way through touch, or even by intention from a distance.

The spontaneous activation of high levels of energy by some NDErs and by the disciples of Jesus long ago also bears strong resemblance to the phenomenon known, especially in the East, as a "kundalini awakening."[81] While not at the point of death or in a lifeless state, those who experience a kundalini awakening sense the movement of energy through the spine in such a way that it dramatically affects the various chakras (natural energy centers that affect specific parts of the body). This sudden flow of energy can transform the brain and nervous system enough to enable them to function at a much higher level. According to Ring, the spiritual connection between NDEs and the kundalini experience is real: "In full kundalini awakenings, what is experienced is significantly similar to what many NDErs report from their experiences. And more than that: The aftereffects of these deep kundalini awakenings seem to lead to individual transformations and personal world views essentially indistinguishable from those found in NDErs."[82]

In Barbara Harris's case, some of her post-NDE events involved an explosive surge in energy, much like a kundalini awakening, that usually led to severe headaches and flashes of light. What happened at Pentecost also appears to have involved flashes of light or "tongues of fire." But whether the disciples experienced a kundalini awakening at Pentecost or not, they'd had at the very least a powerful transformational encounter with the Holy Spirit, as have many NDErs since that time. Although Harris and other NDErs do not suddenly begin to speak in other languages, they reveal the extent of their spiritual transformation by eagerly using their psychic abilities to administer healing energy to others.

Another closely related psychic gift acquired by some NDErs is the spontaneous ability to see or sense the presence of a serious physical problem *within* the body of another person. For instance, one NDEr who was the father of an eighteen-month-old girl *saw* a tumor in her brain before any symptoms presented themselves. Later, after his daughter experienced an epileptic seizure, a neurosurgeon confirmed the problem.[83] Likewise, NDErs often report being able to see the auras surrounding people's bodies as well as the energy centers known as chakras *within* their bodies, despite having had no ability to do so before their NDEs.

In addition to the various physiological enhancements already mentioned, some NDErs have reported a newly acquired capacity to involuntarily radiate enough electrical energy from their bodies to affect nearby electrical equipment. For instance, computers suddenly fail to operate properly or at all, or automobile electrical systems and household appliances cease to operate for no obvious reason. Especially vulnerable are digital wristwatches worn by electrically sensitive NDErs. Such individuals usually stop wearing wristwatches altogether after replacement watches also stop working.[84]

Spiritual Awakenings

While near-death experiences, as we have seen, generate a variety of significant psychological and physiological changes, spiritual transformations are also noteworthy and have broad implications. In the light, or what many NDErs conclude was the luminous presence of God, experiencers are essentially shown a new, expanded reality that can be the basis of a rebirth. Furthermore, this luminous spiritual presence often remains accessible to NDErs long after the actual event in ways not as apparent to others. As one who went through as many as three NDEs herself, Atwater explains it well: "This intelligent luminosity ... is always available as a non-energetic force, a Holy Spirit capable of moving in and through us once we are ready to surrender to it. Experiencers claim that should we ignore its presence or remain locked in a particular lifestyle that denies our true purpose or 'life mission,' this subtle spirit can forcibly intervene, and if it does, a shift occurs."[85]

Atwater is essentially referring to acts of divine intervention. NDErs often report that such interventions occur in a variety of ways well beyond their near-death experiences. For some, especially children who have had one or more NDEs, paranormal events can become commonplace. These events may include occasional out-of-body episodes along with seeing or hearing spiritual beings or angels with whom they can communicate as one would talk to a friend.[86]

Children who have had such visitations usually describe them as peaceful and non-threatening. Some adult NDErs even report having angelic visitations both while sleeping and during waking hours. These visitations or auditory messages from spiritual beings are usually specific and readily remembered and occur at the most opportune moments during times of stress and uncertainty.[87]

As a whole, NDErs also become more interested in spirituality, meditation, and other expressions of openness to the light. This is coupled with an equal loss of interest in religious orthodoxy and in organized religion in general. A related fact is that those who have NDEs come to realize that one's religion or lack of religion makes no difference in the type of experience they have. It seems not to matter whether a person is a Christian, a Jew, a Muslim, a Buddhist, an agnostic, or an atheist— their NDEs are essentially the same in that they are all embraced by the same unconditional love and indescribable divine light. If near-death experiences prove anything, it is that spreading unconditional love and forgiveness to all human beings and every aspect of God's Earthly creation is both the message and the divine gift that transcends religious dogma and church law.

With this premise in mind, it is worth considering that many individuals who have never had an NDE but who have open-mindedly read and listened to what NDErs and their transformative events have to say have themselves been transformed in ways similar to NDErs. Ring decided to find out how substantially these inquisitive non-NDErs have

changed and whether they, along with those who have had one or more
NDEs, now serve as a catalyst for wider spiritual change. He conducted
a study involving seventy-four NDErs and a control group of fifty-four
individuals who had never had an NDE but were interested in the phenomenon.[88] When examining the changes in beliefs and values that
occurred in both groups, he discovered that the non–NDE control group
showed some of the same changes already demonstrated by NDErs due
to the control-group members' efforts to learn as much as they could
about the nature of NDEs. While the depth and breadth of these life
changes among the control group were lesser than they were for those
who had actually gone through an NDE, the study clearly showed that
the members of the control group did become more appreciative of life,
more self-accepting, more compassionate and sensitive to the needs of
others, more spiritual and less materialistic, more confident that life
continues after death, and less fearful of death.

In other words, they ended up with a set of values very similar to
those of actual NDErs. Furthermore, the changes in values and general
outlook on life reflected in the members of the control group did not
disappear over time. All indications were that these life changes were
permanent, as was the case with those who had actually had NDEs.[89]
In the final analysis, Ring came away convinced that the mere act of
acquiring knowledge about NDEs can, in his words, serve as a "benign
virus" that can spread among others with the same positive results. As
a member of Ring's control group put it, "It is possible to gain all the
knowledge a person learns when they die, without dying. You don't have
to die to get there."[90]

What is especially relevant and meaningful about near-death
experiences as a whole is that their transformative power and purpose
are closely related to what Jesus continuously and passionately taught.
The profound truths of everlasting life, unconditional love, and divine
oneness that he brought as good news to the world are often revealed

to NDErs in the presence of the light. Even as Jesus taught us to love one another and to "do unto others as you would have them do unto you," an equally important message is often imparted to NDErs in the midst of their life reviews by beings of light: As we do unto others, we do unto ourselves.

This stunning realization of how spiritually interconnected we human beings really are, and how consequential our thoughts and actions are to ourselves and others, is potentially the most transformative message of all. The world can move closer to the light by being open to the lessons NDErs and enlightened others—these harbingers of spiritual oneness—bring to us. Like the ancient Hebrew prophets and the early followers of Jesus, they call out for a collective spiritual awakening.

There is great significance in the fact that the increasing numbers of children and adults who are actually seeing life beyond death, and the wide dissemination of their profound revelations, come at this time in human history. Whether these events and the remarkable messages and gifts they bring are divinely engineered or humankind is simply at such a level of consciousness that we are capable of being transformed by them—or both—is still an open question. But what seems certain is that in the increasing numbers of well-documented near-death experiences, we are seeing and experiencing a new spiritual awakening that can lead us beyond what separates us toward global oneness—if we are willing to listen and learn.

CHAPTER 7

Reincarnation: A Reality beyond Religious Boundaries

REINCARNATION ACCEPTED IN EARLY EASTERN AND WESTERN CULTURES

The idea that God's creation is an ongoing, evolutionary process involving the reincarnation or rebirth of souls actually came into human consciousness in many parts of the ancient world well before Western civilization began. Although many people in the West have come to assume that reincarnation was strictly a product of ancient Hindu and Buddhist cultures, the roots of a cosmic system of reincarnation can be found well beyond the East.

For instance, with the advantage of modern anthropological research methods and technology, it is now known that a firm belief in some form of reincarnation existed among the tribal people of Africa throughout their long history.[1] The same has been found to be true on the continent of Australia as well as in the Pacific Islands and the East Indies. In Australia, for instance, all the evidence among native tribes points to the strong probability that such a belief was widespread as far back as the early Aborigines.[2] Likewise, a belief in reincarnation is known to have been a factor in the collapse of Central America's native peoples when they initially welcomed invading Spaniards in the sixteenth century as their transformed reincarnated ancestors.[3]

In North America, according to Daniel Brinton, professor of archaeology and linguistics at the University of Pennsylvania, reincarnation was central to many of the Native American tribes. He says:

> This seemingly extraordinary doctrine [reincarnation], which some have asserted was entirely unknown and impossible to the American Indians, was in fact one of their most deeply rooted and widespread convictions, especially among the tribes of the eastern United States. It is indissolubly connected with their highest theories of a future life, their burial ceremonies, and their modes of expression.[4]

Even beyond the eastern part of America, Native American tribes such as the Dakotas, Huron, and Winnebagos, in the North; the Kiowas of the Great Plains; and the Hopi and Mohaves of Arizona[5] demonstrated a clear belief in the rebirth of souls long before the arrival of Europeans. Likewise, in northern Canada, the history of the Eskimo people plainly indicates that reincarnation was central to their culture as well. Naturalist Vilhjalmur Stefansson, who lived for ten years with a group of Eskimos in northern Canada, discovered that their reincarnationist beliefs were quite similar to those found in India.[6]

Finally, reincarnationist beliefs are now known to have existed among ancient Europeans such as the Scandinavians and Icelandic peoples along with the early Saxons, Celts, and Teutons.[7] A belief in transmigration based on Orphic theology was popular in ancient Greece and Rome as well. In fact, even before Pythagorus taught reincarnation to the Greeks, such ideas existed in ancient Egypt.[8]

Even though some variation in the interpretations of reincarnation existed within all these cultures in many parts of the world, the common element is that they all reflect a confidence in the existence of a soul that experiences many rebirths in physical form. One gets the distinct sense that an awareness of reincarnation evolved naturally and simultaneously throughout the world because as humans we are inherently conscious of the rhythmic and cyclical order of things in the environment and its relationship to the pattern of human life and death.

BIBLICAL REFERENCES TO REINCARNATION

Early Judaic References to Reincarnation

Many Christians in the West are still unaware that both the Old and New Testaments contain references acknowledging the existence of reincarnation. In Jeremiah 1:4–5, the writer refers to these words spoken by God: "Before I formed thee in the belly I knew thee; and before thou camest forth out of the womb I sanctified thee, and I ordained thee a prophet unto the nations." Here it is clearly implied that Jeremiah's soul existed before his incarnation. Another suggestion of reincarnationist belief is found in Psalms 90:3–6, which refers to a prayer of Moses: "Thou turnest man to destruction; and sayest, Return ye children of men. For a thousand years in thy sight are but as yesterday when it is past, and as a watch in the night. Thou carriest them away as with a flood, they are as asleep; in the morning they are like grass which groweth up. In the morning it flourishes, and groweth up, in the evening it is cut down, and withereth."

In this case, it seems the author has chosen to use the seasonal cycles of nature as an appropriate metaphor for the cyclical rebirth of the soul. According to Nobel Prize winner Isaac Bashevis Singer, "The Almighty did not create us just for one season and then send us to die. We are coming back."[9]

In the book of the Wisdom of Solomon, which was one of seven wisdom books contained in the Septuagint Old Testament along with Job, Psalms, Proverbs, Ecclesiastes, the Song of Solomon, and Sirach, one can find this unmistakable affirmation of reincarnation attributed to Solomon: "I was indeed a child well endowed, having had a noble soul fall to my lot; or rather being noble I entered an undefiled body."[10] Implied here is that the noble character of the soul's previous incarnation was carried forward to Solomon's present life. The Wisdom of Solomon was written as early as the first or second century BCE.

A final example from the pre-Christian era comes from the Testament of Naphtali, one of the Testaments of the Twelve Patriarchs written during the first century BCE. In this particular testament, Naphtali says, "God makes the body 'in correspondence to the spirit' and 'instills the spirit corresponding to the power of the body.'"[11] Now it seems that the author makes the distinction between the eternal, undying soul (spirit) and the temporary nature of the body. The whole idea of the body being "instilled" with the spirit points to the phenomenon of reincarnation.

Early Christian References to Reincarnation

When it comes to the Christian era, an even greater number of references in support of reincarnation can be found in various parts of the New Testament among the writings of some of the most important leaders of the early Christian Church.

During the time of Jesus, the two most significant Jewish sects were the Essenes and the Pharisees, and first-century Jewish historian Josephus said both groups believed in reincarnation. He tells us that the Essenes were followers of the Greek philosopher Pythagoras, and it is widely known that Pythagoras taught reincarnation, including the concept of a pre-existent, eternal soul.[12] Then, too, since the Pharisee sect represented a preponderance of the first-century Jewish community, it is fair to say that most of the Jews living in Palestine at that time believed in reincarnation. In addition, Jesus would more than likely have been exposed to Greek thought, including belief in immortal souls and reincarnation, since Greek was the international language of his day.[13]

In the New Testament there are as many as ten references to the second coming or reincarnation of the ninth century BCE prophet Elijah that directly relate to the following statement made near the end of the Old Testament: "Behold, I will send you Elijah the prophet before the coming of the great and dreadful day of the Lord."[14]

At no point does Jesus dispute this prophecy, and at various places in the canonical Gospels he seems to encourage it. For example, he appears to express his confidence in the existence of reincarnation when he says in Matthew 11:7, 10-11, "Verily I say unto you among them that are born of women there hath not risen a greater than John the Baptist ... And if ye will receive it, this is Elias [Elijah] which was to come." He seems to reinforce these claims when in Matthew 11:13-14 he says, "For all the prophets and the law prophesied until John came and if you are willing to accept it, he is Elijah who has come."

Then, in Matthew 17:9-13, Jesus says: "Elias truly shall first come, and restore all things. But I say unto you, That Elias is come already, and they knew him not, but have done unto him whatsoever they listed. Likewise shall also the Son of Man suffer of them. Then the disciples understood that he spoke unto them of John the Baptist [who had already been executed]." Statements similar to these also appear in Mark 8:27-28 and 9:9-13 and in Luke 9:18-19.

Although John the Baptist denies that he is Elias reborn in the first chapter of the Gospel of John, Jesus's emphatic claims to the contrary would seem to suggest that his knowledge of pre-existence was more extensive than John's.

Another example that seems to demonstrate Jesus's acceptance of reincarnation is found in John 9:2–3. Here the author describes the following conversation between Jesus and his disciples about the healing of a man who had been blind since birth: "His disciples asked him, Rabbi, who sinned, this man or his parents, that he was born blind?" The disciples appear to be referring to the widespread Jewish belief that the sins of the fathers will be visited upon later generations in the form of divine punishment, as suggested in Exodus 20:5: "For I, the Lord your God, am a jealous God, visiting the iniquity of the fathers on the children, on the third and the fourth generations of those who hate Me." While this man's blindness appears to suggest some sort of inherited punishment or debt, Jesus disagrees: "Neither this man nor his parents sinned; he was born blind so that God's works might be revealed in him." In this instance, Jesus challenges the commonly held notion that this man's unfortunate condition was the punitive or negative result of some transgression that his soul committed in a previous life or that his parents committed. Instead, Jesus recognizes the positive potential for enlightenment on the part of the blind man and those with whom he interacted.[15]

The contrast is clear between the common interpretation of the reincarnationist concept of karma as a cosmic system of punishment and rewards for past-life deeds and Jesus's appeal to go beyond the mere balancing of punishments and rewards. Jesus seems to acknowledge the existence of the so-called law of karma in his Sermon on the Mount, when he says in Matthew 7:2, "With the judgment you make you will be judged, and the measure you give will be the measure you get," and in Matthew 7:12, "In everything do to others as you would have them do to you; for this is the law and the prophets." However, he is not fatalistic when it comes to karma. He continually makes it known to us that we are eternally capable of transcending karmic debts through acts of love, compassion, and forgiveness because God is merciful as well as just. In essence, Jesus must have seen karma as the opportunity for redemption and spiritual growth rather than punishment. It is also important to recognize that at no point in the New Testament does Jesus dismiss the basic idea of reincarnation.[16]

REINCARNATIONIST VIEWS OF EARLY CHURCH LEADERS AFTER THE DEATH OF JESUS

During the period between Jesus's death and 553 C.E., when the Orthodox Church implemented a purge against all Christians professing to believe in reincarnation, some of the most distinguished leaders of the emerging Christian Church also supported reincarnation through their teaching and widely distributed writings. They included bishops and theologians such as Justin Martyr, Clement of Alexandria, and Origen Adamantius (also known as Origen of Alexandria), from the second and third centuries, along with Synesius, Bishop of Ptolemais, and Nemesius, Bishop of Emesa, from the fourth and fifth centuries. Also supportive of reincarnation were certain Gnostic Christians of the second century such as Basilides, who founded the Basilidean sect of Alexandrian Gnostics, and Valentinus, whose ideas spread through North Africa, the Middle East, and Europe.[17]

Bishop Origen's Writings in Favor of Reincarnation

Perhaps the individual on this list who was the most prominent in his views regarding the pre-existence and reincarnation of souls was Origen of Alexandria. He writes:

> Is it not more in accordance with common sense that every soul for reasons unknown—I speak in accordance with the opinions of Pythagoras, Plato and Empedokles—enters the

body influenced by its past deeds? The soul has a body at its disposal for a certain period of time which, due to its changeable condition, eventually is no longer suitable for the soul, whereupon it changes that body for another.[18]

Biblical scholars have described Origen as "the most distinguished and most influential of all the theologians of the ancient Church, with the possible exception of Augustine."[19] He was the author of almost two thousand books, and his ideas were endorsed by many early Christians— even as his writings were attacked, declared heretical, publicly cursed, and burned on orders from the Church's orthodox bishops in the sixth century, long after Origen's imprisonment, torture, and subsequent death in 254 CE. Fortunately, the Church failed to eliminate his writings altogether. His ideas and fame eventually spread to many parts of the Roman Empire.

Although Origen was influenced by Neoplatonist ideas, he did not agree with the Greek Stoics' idea that the soul's cycle of rebirths was perpetual and never-ending. Instead, he believed that reincarnation was an upward-evolving process leading to a gradual maturing of individual souls and the world as a whole on the way to ultimate union with God. To him, reincarnation was the key to salvation in the sense that spiritual progress was based on individual effort and moral responsibility. He saw this happening over time by means of the soul's reincarnating in several successive bodies. He was also influenced by Christian and Jewish scriptures (before the New Testament existed) in addition to the ideas of Plato, Gnostic writers such as Paul the Antiochene, the Neoplatonists, and Clement of Alexandria, and possibly his belief that Jesus's secret teachings included reincarnation.[20]

Origen's best-known document, *On First Principles*, did much to present his case in favor of reincarnation. According to him, the two most important principles were, first, that "God is just" and, second, "that human beings have free will."[21] When considering the cause of anyone's unfortunate physical disability or other misfortune at birth, Origen argued that the basis for such a handicap can be found in his or her past-life actions rather than in some arbitrary or capricious decision on the part of God. Likewise, Origen recognized that our free will, granted to us by God, often leads to unfortunate circumstances caused by the unwise choices we all make at times but that the alternative to God's gift of free will is predestination without any opportunity for a soul's growth and enlightenment.

Unfortunately, the approach that many present-day fundamentalist Christians take tends to distort Origen's first principle while ignoring the second. In other words, the assumption is often that all our misfortunes throughout life are caused by some previous sin or sins that we have committed—an attitude not unlike those of the biblical "friends" of Job.

MODERN SCIENTIFIC STUDIES OF REINCARNATION

In the modern world, particularly over the past century, reincarnation has been the subject of numerous case studies conducted by highly respected researchers in the fields of psychology and psychiatry as well as theology. As a result of this ongoing research, we have much more evidence to suggest that reincarnation is real and quite relevant to the evolution of human consciousness.

Perhaps the best-known and respected person in the field of reincarnation research was the late Dr. Ian Stevenson (1918-2007), who was Carlson professor of psychiatry and director of the division of parapsychology, in the Department of Behavioral Medicine and Psychiatry, at the University of Virginia School of Medicine. For a period of forty-six years, he collected and documented more than three thousand cases of reincarnation, specifically among children.

Although Dr. Stevenson wrote several books and articles on the subject, I mainly refer to the second edition of his 1966 book, *Twenty Cases Suggestive of Reincarnation*, as it's one of the most important sources of evidence in support of reincarnation. According to Stevenson, the twenty cases cited in his book provide a representative sample of the nearly six hundred cases he had documented by that time. Stevenson's thorough and time-consuming methods of investigation were legendary and exemplary. Much of his time was spent examining records, independently interviewing family members and others associated with the person or persons suspected of being reincarnated, and comparing the results against possible alternative explanations.[22]

Stevenson had the reputation of leaving nothing to chance. He usually chose not to gather evidence from New Age sources, past-life readings, or hypnotic regressions, although other respected researchers consider some of these methods legitimate when used carefully and objectively.[23] Stevenson chose mostly children as his study subjects because their memories of previous incarnations had had less time to fade than adults' memories and were less "contaminated" by adult ideas and cultural indoctrinations. He also chose to study young children because their spontaneous past-life memories could be investigated scientifically. When doing so, he carefully recorded a child's recollections about a previous life, and then he identified the deceased person the child claimed to have been. Finally, he gathered the facts of the deceased person's life to see if they conformed to the child's memory.

In some cases, Stevenson was even able to match birthmarks and birth defects on the living children to wounds or scars on the bodies of the deceased people they remembered being, as established and verified by medical records.[24] The living children usually could remember how they died in their previous life in vivid, sometimes grim detail that explained the nature of the marks.

Stevenson also discovered that most of the children whose cases he documented had lived previous lives only a few years before their present incarnations. In other words, it seemed that children who died at an early age tended to reincarnate sooner than those who were older. At least this seemed to be the case in those areas of the world where Stevenson conducted his investigations. Most of the children Stevenson interviewed before the publication of his *Twenty Cases Suggestive of Reincarnation* were from India, Ceylon, Brazil, Alaska, and Lebanon.[25] The following case, involving the alleged rebirth of a young boy from India, was investigated by Stevenson in 1961. The case is quite similar in its details to many other cases he examined.

The Case of Nirmal and His Later Reincarnation

In April 1950, a ten-year-old boy named Nirmal died of smallpox in the town of Kosi Kalan. Sixteen months later, in August 1951, an infant boy named Prakash was born in another town in India called Chhatta. Stevenson reported:

> As an infant Prakash was noted to cry much more than other children, but otherwise he showed no unusual behavior until the age of about four and a half. At that time he began waking up in the middle of the night and running out of the house to the street. When stopped, he would say he "belonged in" Kosi Kalan, that his name was Nirmal, and that he wanted to go to his old home. He said his father was Bholanath.[26]

Prakash insisted on being called Nirmal and sometimes would not respond when called Prakash. He told his mother she was not his mother and complained about the mediocrity of the house they lived in. He talked of "his father's" shops, his iron safe, and the members of the previous family. Often he would weep abundantly and go without food during the period of his pleadings to go to Kosi Kalan. One day Prakash took a large nail and started off in the direction of Kosi Kalan. Members of the family went in search of him and found him half a mile away, in the direction of Kosi Kalan. When asked what the nail was, Prakash replied: "This is the key of my iron safe."[27]

Then in 1956, Prakash pleaded so persistently to be taken to Kosi Kalan that his uncle took him on a bus he thought was traveling to Kosi Kalan but was actually headed to the town of Mathura. Five-year-old Prakash, however, "immediately pointed out the error and cried to go to Kosi Kalan. His uncle then put him on the correct bus and took him to Kosi Kalan."[28] Nevertheless, after arriving in Kosi Kalan, he was unable to meet anyone from Nirmal's family.

In the summer of 1961, the father of the deceased Nirmal traveled to Chhatta on business with one of his daughters, Memo. Since he had heard by that time that a young boy in Chhatta named Prakash was claiming to be Nirmal, he decided to meet him without any notice. When the two met for the first time, Prakash immediately recognized Nirmal's father by name but misidentified the daughter as Vimla, a sister to Nirmal.

During the course of his investigation, Stevenson noted that no members of either of the two families had met before this initial exchange and that the two families "are of slightly different subcastes and this would make more unlikely their having acquaintanceship or mutual friends."[29] Stevenson added:

More difficult to explain are Prakash's correct recognitions of numerous members of the Jain family [Nirmal's family] and their neighbors, sometimes giving proper names as well as correct relationships or other identification. Two of the persons recognized were ladies in purdah [in seclusion from men or strangers]. Prakash, moreover, had information about the rooms of the Jain house and some shops accurate for the time of the life of Nirmal, but out of date at the time of his visit to Kosi Kalan.

Such items and his error in mistaking Memo (who had not been born when Nirmal died) for Nirmal's other sister, Vimla, suggest previously acquired knowledge of past events rather than recently acquired knowledge as the source of Prakash's information about people and places in Kosi Kalan.[30]

After thoroughly investigating this case, Stevenson concluded that there was no possibility that either family had perpetrated a hoax.[31]

Stevenson's Conclusions about the Reincarnation of Children

Stevenson documented hundreds of cases similar to this story over the course of his many years of research. In such cases, children he interviewed clearly remembered their former lives as adults, including the nature of their deaths. They often remembered the names and details of their former husbands or wives, children, in-laws, friends, and so on. This was particularly interesting when the incarnated children were able to meet and easily identify their former spouses as well as other previous family members!

In a relatively small number of cases, Stevenson was able to disprove the accounts given to him because of unreliable information or discrepancies in the stories given by witnesses. However, a substantial number of cases still remain credible and well-supported by the facts. in *Twenty Cases Suggestive of Reincarnation*, many of them are explained in much greater detail than is possible to present here. To date, no other credible explanation has been found to account for these cases other than reincarnation. Stevenson discovered as well that children's initial memories of previous lives almost always fade away between the ages of five and ten and are seldom a cause of concern in their adolescent and adult lives.[32]

OTHER REINCARNATION STUDIES BY STEVENSON

Links between Birthmarks and Past Lives

In a 1988 interview conducted by *Omni* magazine, Stevenson said he was working on a large number of cases that involved birthmarks and birth defects among children in Burma, Turkey, Lebanon, and the American Northwest.[33] He revealed that he had documented about two hundred cases in which raised or depressed birthmarks could not be distinguished from the scars of wounds originally inflicted on the deceased individuals the children claimed they had been in a previous life. Stevenson was able to verify several of these matches by obtaining autopsies and other medical records.[34]

One such example that appears in the book *The Soul Genome: Science and Reincarnation,* by highly respected researcher Paul Von Ward, is the case of a child who insisted that he had died of gunshot wounds in a previous life. After examining autopsy reports of the child's "former self" it was discovered that the deceased person was, in fact, shot to death and that the two birthmarks on the living child's body perfectly matched the size and locations of the two bullet wounds on the deceased person's body.[35] According to Stevenson, this particular case was not unique; he was able to document several other cases of a similar kind. He was convinced that in these instances, coincidence was not a viable explanation.

Stevenson's discoveries along these lines eventually resulted in the 1997 publication of his book *When Reincarnation and Biology Intersect.*

The Child-Prodigy Phenomenon

Another phenomenon Stevenson studied extensively was that of predispositions in which children show exceptionally strong interests and certain superior skills not typical of most children. He acknowledged that environmental influences can be a factor in some cases but said that in many child-prodigy cases, such skills and dramatically advanced abilities at an early age cannot be explained by environment, heredity, chance, or coincidence. On the basis of his research, Stevenson seemed convinced that in these extraordinary cases, the deliberate retention of certain knowledge and abilities from previous incarnations seems to be the only reasonable conclusion.[36]

Views Concerning Past-Life Regression Hypnosis

Throughout his years of research, Stevenson remained convinced that hypnosis was not a reliable device for recalling previous personalities, but he acknowledged that in some rare cases, hypnosis yielded legitimate evidence in support of reincarnation. For instance, he referred to the case of the wife of a Methodist minister who suddenly began to speak German after he hypnotized her despite having had no knowledge of the language before hypnosis. He acknowledged that this spontaneous ability to speak an unlearned language, known as xenoglossy, could very well stem from a past-life experience and that no alternative explanation serves to provide a better answer in this and other cases in which the hypnosis process is properly and responsibly administered.[37]

Links between Gender and Reincarnation

During the 1988 interview, Stevenson also had some things to say about the fact that a soul's sex can change from one incarnation to another. He revealed that among the one hundred sex-change cases he encountered, sixty-six involved girls who recalled previous lives as boys. In other words, in cases where a change in gender occurred, it tended to involve a male-to-female change more often.[38] Stevenson was questioned further about the possible implications he thought this might have regarding the issue of homosexuality. He agreed that it brings a whole new dimension to the matter. In the end, Stevenson seemed convinced that reincarnation should be given serious consideration as a possible cause, just as most people in Southeast Asia do.[39] So, when it comes to Southeast Asian children, there appears to be no overblown, judgmental reaction to gender-identity confusion as there is in America, especially in its Christian communities.

Reason for the Loss of Memory of Previous Lives

When asked in his 1988 interview what advice he had for most of us who have no memories of previous lives, Stevenson responded:

> Some persons have said it is unfair to be reborn unless you can remember details of a previous life and profitably remember your mistakes. [This was one of the points raised by the early Orthodox Church polemicists against the Christian reincarnationist bishops.] They forget that forgetting is essential to successful living in the present. If every time we walked, we were to remember how we stumbled, we would fall again.

He went on to say, "The memories they [children] have are often more of a handicap than a blessing; and nearly all become happier as they grow older and forget their previous lives. To paraphrase Jesus Christ, sufficient unto one life is the evil thereof."[40]

The Evolutionary Purpose of Reincarnation

Finally, Stevenson was asked if he thought reincarnation had a higher purpose and he replied, "Well, yes I do. My idea of God is that he is evolving. I don't believe in the watchmaker God, the original creator who built the watch and then lets it tick. I believe in a 'self-maker God' who is evolving and experimenting; so are we as parts of him. Bodies wear out; souls may need periods for rest and reflection. Afterward, one may start again with a new body."[41]

THE 'SOUL GENOME' THEORY OF REINCARNATION

In addition to Stevenson, Paul Von Ward has gathered valuable evidence in support of reincarnation using scientific methods of investigation that have withstood the test of serious scrutiny. In his book *The Soul Genome*, he establishes what he calls an "integral model" that provides one possible reason behind what he calls the mounting evidence that makes the concept of reincarnation increasingly credible.[42] The types of evidence that Ward refers to are those that cannot be explained away by present theories concerning genetic and personality development. As a result of his research, he believes it is possible that "your physical appearance, the way you think, how you react emotionally to life events, the way you interact with other people, and the creative activities and vocations you choose may be predisposed by the experience of one or more humans who lived in the past." He adds, "Even if you don't know who they were, you may find what appears to be their 'soulprint' in the person you are today and the manner in which you live."[43]

Ward is convinced that reincarnation involves a sequential retention of inherited data from lifetime to lifetime in some kind of "nonmaterial it." He refers to this "it" as psychoplasm. In his opinion, psychoplasm is essentially "a genome-like energetic and information biofield that embodies a single being's knowledge, feelings, and behavior patterns that transcend space and time."[44] For the most part, his research has been conducted for the purpose of answering his following questions:

> Where does a prodigy's amazing knowledge originate? How can we explain a child's knowledge or behavior that has not been taught? How can we access memories of knowledge and experiences that are not our own? Whence do dreams and visions of possible former lives and historical eras come? Why does past-life therapy help people heal chronic psychological and psychosomatic problems? Why do individuals living today look just like unrelated individuals who lived many years before they were born?[45] [In the latter case, Ward is referring to more than common, superficial similarities.]

As a means of doing so, his work has been directed toward the analysis of alleged reincarnations that involve comparing all aspects of the life of a well-known, deceased individual with those of a living person who resembles the deceased person in so many respects that mere coincidence probably did not account for them. For instance, Ward believes there is ample evidence to prove beyond a reasonable doubt that a Dutch artist living in America is the reincarnated soul of nineteenth century French artist Paul Gauguin. Moreover, additional data gathered about this case strongly suggests that the living artist's wife was formerly Gauguin's wife, Mette.[46]

Other currently living individuals have been similarly matched with well-known deceased persons such as Civil War General John B. Gordon, Marilyn Monroe, eighteenth century British writer Samuel Johnson, and at least one of America's founding fathers, James Madison.[47] Since in many cases accurate information about deceased historical figures is readily available through improved computer imaging and data-gathering techniques as well as painted portraits and photographs, more credible comparisons can be made with living individuals who may be their current incarnations. The many comparative cases cited by Ward and his colleagues and the wide range of credible data they have carefully gathered and compiled in the process leads him to believe that each newborn child begins life with a past-life legacy.[48]

To make credible comparisons, Ward's work focuses on identifying and evaluating five major factors contained within what he calls an individual's psychoplasm, or "soul genome." They are:

A person's physical characteristics, or what he calls the "genotype/phenotype"

The cognitive "cerebrotype," or a person's "mental style and capacities"

The emotional "egotype," or the factor that determines how a person copes with the environment

The social "personatype," which refers to how a person relates to others

The behavioral "performatype," which refers to the creative traits an individual displays when engaging in work and play.

Using these factors as a foundation for his research, he and his colleagues concluded that the five factors of certain living people so closely matched those of genetically unrelated deceased people with readily available historic and personal information of a credible nature that no chance happenings or normal causes could account for them.[49]

A typical example of such a close match can be seen in the genotype comparison between photographs of Marilyn Monroe, who died in 1962, and a woman living today who appears to be her soul's reincarnation. The detailed biometrics of their faces vary by such a small amount that the woman who appears to be Monroe's reincarnated personality would be recognized by a highly accurate photo-ID computer as Marilyn Monroe.[50] Along with other consistent similarities between the two women, this biometric match exists despite the fact that the woman who is alive today was born a year after Monroe's death.

In the end, Ward is convinced that further scientific study into the nature of reincarnation is more than justified. "If less than a 10 percent probability exists that reincarnation is a real phenomenon, society should assign it at least a fraction of the billions it allocates to research in physics, psychology, and genetics," he says. "Discoveries about reincarnation may be as relevant to our development and species survival as any of those three areas."[51]

PAST-LIFE REGRESSION HYPNOSIS STUDIES BY DR. HELEN WAMBACH

Well-known psychologist Dr. Helen Wambach also began to gather convincing evidence of the existence of reincarnation, but this time through the use of hypnosis that enabled her patients to revisit and vividly experience one or more of their previous lives. Her purpose in using this technique, known as past-life regression, was to focus on the demographic consistency of past-life memories. The reports she was receiving from her hypnotized patients persuaded her that their recalled information needed to be compared with the anthropological, sociological, and archaeological information already available by way of earlier studies of the particular cultures her patients were describing.[52]

Wambach's purpose was to determine if there was any demographic consistency in their recollections under hypnosis. To establish the degree to which her patients' stories were real or imaginary, she recorded specific details about their past-life gender, race, and economic status along with ordinary details of everyday life that anyone in that earlier time might have observed in the home, on the street, or in conversations with other people. Over a ten-year period, she recorded this type of information gained from more than a thousand patients,[53] and she found that the information was consistent with what was known about the demographics of the cultures described by her patients. The following three examples seem to prove the point.

Gender Changes

Given the fact that the majority of the subjects Wambach worked with were women, her expectations were that they would recall being females in their previous lives, but to her surprise a disproportionate number recalled being males. Even though a smaller proportion of her male subjects remembered being women in their previous lives, gender changes were clearly apparent in both cases. The facts seemed to indicate that the past-life "memories" of her subjects were authentic.

Past-Life Social Status of Most Subjects

When it came to the matter of social classes, here again Wambach discovered a close consistency with documented demographic information. She asked her subjects under hypnosis to identify whether they had been poor, middle-class, or upper-class individuals in their previous lives. While she expected most to say they'd come from upper-class or historically famous stations in life, fewer than 10 percent of her subjects recalled living affluent lives of this sort. Instead, most recalled living rather mundane, even poverty-stricken lives. From 25 percent to 30 percent remembered being middle-class merchants or artisans. This, too, turned out to conform rather closely to sociological studies of the same periods identified by the subjects.[54]

Recalling Past-Life Environmental Details

Wambach also found that her subjects were able to describe such common, ordinary things as architectural details, styles of clothing and footwear, types of coins, the foods that were eaten and how they were prepared, types of eating utensils, and other common items in use during the time periods they identified. In every case, they were consistent with what archaeologists know about those time periods and regions. The fact that her subjects were often able to describe these simple items from previous lifetimes in intricate detail despite the subjects' lack of exposure to any information about them in their current incarnations seemed to dispel any notion that the subjects were able to construct elaborate, well-maintained imaginary stories.[55] Again, Wambach was convinced that the quantity and quality of the data pointed to reincarnation as the only feasible explanation. Although skeptics have questioned her conclusions and her methods, no one has been able to deny that her studies have produced remarkable results, and, according to reincarnation researcher Jeffery Danelek, the data she has compiled constitutes "one of the best and most objective pieces of evidence for the validity of reincarnation in existence."[56]

RESEARCH INTO THE NATURE AND PURPOSE OF REINCARNATION

Dr. Michael Newton, a member of the American Counseling Association and a state-certified master hypnotherapist, has also been engaged in the practice of hypnotic age-regression therapy along with other investigative methods for many years. He has not only uncovered the past lives of his subjects but has focused his attention on the educational experiences of deceased discarnate personalities during the periods between their last incarnations and their subsequent rebirths.

On the basis of his research, Newton is convinced that our soul—our larger or higher self—is the totality of our being that is far more than what encompasses our present incarnated personality living on Earth. So, in reality, we are much more than our current physical being. In effect, you and I are personalities that are experiencing life in physical form on Earth today as extensions or emanations of our souls, which in turn, are extensions or emanations of God, the Ultimate Source.

Another way of explaining it is to say that each of us is a packet of light energy released from, but belonging to, the total light energy of our soul. This is akin to saying we are fractals of a larger whole and bear the imprint of the whole, which in this case is our soul.

The holographic analogy applies in the sense that each portion of a holographic image (a personality, in this case) recorded on holographic film is a replication of the whole (the soul). Since the total light energy of a soul is far greater than what a physical body can accommodate, each of us experiences physical life on Earth having only a portion of our soul's total energy. In essence, our soul has extended itself in the form of different incarnated personalities many times and continues to do so.[57]

Such personalities represent our past, present, and future lives on Earth (or in other locations in the universe). Some of our past-life personalities appear at times in the midst of sleep and dreaming, but also at opportune times while we're awake. Dutch psychologist and reincarnation researcher Hans TenDam refers to these past personalities (or personality) most closely connected to our present life as "feeding" personalities that are reflected to a greater or lesser degree in our particular moods, general outlook, and special abilities or interests.[58]

However, each of the incarnate personalities of our soul is always given complete freedom in how it governs its earthly life. In essence, each personality of a particular soul is incarnated at a particular time and place so that it may learn, grow, and evolve experientially. This is for the purpose of addressing the soul's needs and intentions in harmony with God's loving will.

By experiencing earthly life in physical form with all the tribulations, joys, and challenges that human relationships bring, the soul is able to evolve intellectually and emotionally by gaining in knowledge, understanding, compassion, and love. Growth is also attained in this way by experiencing independence (separation) and the freedom to make wise and unwise choices, with all their natural consequences. Despite its vast cosmic perspective, the soul recognizes that it remains incomplete without directly experiencing the dichotomies of sickness and health, youth and old age, male and female genders, love and fear, and so on that are made possible over the course of several earthly incarnations.

The evidence available from an expanding number of past-life case histories appears to indicate that for every incarnated personality, there are many other discarnate personalities existing in spiritual form from previous lives enfolded into, or belonging to, one's soul or larger self. But while each of us, in our present life on Earth, is a reincarnation of our soul, we are not a composite or continuation of our past personalities. We may, as said before, retain or inherit certain qualities, abilities, and knowledge from the past-life personalities of our soul, but they remain more or less independent of our current personality. Likewise, even though communication between our discarnate or past personalities and our present personality is possible at times, such spiritual entities continue to exist independently as part of the larger self. This is why those who have had near-death experiences often report having met deceased friends, family members, and soul mates on the "other side."

In other words, our spiritual communication and connection with our soul's other personalities, whether at the conscious or unconscious level, is much like that which exists between family members or friends whom we have known and had a deep connection with. In fact, there is every indication that our own behavioral changes, which sometimes occur in the midst of unique circumstances or because of age, may be due in part to such influences.[59]

Nevertheless, if multiple personalities emanate from a given soul over a period of hundreds or even thousands of Earth years (the soul exists outside of time and space), can the soul remain a distinct entity or individual? Some research has suggested that the soul integrates its various sub-personalities in such a way that a "superpersonality" emerges within the evolving soul even while it retains the individuality or uniqueness of each sub-personality. In this way, each of the soul's many past personalities shape its spiritual growth.[60]

When each successive personality or extension of the soul returns to the spirit world after its particular time on Earth, it begins what could be called an "intermission," a period of time during which healing, restoration, and education take place with the loving assistance of spiritual teachers and guides before the soul is ready to reincarnate once more. Based on Helen Wambach's 1978 research, intermissions can be as little as four months to more than two centuries with the average being about fifty years, depending on the circumstances associated with the end of the previous personality's life and the overall spiritual goals that remain.[61]

Ian Stevenson discovered, however, that intermissions for children who died prematurely ranges from only a few years to twelve years.[62] Cases of near-death experiences have shown that each of us, after completing our life on Earth, will have the opportunity to review every experience of that life. Gary Zukav, reincarnationist researcher and visionary, believes intermissions enable souls to see their earthly lives in total so that "their causes, their reasons, and their contributions to the evolution of the soul, and to the evolution of the souls with whom the soul shared its life, are revealed."[63]

Intermissions are also a time for reunion with family members, friends, and those we have known before, on both the spiritual and earthly planes. Loving and caring relationships among souls (soul extensions) endure and grow in the spirit world as on Earth. Furthermore, souls tend to reunite in groups of varying sizes and remain together as they reincarnate time and time again in earthly lives that offer important opportunities appropriate for their spiritual needs and desires.

It all simply amounts to a translocation of energy. Each soul has a specific pattern of energy that becomes an eternal "blueprint of its character" that carries on through successive reincarnations.[64] Nothing is lost in the process, cosmically speaking. Since the essence of God is love, the relationships developed and sustained in love are eternal. Here again we have an unmistakable connection, it seems, between the translocation of spiritual energy mentioned above and the concept of a holographic universe involving the flow of intelligent energy to and from the implicate and explicate orders as described by Bohm and Pribram.

As mentioned earlier, there is ample evidence to suggest that souls change genders according to their reincarnation goals and life plans. Each of us either has already or will eventually change our gender in order to contribute to our soul's evolution. In fact, the data suggests that gender changes between one reincarnation and the succeeding one occur about 20 percent of the time; when considering the span of several lifetimes, the chances of experiencing some lifetimes as a female and others as a male rises considerably.[65] It is also true that souls will tend to choose one particular gender more often than the other. So it is important for every man currently alive to realize that he has spent, and will most likely spend, other lifetimes as a female. Of course, the reverse is equally true. How else could human life in its totality be truly understood and appreciated? Among other things, this seems to suggest the certainty of moral justice as well as spiritual enlightenment.

The phenomenon of gender change seems particularly relevant to the issue of homosexuality as suggested by Stevenson. Since it has become clear that a soul chooses when, where, and how it will reincarnate in terms of its next genetic makeup and gender, it is quite possible that an opposite-sex incarnation could also result in the retention of some of the sexual proclivities associated with its previous life. Such a radical change as a shift in gender might, in some cases, require more than one incarnation to achieve the needed adjustment to a new sexual orientation. Therefore, it would be a mistake to conclude that a life as a homosexual or bisexual is unnatural or incomplete, since it may serve a specific spiritual purpose or soul agenda by providing special opportunities for spiritual growth.

As Stevenson and others have discovered, reincarnation can be meaningful and fulfilling regarding each soul's needs and intentions while on Earth only if conscious memories of previous lives and their personalities are erased by the soul, usually in the fetal stage or shortly thereafter. It amounts to having a fresh start and a clean slate that is free of spiritual "baggage" and possible guilt that would undoubtedly be carried over from earlier mistakes.

Without this God-given gift of initial amnesia, it would seem less likely that each of us could begin a new life with fresh eyes and open minds. As a way of illustrating this truth, it has been said that each incarnate human being, at any particular point in time, consists of two parts. One constitutes the core aspects of the individual, such as his or her aptitudes and natural inclinations, both positive and negative, and the other, which tends to be less deeply rooted, amounts to the individual's outward personality. The core aspects are, in effect, what the soul succeeds in carrying over from one lifetime to the next even as personalities change in accordance with physical variations and different environmental circumstances.[66]

The Issue of Karma

Another aspect of reincarnation that has been the subject of much confusion, especially among Christians, is the concept of karma. Based partly on Origen's idea of God's justice but mainly on Hindu and Buddhist interpretations, karma is assumed by many Christians today to be an uncompromising, arbitrary cosmic law or moral order involving a direct cause-and-effect relationship between a personality's actions in one life and certain inevitable karmic outcomes in one or more future incarnations. In other words, karma is generally thought to be a moral debt that must be paid in full eventually.

Unfortunately, this interpretation can easily lead to the assumption mentioned earlier that suffering or tragic circumstances are the results of sins committed in a present or previous life. While this rather punitive interpretation gives some assurance of ultimate moral justice and highlights the importance of personal responsibility, it also envisions the existence of a rigid debt-and-credit system managed by cosmic auditors and tends to ignore the effects of God's gift of free will and freedom of choice.

In many instances, our misfortunes are caused by the actions of others and circumstances beyond our control. Examples include war's destructive effects on innocent civilians and the maiming and possible death of passengers in planes that crash due to pilot error or mechanical failure. Interactions and interconnections with other human beings continually affect our lives, and their choices as well as our own can affect others either negatively or positively.

The recognition that Christ came to break the bonds of rigid religious laws and requirements has tended to argue against the seemingly rigid cosmic law that karma has been perceived to be. Besides, if experience provides any lessons in this regard, the relatively high recidivism rates among those who have served prison terms in this and other countries suggest that punishment in and of itself seldom brings lasting positive behavioral changes.[67]

Past-life regression therapies tend to present a different picture of karma or the relationship between the actions or deeds of a previous incarnation and a soul's present-life circumstances. The initial circumstances of our next incarnation, such as the fetus our soul will inhabit, its environment, and new family relationships, are freely chosen by the soul with the help of its spiritual guides based on its own assessment and personal judgment about its spiritual liabilities and assets.

No soul, regardless of its past lives, is coerced, but the power of self-judgment in the light of what it sees and learns about itself in the interim is enough motivation to seek the opportunity for spiritual growth through reincarnation. We are always presented with the potential for growth and change through the power of love for ourselves and others, and we can freely choose to accept, reject, or delay. Surely, this is proof of God's everlasting grace. We are given the chance to live again with the hope of transforming ourselves, regardless of what has gone before.

On the other hand, the traditional Eastern view of karma is that life on Earth is a burden that must be endured in a seemingly unending cycle of rebirths before karmic debts are paid in full. From this Eastern perspective, death is a necessary and desirable release from bondage as well as a possible entry into the permanent state of nirvana, wherein the self is absorbed into the One.

By contrast, most Christians believe that life on Earth is a gift from God, which generally leads to a more positive outlook, even while acknowledging that tragedies do occur in life. Among reincarnationists in particular, there is today an overall sense that life on Earth is basically good and that it holds the evolutionary promise of becoming better.

Hans TenDam hastens to remind us that certain assets are always retained from previous lives along with liabilities. He uses the term *dharma* to refer to those positive qualities that serve as a foundation for further spiritual and psychological growth. Here the focus is more on the strengths than the weaknesses of personalities, whether from the past or the present.[68]

THE CHURCH'S HISTORY OF OPPOSITION TO REINCARNATION

Today the subject of reincarnation is often dismissed, ridiculed, or avoided altogether in most Catholic and Protestant churches. The source of much of this resistance can be traced to the early centuries of Christian history. For instance, despite some initial support for Origen's reincarnationist ideas by some of the early bishops, other church leaders such as Irenaeus of Lyon, Tertullian, and, in the sixth century, Emperor Justinian mounted a persistent campaign against Origen's teachings.

The opposition initially launched against Origen was in essence a microcosm of the larger conflicts that raged well beyond his lifetime between orthodox polemicists and the so-called "heretics" believed to be associated with Origen and his successors. In her book *Reincarnation: The Missing Link in Christianity*, Elizabeth Clare Prophet points out that for almost three hundred years, the Church largely silenced those deemed to be heretics "as it codified doctrine and defined Scripture, substituting order for illumination."[69]

The objections that orthodox defenders of the Church raised against Origen's teachings came to a head well after Origen's death when the Church's Fifth Ecumenical Council met in 553 CE. A major issue concerned the growing interest among the faithful in Origen's belief in the pre-existence of souls, a prerequisite for reincarnation.[70] Origen's thinking was compatible with the third century Neoplatonist theory of the origin of the universe as an emanation from God. To

Origen, this implied a direct link between God and the human soul or, as the third century Neoplatonist Plotinus suggested, "an extension of God."[71] In essence, Plotinus favored the pre-existence of souls—which is to say, life before incarnation. Origen could say as well that the soul exists before it takes on bodily form and must, therefore, exist independently of the body.

Ultimately, the council issued an official ban against Origen's reincarnation-related teachings altogether, including his belief in the pre-existence of souls. With Justinian's blessings and urgings, the ban stated, "Whosoever teaches the doctrine of a supposed pre-birth existence of the soul, and speaks of a monstrous restoration of this, is cursed."[72] Justinian's compliant bishops in attendance argued against the possibility of pre-existent souls by claiming that souls are created at the same time as the body.

Furthermore, they insisted that the human soul had never been a part of God, and since it belonged to the material world—that which God supposedly created out of nothing—it was separate from God. In choosing to separate the human soul from the divine, they not only moved toward a theology of separation but also called into question the humanity of Jesus by claiming that Jesus was God (as implied by the Nicene Creed), separate from all humankind. In essence, their position was that no human could also be divine.

To suggest, as reincarnationists did, that each human soul came from God and had the potential and the assurance of evolving in Christlike fashion to return to God was heretical in the opinion of the early orthodox bishops.[73] This early orthodox view still endures in the higher circles of the Church today as illustrated by the following statement that appears in the *New Catholic Encyclopedia*: "Between Creator and creature there is the most profound distinction possible. God is not part of the world. He is not just the peak of reality. Between God and the world there is an abyss."[74] Of course, what is not too subtly implied is that the only way to cross the abyss is through the Church—that is, if the soul is worthy of admittance.

Since, in the opinion of the council's sixth century bishops, the soul and the body were inseparable, they could also insist that Jesus's resurrection was in bodily form rather than spiritual as claimed by the advocates of reincarnation. The Church's position was that since the body and soul are one, our physical bodies would eventually be restored at a future second coming of Christ when all the saved would be resurrected into immortality. Again, to suggest otherwise was to invite an accusation of heresy.

Another issue that drew the ire of the Church's early polemicists was Origen's claim that God's Creation is a cosmic evolutionary process in which souls are given free will and endless opportunities in successive earthly lives to grow experientially through personal effort and moral responsibility. For one thing, the Orthodox Church's point of view was that this represented a direct threat to its authority, since it seemed Origen was claiming that the soul's salvation could be determined through its own independent initiative. Certainly by the sixth century, the Church had placed a high priority on subservience to its authority and considered the reasoned and thoughtful inquiries of Origen and other reincarnationists to be dangerous and arrogant. This persistent fear of inquiry on the part of the Church is clearly reflected in this statement from Augustine's *On the Soul and Its Origins* (4.4.5): "Seek not the things that are too high for thee, and search not into the things that are above thy ability, but the things that God hath commanded thee; think of them always and in many of his works be not curious."[75]

Sadly, this call from the sixth century to "be not curious" still characterizes much about the modern Church's attitude toward reincarnation and other views arising from recent biblical research that challenge long-standing, traditional understandings. Also related to the Orthodox Church's rejection of the reincarnationist idea of a spiritual evolutionary process was its insistence that God's creation of the world was a single event completed long ago, as described in Genesis. This left no room for any concept of a divine creation that was ongoing, including the evolution of souls. From the orthodox bishops' perspective, an evolutionary view of creation also eliminated the stability, order, and permanence that were naturally associated with their theistic understanding of God.

Since at least the fifth and sixth centuries, when the Orthodox Church was firmly in place, the Christian Church as an institution has also been successful in persuading most Christians that they have but one life to live on Earth and that when that single life span ends they go either to hell or to heaven—or, according to Roman Catholic doctrines, to an intermediate state of existence known as purgatory. According to church tradition, these outcomes are based on the final and irrevocable judgment we receive from God.

Likewise, many Christians are still told that entrance into heaven is conditional and dependent on one's unwavering faith in Jesus Christ. However, individuals who live only for a brief time on Earth—such as the child who dies at birth or shortly thereafter or the young child or teenager who dies in a car accident or a natural disaster or of sickness—would have little opportunity to develop such a strong Christian faith. In these instances, there would seem to be little or no basis for a final divine judgment. If young people such as these never have a chance to live out their potential for better or for worse during their one and only chance at living an earthly life, the whole concept of a single life on Earth raises doubts about the real purpose or value of physical existence.

Nevertheless, there are Christians today, such as Catholic Deacon Gerald DuPont, from St. Mary's Seminary in Houston, who will readily refer to Paul's Epistle to the Hebrews 9:27, which says, "It is appointed unto men once to die, but after this the judgment." According to the Rev. DuPont, the Catholic Church as a whole flatly rejects reincarnation because, as he says, "the doctrine of reincarnation reduces the seriousness

of God's grace and of human liberty, exercised in one life that is termi-
nated by a once-and-for-all death."[76] Cardinal Francis Arinze, president
of the Pontifical Council for Inter-Religious Dialogue, also warns that
believing in reincarnation "is a major challenge, if not a conscious or
unconscious undermining of the Christian worldview."[77]

The claim that Paul's statement in Hebrews rules out the possibility of reincarnation is based not only on the assumption that men
die only once but also on the phrase "after this the judgment," which
implies a single, *final* judgment. However, biblical scholar Geddes
MacGregor claims that while it is true that our present bodies will
die just once, Paul's statement does not rule out the fact that our soul
lives on and will reincarnate in a new and different body at some point
in the future. He is also quick to explain that the Revised Standard
Version of the Bible presents a slightly different translation of this
verse. Here Verse 27 reads, "It is appointed for men to die once, and
after that comes judgment."[78]

This interpretation is not at all inconsistent with the concept of reincarnation, since the whole idea of karma implies judgment, particularly
self-judgment as experienced by those who have gone through a life
review in connection with an NDE. In addition, Anglican priest Thomas
Strong of England points out that Hebrews was not written for the
purpose of either discrediting or defending reincarnation in the first
place. It had more to do with Paul's message to new Jewish converts to
Christianity that since Jesus's return was imminent, traditional temple
sacrifices were no longer needed—another subject entirely.[79]

Another long-standing objection to reincarnation is based on the
assumption that if the soul is given the opportunity to evolve through
several life experiences on Earth, the incentive for a person to do
good during any particular incarnation is weakened. Jeffrey Daneleke
addresses the issue of incentive differently:

In effect, if people delay learning their spiritual lessons in this lifetime, they will not evolve spiritually regardless of whether they believe in reincarnation or not. They will remain, by their own choice, in a spiritually primitive state not because reincarnation encourages it—it clearly does not—but because apathy is the truest reflection of their spiritual state. The ultimate goal of reincarnation is for the soul to evolve spiritually.[80]

Likewise, many Christians reject reincarnation precisely because it is thought to provide an escape from, or at least a delay in, moral justice. Because it is understandable that liabilities or karmic issues from previous lives can clearly be judged to exist for those who have committed the worst crimes against individuals and humanity as a whole, one might think that being given a chance of redemption in a new life free of some eternal punishment makes a mockery of justice at any level.

The truth is that the harshest form of judgment results from the genuine realization of one's own treatment of others while on Earth—experiencing it from the others' perspective as well as from the broader perspective of one's soul. We have seen that those who have had life reviews on the "other side" as a result of their near-death experiences report how completely devastating and remorseful such an experience would be were it not for the spiritual guides and teachers who seek to heal and restore damaged souls so they may willingly atone for the betterment of all. The goal in the spirit world is not retribution but healing and redirection in line with the soul's true purpose of evolving toward ever-higher levels of consciousness and spiritual maturity. Although the Old Testament is filled with examples of divine punishments administered to individuals and whole nations for a variety of supposed offenses against God, and the basic principle of "holy" retributions has been instilled as the "Word of God" in all three of the major religions, reincarnation provides an essential message to the contrary. The message of reincarnation is that an "eye for an eye" form of morality does nothing to end continually descending cycles of violence and separation.

In addition to the reasons already given for the Church's condemnation of reincarnation was the assumption made by some of its early orthodox leaders that reincarnation necessarily involves the transmigration of souls, or the idea that the soul may return to earthly life as an animal, insect, or other nonhuman life form. In the fourth century, for instance, Basil the Great insisted, "Avoid the nonsense of those arrogant philosophers who do not blush to liken their soul to that of a dog, who say that they have themselves formerly been women, shrubs, or fish."[81] By the same token, Gregory of Nyssa said the following in 379: "If one should search carefully, he will find that their doctrine [reincarnation] is of necessity brought down to this. They tell us that one of their sages said that he, being one and the same person, was born a man, and afterward assumed the form of a woman, and flew about with the birds, and grew as a bush, and obtained the life of an aquatic creature."[82] Even today, DuPont basically makes the same assumption in arguing against reincarnation on behalf of the Catholic Church: "According to this belief the soul pre-exists its embodiment and after death exists in a disembodied state before animating once again a body of the same or different species."[83]

However, no one in the East or West has provided a plausible reason why any soul, having reached the level of self-consciousness, would wish to descend to the level of simple consciousness characteristic of animals or other nonhuman species. It is fair to say that most who endorse reincarnation in both the East and West today recognize it as an upward or ascending evolutionary journey aimed at achieving an ever-expanding cosmic consciousness and sense of self in union with all that exists in God. If the main purpose of each soul's journey through multiple reincarnations is to evolve spiritually in harmony with God's benevolent will, our personal effort and responsibility must be directed toward self-sacrificing love that can exist only in the form of caring, constructive relationships with other human souls as modeled by Jesus.

It is here, however, that the orthodox Christian doctrine of atonement comes into conflict with the need for personal initiative and responsibility to achieve spiritual growth (salvation). As a consequence of believing that Christ paid for our sins through his death on the cross, this has become, in the minds of many, a means of escape from being responsible for their own salvation. Reincarnation teaches us instead that God's forgiveness allows us to overcome our sins of self-above-others *by experiencing the consequences of such sins.* Regardless of Jesus's willingness to accept the cross, we cannot avoid the consequences of our own acts, whether on Earth or in heaven. Thankfully, reincarnation enables each soul to experience a variety of earthly lives with which to achieve redemption for its various shortcomings, no matter how serious and damaging they might be.

Whether the Church ever adjusts to the fact that reincarnation is a reality and that the ancient orthodox concept of a single life on Earth and final judgment is not credible is perhaps beside the point in the long run. As Jeffrey Daneleke says, reincarnation "permits us the dignity of securing our own salvation not through some carte-blanche absolution resulting from membership in a particular religion or by professing a specific creed, but by taking responsibility for our own lives and actions and learning to grow beyond our very human frailties and weaknesses."[84]

POSITIVE BENEFITS OF ACCEPTING THE REALITY OF REINCARNATION

In addition to the basic purposes and characteristics of reincarnation that have already been examined in the light of modern scientific and historical research are the practical as well as broader implications of reincarnation for individuals and for the world in general.

From a practical standpoint, past-life therapies conducted by a growing number of holistically inclined medical professionals are helping their patients overcome certain physical or psychological problems generally triggered by emotional situations in their lives. Use of past-life regression therapy treatments where more traditional medical approaches have failed has eased and in some cases eliminated problems such as dermatitis, ulcers, hypertension, and various gastro-intestinal disorders.

In this case, the key to successful past-life therapy treatments is to find the root cause of a patient's problems in a past-life event or series of events. Psychiatrist Dr. Raymond Moody (the author of *Life after Life*) cites one case in which he used the past-life regression procedure to help a woman in her thirties overcome a serious problem with asthma that standard medical treatments had not relieved. During her past-life regression session, she vividly recalled a former life in nineteenth century England during which she was murdered by a male intruder who forced his way into her London apartment. Moody later described what she experienced under hypnosis: "She fought to escape, breathing rapidly and thrashing on the couch in front of me as she described the battle. The fight was to no avail. Soon he was on top of her and in a flash her face was covered with a pillow and she was being suffocated."[85]

As a result of her past-life recall, Moody's patient was able to face the trauma that had caused her lingering subconscious fear of suffocation, which manifested as asthma. After her treatment, the frequency and intensity of her asthma attacks declined dramatically, as did her dependence on various medications. The increasing utilization of this nontraditional type of therapy by other medical professionals shows an equally important willingness on their part to accept reincarnation as a legitimate phenomenon.

The issue of suicide can also be meaningfully addressed within the context of reincarnation. If the basic causes for some illnesses or addictions can be traced to various past-life problems or traumas through the use of past-life therapies, it seems reasonable to assume that the despair that leads in some cases to attempted suicides could also have a past-life source. Having knowledge of the possible past-life origins of a present life crisis can broaden one's perspective on life to the point of seeing that no situation in life is beyond hope. If suicide does prevent certain spiritual lessons to be learned in one life, the circumstances that are needed to learn the same lessons are likely to be presented again in subsequent reincarnations so that progress and ultimate resolution can be achieved.

Corroboration for such a claim comes from those who have had near-death experiences after suicide attempts. They generally report that their "deaths" did not eliminate the issues that drove them to suicide. In addition, these NDErs tell of experiencing profound regret for their life-ending act when they saw the resulting pain and misery suffered by their friends and family members.[86]

Nevertheless, it is equally important to realize that based on the reports of NDErs, suicide is not a punishable act in the cosmic scheme of things and that the perceived need to end one's life will be addressed and overcome with the loving assistance and understanding of spiritual teachers on the "other side," regardless of how long it takes.[87] Past-life therapies can also serve as a way of revealing this truth.

An acceptance of reincarnation as a natural phenomenon can also lead to a better understanding of the nature of good and evil. For instance, it is not beyond the realm of possibility that many people who are now living in miserable conditions may have chosen to do so for the "soul purpose" of challenging and awakening the moral conscience of humanity. However, this does not give us a reason to assume that their unfortunate situation is "their problem" and not ours. If we fail to reach out to "the least of these" in love and understanding, we fail to recognize that their souls may be seeking to affect our spiritual growth as well as their own. As Jesus said, "Neither this man nor his parents sinned; he was born blind so that God's works might be revealed in him" (John 9:3).

We have only to remember the example of Jesus himself. He freely chose the cross in response to evil because of his passionate need to affect the spiritual growth and enlightenment of the world. Neither does this amount to some sort of acceptance of social injustice. The victims of social injustice are, indeed, innocent victims, but not as a result of God's will or intention. They are not enduring some cosmically imposed punishment for imagined sins. Neither is their misery (and the suffering of all others, regardless of circumstances) the result of some form of punitive karma. The victims of social injustice suffer instead from the greed, intolerance, and indifference practiced by those, often in positions of political or corporate power, who separate themselves from God as a consequence of their lack of spiritual growth and maturity.

In the end, knowledge and acceptance of reincarnation brings with it the realization that we are much more than we think we are from our limited, immediate perspective. Through the mechanics of reincarnation, we are all on an evolutionary journey that has taken us through the entire span of human history, with more to come.

There are many "old souls" among us—some of whom are the children we see today. Since in the spiritual realm there is no time or space, only an eternal "now," we should be aware that genetic age and environment have less to do with our true spiritual maturity than the kinds of inner traits, abilities, and knowledge we have retained from several previous lives. This is why we should avoid judging others too harshly based on appearances; in many cases, we will meet and engage with one another again in future lives as we have in the past, albeit in different roles and under different circumstances.

Reincarnation also offers hope for those burdened by disappointment and regret over what they perceive to be unfulfilled or wasted lives. Nothing is lost, never to be experienced again, because death is only the closing of a chapter and the beginning of the next in our eternal adventure. Issues that remain to be resolved in future lives, if not in this one, *will be addressed* with the help of God's grace, free of retribution and pointless punishment. Such is the nature of reincarnation.

CHAPTER 8

The Evolution of Human Consciousness: A General Background

While the previous chapter focused on reincarnation as a means of ensuring the evolution of human consciousness toward greater levels of spiritual maturity, this chapter will focus on the *ways* human consciousness has evolved. In more specific terms, the goal will be to look at ways human beings perceive the world in relation to themselves and to others as observed by certain scientists and modern visionaries.

THE WORLD FROM A DIFFERENT PERSPECTIVE

It often seems, from our limited perspective of time and space, that history simply repeats itself with little or no indication of positive changes in human consciousness and behavior. For instance, in various parts of the world at any given time, wars continue to occur, large numbers of people still struggle with poverty, and various acts of cruelty, greed, and indifference are shamefully committed.

Generally less discernible is that forward leaps of human consciousness toward global integration and interdependence have been occurring throughout the history of our species and will continue to occur as time goes on. Such dramatic shifts or awakenings as the emergence of Judaism, the classical age of ancient Greece, Buddhism, Christianity, Islam, the Renaissance, the Protestant Reformation, the Enlightenment, the organization of the United Nations, the human rights movement of the 1960s, and more recent cooperative ventures into outer space are but a few examples.

As we consider how far we as a species have come on this journey in our divinely sanctioned quest for a more integral world, it is important to realize that souls do not necessarily evolve in the same way at the same time. The reality is that a certain level of human consciousness tends to dominate at a given time or exist alongside other less widely adopted ways of thinking and acting. In other words, souls can be at different places on the path toward enlightenment at any particular time. As a whole, however, the divine imperative is for an ascending evolutionary journey through time at a rate necessary for lasting growth.

According to Teilhard de Chardin, author of the well-known book *The Phenomenon of Man*, human intelligence on a worldwide scale could be considered to be an interrelated superorganism that he called the "noosphere." *Noos* is derived from the Greek word *nous*, which means "mind," so in Chardin's opinion the noosphere consists of all the spiritual, cultural, social, and technological expressions of humanity.[1] While it appears that humanity hasn't changed much from a biological standpoint over the past two thousand years, Chardin observed that our larger social body—the noosphere—has expanded greatly.[2]

This becomes obvious to anyone who has been around for the last three-quarters of a century, as I have. Just within this period of time, our shared intelligence and capacities as a people have enabled us to venture into outer space and walk on the moon; transmit television images instantaneously around the world; split the atom and produce nuclear energy (for peaceful purposes as well as for weapons of mass destruction); and produce computers, the Internet, cell phones, iPods, and countless other wireless communications devices and programs.

All these technological developments clearly indicate the extent to which the capacity of the human mind is expanding, but they say nothing about the expansion of the human heart. What evidence is there that would suggest humanity has evolved to a higher moral and ethical level in conjunction with its amazing technological advances? In other words, how mature has humanity become from a spiritual perspective?

In her book *Conscious Evolution: Awakening the Power of Our Social Potential*, Barbara Marx Hubbard begins to address these questions by comparing human beings to Earth. In her opinion, both have always been living organisms with encoded plans or programs that guide them from conception through birth to eventual maturity and death. This suggests that planets, solar systems, and galaxies follow life cycles similar to the human biological life cycle. However, she's quick to point out that these so-called encoded evolutionary plans for all living things are *pre-patterned* rather than predetermined. In other words, while these plans or evolutionary paths may exist for both human beings and Earth, there is room for change and variation along the way with the possibility of different outcomes. At the same time, she observes that humanity's evolutionary path moves inexorably toward a higher, more expanded consciousness.[3]

THE ASCENT OF HUMAN CONSCIOUSNESS

Given what we now know from modern scientific research, such an inbuilt evolutionary plan or design that encompasses the entire universe is quite plausible. Hubbard maintains that a "new story of evolution" is emerging as a result of the combined efforts of scientists, historians, spiritual leaders, and uniquely informed visionaries.

One such visionary was Richard Maurice Bucke, who in the waning years of the nineteenth century, at the age of thirty-six, had the powerfully transformative experience of being momentarily elevated to a higher state of consciousness. In his 1901 book *Cosmic Consciousness*, he described what he learned and experienced during a few brief moments. Here he refers to himself in the third person while recounting the event:

> All at once, without warning of any kind he found himself wrapped around as it were by a flame-colored cloud … The next he knew that light was within himself. Directly afterwards came upon him a sense of exultation, of immense joyousness accompanied or immediately followed by an intellectual illumination quite impossible to describe. Into his brain streamed one momentary lightning flash of the Brahmic Splendor which has ever since lightened his life …

> He saw and knew that the Cosmos is not dead matter but a living Presence, that the soul of man is immortal, that the universe is so built and ordered that without any peradventure all things work together for the good of each and all, that the foundation principle of the world is what we call love and that the happiness of everyone is in the long run absolutely certain.[4]

This experience eventually led Bucke to conclude that the natural processes of life include a series of ascending leaps of consciousness. For instance, when considering the full scope of life on Earth, beginning with the inorganic level and continuing forward, he envisioned three distinct stages of awareness.

He identified the first as "simple consciousness," or that level of awareness typical of higher animals. At this stage, consciousness is largely instinctual and sensory, characterized by embryonic forms of thinking.[5] Bucke realized that while some individuals are at this level,

most of humanity has evolved to a second stage of awareness he called
"self-consciousness." He observed that human self-consciousness
emerges with the ability to communicate through language, which, in
turn, enables humans to engage in abstract reasoning. A person at this
stage of consciousness is also aware that he or she is a unique individual.[6]
At this level of thinking, the individual is also capable of judging, comparing, reflecting, and imagining.[7]

Bucke identified the third and ultimate stage of human consciousness as "cosmic consciousness." At this point, even as human beings continue to possess simple and self-consciousness, they will become aware
of "the life and order of the universe."[8] He went on to say that cosmic
consciousness also enables one to recognize that the cosmos is "not of
dead matter governed by unconscious, rigid, and unintending law ... but
that it is ... entirely immaterial, entirely spiritual and entirely alive."[9]

Also at this cosmic stage of development, a kind of dual consciousness, both human and spiritual in nature, will emerge. As Bucke explained
it, "Churches, priests, forms, creeds, prayers, all agents, all intermediaries
between the individual man and God will be permanently replaced by
direct unmistakable intercourse."[10] Moreover, "there occurs an intellectual enlightenment or illumination which alone would place the individual on a new plane of existence—would make him almost a member
of a new species."[11]

Along with his certainty of the existence of cosmic consciousness,
Bucke was equally convinced that every human being will eventually
evolve to this level, just as earlier humans had passed from simple to
self-consciousness: "As a race we are approaching nearer and nearer to
that stage of the self-conscious mind from which the transition to the
cosmic conscious is effected."[12]

Overall, what's so important about Bucke's views is that they represent the beginning of a concerted effort on the part of scientists in

subsequent years to explore the evolution of human consciousness—that is, the gradual ascent from simple consciousness through various sub-stages of self-consciousness to cosmic consciousness.

THE SPIRAL-DYNAMICS MODEL OF EVOLUTION

A significant step in this exploration was made in the 1950s when the late Dr. Clare Graves, psychology professor at New York's Union College, became engaged in the study of the development of human nature. His research ultimately led him to the following theory:

> What I am proposing is that the psychology of the mature human being is an unfolding, emergent, oscillating, spiraling process marked by progressive subordination of older, lower-order behavior systems to newer, higher-order systems as man's existential problems change. Each successive stage, wave, or level of existence is a state through which people pass on their way to other states of being. When the human is centralized in one state of existence, he or she has a psychology which is particular to that state.[13]

Eventually, his pioneering efforts formed the theory behind the spiral-dynamics model for the evolution of human consciousness that became widely known in 1996 after the publication of *Spiral Dynamics: Mastering Values, Leadership, and Change*, by Don Beck and Christopher Cowan, who had been students of Graves before collaborating on their groundbreaking book.

In writing their book, Beck and Cowan chose to use the term ᵛ*MEME*—for "values meme"—when referring to various commonly held worldviews, conventional beliefs, or levels of human consciousness in general.[14] ᵛ*MEME* is a variation of the word *meme* (a derivative of the Greek *mimeme*), which was introduced in the twentieth century by Richard Dawkins when referring to units of cultural information. Dawkins considered memes to be the information units of our psycho-cultural DNA that function much the way biochemical genes instruct our physical body. Likewise, Beck and Cowan believe memes contain "behavioral instructions that are passed from one generation to the next, social artifacts, and value-laden symbols that glue together social systems."[15]

However, Beck and Cowan thought in broader terms when referring to the ᵛMEME, since they meant to identify a larger organizing principle that acts like an attractor for various cultural memes. In their opinion, ᵛMEMEs "are the amino acids of our psychosocial 'DNA' and act as the magnetic force which binds memes and other kinds of ideas in cohesive packages of thought … They reach across whole groups of people and begin to structure mind-sets on their own."[16]

References to memes or ᵛMEMEs on the part of Dawkins, Beck, and Cowan, however, should not be confused with the more popular memes featured on Facebook and in other social media today. References to memes within social media tend to be associated with passing fads, such as preoccupation with certain clothing styles, unconventional personal behaviors, and public demonstrations. In some cases, however, these social media memes do tap into broader societal undercurrents. Therefore, to avoid confusion, I will refer to Beck and Cowan's ᵛMEMEs as stages or levels of human consciousness from this point on.

When designing their particular theory of spiral dynamics, Beck and Cowan settled on a series of eight distinct levels of consciousness even while allowing for the possibility that even higher levels could emerge. They referred to these eight levels as increasingly "complex" rather than "better" or even "higher," since they recognized that every level of human consciousness is appropriate to the changing needs of individuals and societies. For instance, every person represents an accumulation of what has come before—the roots necessary for lasting change.

While the spiral-dynamics model clearly suggests a graduated hierarchy of consciousness, there's no denying the necessity for every human being to experience each of the stages within the ascending and expanding spiral of human consciousness. For one thing, it is true that individuals and societies are capable of reverting, at least temporarily, to earlier levels of thinking and behaving when faced with a crisis or changing conditions. Likewise, any shift to a higher level of consciousness requires having the foundational experiences of the previous level.[17] Hubbard uses a perfect analogy for this phenomenon:

> Let's compare our situation with the metamorphosis of a caterpillar into a butterfly. When the caterpillar weaves its cocoon, imaginal disks begin to appear. These disks embody the blueprint of the butterfly yet to come. Although the disks are a natural part of the caterpillar's evolution, its immune system recognizes them as foreign and tries to destroy them. As the disks arrive faster and begin to link up, the caterpillar's immune system breaks down and its body begins to disintegrate. When the disks mature and become imaginal cells, they form themselves into a new pattern, thus transforming the disintegrating body of a caterpillar into a butterfly. The breakdown of the caterpillar's old system is essential for the breakthrough of the new butterfly. Yet, in reality the caterpillar neither dies nor disintegrates, for from the beginning its hidden purpose was to transform and be reborn as the butterfly.[18]

In other words, social resistance to new, more expansive and holistic ways of thinking have always been characterized by a gradual or sometimes-rapid disintegration of previously accepted social structures, institutions, perceptions, and ways of interacting. The result is a transitional period that is necessarily unstable, fearful, and often chaotic. For example, the period from 1860 to 1965 in America was a time in which accepted attitudes and laws about race changed dramatically only after extreme divisiveness, violence, and the collapse of the institution of slavery had occurred. A costly civil war, the assassination of President Lincoln, many years of Ku Klux Klan terrorist activity, and the intense civil rights struggles of the 1960s eventually led to the Civil Rights Act of 1965.

In every case, efforts to bring human consciousness to a new level of racial tolerance and understanding were met with passionate resistance from fearful and resentful whites who saw their segregationist world collapsing. But this is not to say that racist attitudes no longer exist in America. Even now, in the second decade of the twenty-first century, we still see race-fueled violence and injustices in places like Ferguson, Missouri; Baltimore; and Charleston, South Carolina. Nevertheless, the fact that racism as an institution is no longer viable is evidence of at least one important paradigm shift in human consciousness. Today, the world as a whole is in the midst of an even broader, more encompassing transitional period of unrest and uncertainty, which will be the subject of the final chapter of this book. With Hubbard's analogy in mind, we shall consider the structural aspects of the spiral-dynamics model.

EXAMINING THE SPIRAL-DYNAMICS MODEL

Ordinarily, new ways of collective thinking emerge slowly, among a small percentage of the population, before building to a critical mass that results in a paradigm shift. When such an accepted way of thinking is eventually found to be inadequate in the face of changing circumstances and discoveries, it too will come to be replaced by newer, more expanded systems of values and understandings of the world associated with the next level of the ascending spiral.

In the years that followed the introduction of this concept of human development and the publication of *Spiral Dynamics*, Beck and Cowan's theory came to be validated and accepted by most researchers in the field of human development. In fact, by the year 2000, the Graves model had been tested in more than fifty thousand people worldwide and no major exceptions were found with the model.[19]

As we begin to examine the various levels of human consciousness that constitute the spiral-dynamics model, I wish to emphasize once again that, first, the concept as a whole involves a spiritually driven, ascending, and expanding evolutionary process toward an integral, holistic state of existence, and second, that as a divine imperative, each of us has within us the accumulated knowledge and experience derived from previous levels of existence. Furthermore, if our current level of consciousness is an accumulation of previous levels of existence, then differences regarding race, economic status, and political power should be less important than any particular stage of development for an individual or a culture. "The focus is not on types *of* people, but types *in* people," Beck says.[20] I am also convinced that the spiral-dynamics theory of human evolution essentially depends on the existence of reincarnation. How else can humanity evolve without remembering or at least retaining what has been learned before, if only at the DNA level?

Within the spiral-dynamics model of eight progressively expanding mind-sets, the first six are the "subsistence levels" and represent "first-tier thinking." Those associated with "second-tier thinking" begin at the seventh level and progress through the eighth. The progression from the sixth level to the seventh level represents a major shift in consciousness involving significant developmental changes.[21] What follows are the various stages in the evolution of human consciousness as identified by Beck and Cowan and briefly defined in an article by Steve Dinan of the Esalen Institute titled "Summary of Spiral Dynamics, by Don Beck and Christopher Cowan."

First-Tier Thinking

1. Survival/Sense or the Instinctive level [22]

"Semi-Stone Age ... Dominated by nature and basic survival instincts, acting much as other animals. Results in loose, clan-based survival groups."[23]

2. Kin Spirits or the Clannish level [24]

"Tribal animistic, magical, spiritualistic, close to the earth and cyclic outlook. This leads to tribal groupings, focus on rituals to appease ancestral spirits. Blood bonds are strong ... Respect for clan rules and allegiances"[25]

3. PowerGods or the Egocentric level [26]

"Rugged authoritarianism, finds expression in slavery or virtual slavery, exploitation of unskilled labor. Generally run by a Top Boss and series of proxies, strict division of have's and have not's. Assumption is that people are lazy, must be forced to work."[27]

4. TruthForce or the Purposeful level [28]

"Purposeful and patriotic, leads people to obey authority, feel guilty when not conforming to group norms, try to serve the greater good through self-sacrifice. Works very well in industrial economies ... Moralistic-prescriptive management techniques. Organizational structure is pyramidal."[29]

5. StriveDrive or the Strategic level [30]

"Entrepreneurial Personal success orientation, each person rationally calculating what is to their personal advantage. Motivations are largely economic, people are responsive to perks, bonuses, money rather than loyalty, group belongingness, or life employment … Competition improves productivity and fosters growth … Main concerns are autonomy and manipulation of the environment."[31]

6. *HumanBond* or the *Relativistic level* [32]

"Communitarian Sensitive and humanistic, the focus … is community and personal growth, equality, attention to environmental concerns. Work is motivated by human contact and contribution, learning from others. Being liked is more important than competitive advantage, value openness and trust, fear rejection and disapproval. Leaders become facilitators, less autocratic. Hierarchies blur in the move towards egalitarianism with a resulting tendency towards inefficiency and stagnation."[33]

Second-Tier Thinking

7. *FlexFlow* or the *Systemic level* [34]

"This is the first [level] of the second tier in which there is a quantum shift in the capacity to take multiple perspectives in life. [It] is motivated by learning for its own sake and is oriented towards integration of complex systems. Change is a welcome part of the process in organizations and life … It is characterized by systems thinking, an orientation to how parts interact to create a greater whole … It is also ecologically oriented, but in a more subdued, behind the scenes way"[35]

8. *GlobalView* or the *Holistic level* [36]

"Holistic Focused on a global holism/integralism, attuned to the delicate balance of interlocking life forces. Synthetic and experimental, emerging focus on spiritual connectivity. Work must be meaningful to the overall health of life … Conscious of energy fields, holographic links in all walks of work and life."[37]

AN 'INTEGRAL VISION'

Among those impressed with Beck and Cowan's spiral-dynamics model was American philosopher and modern visionary Ken Wilber. He came to agree that second-tier thinking, as represented by Levels 7 and 8, is just now beginning to emerge in the world as a kind of revolutionary leading edge. Wilber also believes there are some indications that an integral-holistic ninth level may be on the horizon as well.[38] More important, he is convinced that a paradigm shift to second-tier thinking will be essential in this century if humanity is to avoid global calamity in which various first-tier levels of consciousness resort to divisive competition and mutual destruction in the absence of substantive change.[39]

Wilber launched what he called the Human Consciousness Project in 2000. The purpose of the project was to "map" each of the many aspects of human consciousness.[40] He came to the conclusion at that time that only about 2 percent of the world's population was capable of second-tier thinking; most people in the world were still functioning within the TruthForce, StriveDrive, and HumanBond levels. Now, more than a decade later, it seems evident that the state of affairs remains much the same. Nevertheless, Wilber seemed optimistic in one sense: "We have had three decades [as of 2000] of the green meme [HumanBond level] as a substantial percentage of the population, and it has mightily tilled the soil for such a transformation."[41]

Based on his holistic philosophical outlook, he went on to construct what he called an "integral vision" founded on the fact that hierarchies are a natural part of the universe at all micro and macro levels.

Even though it is often assumed that hierarchies are rankings based on degrees of value from the least to the greatest, Wilber made a distinction between "dominator hierarchies" and "growth hierarchies."

As he sees it, dominator hierarchies are characterized by religious and secular power structures or social rankings—all of which retard the growth of human consciousness. Meanwhile, growth hierarchies are those that make crucial contributions to an entire sequence of nesting hierarchies. For instance, one system of sequential growth hierarchies that happens to form the basis for the natural world can be seen in the fact that "subatomic elements are parts of atoms, which are parts of molecules, which are parts of cells, which are parts of organisms, which are parts of ecosystems, which are parts of the biosphere."[42] No matter how unimportant each separate unit may seem to be in this example, the growth of the entire sequence would fail in the absence of any one unit. In fact, the interconnected, interdependent nature of growth hierarchies reveals a true integral world.

By the same token, growth hierarchies are found in all other aspects of existence beyond the material ones just mentioned. We are referring, of course, to hierarchies of human consciousness, both individually and collectively. Each stage incorporates all previous stages even while adding new elements. In other words, every stage or unit of consciousness along the continuum of growth hierarchies is essential for the continued growth and existence of all the others that constitute the whole of humanity.

But in the end, reality is composed of neither wholes nor parts, according to Wilber. Instead, he envisions our world consisting of whole/parts that he calls "holons," which by definition are wholes that are part of other wholes.[43] This picture of the world essentially suggests that every hierarchy contains progressively smaller and larger holons, with everything connected to everything else—an unending, unbroken string of relationships spiritually engineered and maintained.

Since growth hierarchies are composed of interconnected holons, one could, by extension, think of the progressive, spiraling levels of individual and collective human consciousness as holons. According to Wilber, when the various holons or levels of human consciousness are considered collectively, this conglomerate, or spiral-dynamics model, could be called a "holarchy." He explains it this way: "The Kosmos is a series of nests within nests within nests indefinitely expressing greater and greater holistic embrace—holarchies of holons everywhere ... In the end, all of these holarchies intermesh and fit perfectly with all the others."[44]

This, in a nutshell, is the main premise of this book, which is that humanity is slowly awakening to the reality of a spiritually interconnected, evolving world, with all the implications for progressive change that it brings. Furthermore, the cosmic interconnections described by Beck, Cowan, Wilber, and others have already been confirmed by modern discoveries in the field of quantum physics, including the enfolding and unfolding nature of what appears to be a holographic universe. Likewise, there is now a greater possibility that humanity will come to understand and accept reincarnations as holons within soul holarchies. They are part of the overall spiritual fabric of growth hierarchies contributing to the evolution of human consciousness. Finally, the profound messages coming from more and more people who have had near-death experiences or other authentic out-of-body contacts with the spirit world seem to suggest that heaven is perhaps the ultimate holarchy.

A CALL TO HEAL, UNIFY, AND LIBERATE

In his book *A New Kind of Christianity: Ten Questions That Are Transforming the Faith*, Brian McLaren seems to endorse the spiral-dynamics model even if in a more concise way with fewer levels and different color identifiers. Despite some variations in his descriptions of the various levels, his spiritually oriented interpretations are largely compatible with Beck and Cowan's model and are especially relevant to today's world. For instance, when referring to the newly emerging sixth mind-set or level of human consciousness as a tendency to finally be more honest about the harmful as well as constructive aspects of modern capitalism, materialism, and individualism, McLaren points with hope toward a further, more important inclination to "heal what we have so disastrously broken, ... to unify and liberate what we've tragically divided and conquered, and ... to rediscover a larger and more beautiful whole rather than pit part against part."[45]

But perhaps McLaren's passionate call to include and transcend is his most important message as we find ourselves at a crossroads in the new millennium: "If we don't transcend a stage in the fullness of time, we experience a kind of stagnation and stuckness. We only look backward, congratulating ourselves for how we are superior to those who came before, but never looking forward to see the next stage before us. Our pride thus prepares us for a regression."[46]

He challenges us "to see all previous zones as appropriate and adequate for their context, just as we consider infancy, childhood, and adolescence as appropriate and adequate to their time, not bad, evil, or wrong."[47]

Now in the second decade of the new millennium, the reality of an evolving world and the impetus to transcend previous levels of human consciousness can be plainly seen in unprecedented ecological and social changes happening everywhere. Just what are the unique aspects of these changes and what prospects do they hold for the future, whether in negative or positive terms? Even more important, what underlying spiritual implications do they have and what realistic reasons are there to hope for a significant leap of human consciousness in the coming decades? These questions will be the focus of the final chapter.

CHAPTER 9

At a Crossroads in the New Millenium: A World in Transition

GLOBAL COLLAPSE OR SPIRITUAL AWAKENING?

Since the beginning of the new millennium, the world's population has felt a sense of uncertainty and insecurity in almost every sector of human life. The news from many parts of the world is of violence arising from narrow religious and material interests, which at the same time threaten the long-term health of the planet. An unsustainable gap between the world's poorest and wealthiest nations also continues to exist despite efforts to solve this seemingly intractable problem.

Nevertheless, there are important parallel developments of a different and more encouraging kind, and they hold the potential for a dramatic shift in human consciousness toward a more integral, holistic world. Such developments include:

A growing understanding and appreciation for the spiritual energy of human consciousness and metaphysical phenomena

The advent of a global electronic communications network

The unprecedented rise of humanitarian aid organizations worldwide

The emergence of global ecological movements to restore and maintain the health of the planet

The disintegration and decline of conventional social, political, and economic systems that have failed to serve the common good

The decline of exclusivist religious orthodoxies and objectives in favor of more inclusive and experiential forms of spirituality.

The world is essentially in a period of transition—perhaps the most significant in the history of humankind. According to Edmund J. Bourne, author of *Global Shift: How a New Worldview Is Transforming Humanity*:

Humanity finds itself in the midst of a major shift in worldview. Such a shift involves a fundamentally new way of perceiving the world, the environment, each other, and ourselves. Accompanying this perceptual shift are fundamental changes in values, and priorities, in what is deemed important. Stated most briefly, the shift involves a movement away from a material view of the universe and our place in it to a more spiritual view. Instead of the ultimate "stuff" of reality being material, with consciousness secondary and derivative, consciousness is coming to be understood as the underlying foundation of reality, out of which the entire cosmos arises. Nature is no longer merely a neutral object for scientific investigation or a resource for industrial exploitation. It is a sacred order infused with intelligence and purpose—one with which humanity needs to cooperate.[1]

Widespread changes of this magnitude inevitably lead to unrest and a crisis of confidence, as we are seeing, but every crisis also leads to opportunities for growth and learning by virtue of God's grace. Barbara Marx Hubbard's analogy of the caterpillar's metamorphosis into a butterfly again comes to mind:

> We can view the reactive and conservative ways of the past few decades as a survival mechanism—as the caterpillar's immune system rigidly holding on to old structures until new social systems are mature enough to function. As we enter the 21st century, millions of people are awakening in every field, culture, and ethnic group. The imaginal disks are linking up, are becoming imaginal cells, and are beginning to proliferate throughout the social body.[2]

Biologist Lynne Margulis discovered there is actually a scientific basis for this human evolutionary process described metaphorically by Hubbard. In 1967, Margulis found that at a very early stage in the history of the Earth, a nucleated cell known as the "eukaryote" was formed and subsequently served as the basis for all advanced forms of life that followed, including the human species.[3] But in studying this evolutionary phenomenon that she called "symbiogenesis," she discovered something even more important. The formation of the eukaryote was the result of *cooperation* among bacterial organisms. In other words, cooperation among bacterial entities proved to be the key factor in their survival rather than competition in this and all future evolutionary events.[4]

Evolutionary biologist Elisabet Sahtouris agrees with Margulis and explains how profoundly relevant this "symbiogenesis" process is to our human condition now and for the future:

> The nucleated cell—an entirely new life form about a thousand times larger than an individual bacterium—was formed, as the bacteria took on divisions of labor and donated part of their unique genomes to the new cell's nucleus. Thus, the nucleated cell—the only kind of cell other than bacterial ever to evolve on Earth—represents a higher unity than the bacteria achieved after eons of tension and hostilities, as they engaged in successful negotiations and cooperative evolution. This process—whereby tension and hostilities between individuals lead to negotiations and then ultimately to cooperation as a greater unity—is the basic evolutionary process of all life forms on our planet, as I see it.[5]

Perhaps one of the best ways to understand and appreciate our present global predicament is to recognize, as Sahtouris does, that stress actually creates evolution. In fact, in her words, "Stress is the *only* thing that creates evolution."[6]

SIGNS OF AN EMERGING NEW PARADIGM

From a historical standpoint, the world has been experiencing the consequences of two major developments of the mid-twentieth century. The first began with the splitting of the atom and the harnessing of atomic energy for destructive as well as constructive purposes. The second pivotal development came with the realization by numerous scientists and non-scientists alike that such a profound technological breakthrough meant that humanity was capable of permanently damaging if not destroying the Earth's environment. For the first time, the future survival of the Earth was in question. Now, as we enter the new millennium, there is also a growing realization that the world's insatiable appetite for material gain and consumption through competitive industry and technology poses a real and present danger to humanity and must be addressed.

Physicist Duane Elgin has described this newly emerging shift in human consciousness as a "reflective/living systems" paradigm that sees the universe as a living, unified system characterized by wholeness and interconnection.[7] As we have already seen, Beck and Wilber reason that this represents a transformation to second-tier thinking. In either case, the emerging paradigm will contrast sharply with the world's prevailing materialistic, egocentric mind-set that believes in a universe that is mostly empty space and lifeless matter characterized by separation and isolation.

If everything is interconnected as we are beginning to realize, building cooperative relationships can and must be the overarching goal. There is a great potential for the emerging paradigm or second-tier levels of thinking to bridge differences among races, sexual orientations, genders, ideas, and other kinds of human relationships. The natural impulse will then be to celebrate diversity and to function in ways that foster a more harmonious, holistic world.

This critical evolutionary shift in human consciousness has been underway since at least the 1960s. The conventional wisdom of the decades leading up to the sixties was severely challenged by calls for social change and a reexamination of personal and collective values. Various grass-roots initiatives such as the environmental movement, the anti-war movement, the women's movement, the civil rights and human rights movements, and the use of mind-expanding drugs all contributed to a "disintegration" of established social systems.

Despite some narcissistic aspects of the developing drug culture, these social-change movements were, overall, the impetus for such social goals as better education, universal health care, economic justice, racial equality, and other efforts aimed toward achieving a more humane society.[8] While a number of these goals have not been entirely fulfilled, there is evidence that the following evolutionary developments are moving us closer toward achieving a more humane and holistic world.

Growing Interest in Spiritual Energy and Metaphysical Phenomena

There now seems to be a greater awareness that our problems as a species stem mainly from the fact that our spiritual progress, the maturation of consciousness, has not kept pace with our advances in technology. Evidence is found in the proliferation of books and articles dealing with the subject of consciousness as well as the rapidly growing scientific interest in this area. In fact, statistical results from many scientific studies conducted since the 1950s have verified the existence of such paranormal phenomena as telepathy (perceiving the thoughts of others), clairvoyance ("seeing" nonlocal objects, people, or occurrences), precognition (awareness of future events), and psychokinesis (moving or affecting objects through the application of concentrated mental energy).[9]

Furthermore, Dean Radin of the Institute of Noetic Sciences has proved through his study of "field consciousness" that the collective thoughts of small or large groups of people can especially affect the physical world. In his 2006 book, *Entangled Minds*, Radin said he is also convinced that telepathy is essentially the result of an entanglement of minds closely related to the quantum-entangled particles in quantum physics.[10]

The dramatic growth in understanding of and appreciation for the power of human consciousness and spiritual energy has been transforming the field of medicine as well, particularly in the global West. The increasing acceptance of "holistic" or "alternative" medical practices that has occurred in America since the 1960s among medical professionals such as Deepak Chopra and Andrew Weil demonstrates a new recognition of the importance that emotions, attitudes, and the soul play in the treatment of disease and health management.

Whereas conventional medicine in Europe and America has mainly tended to combat disease and other medical disorders through the use of surgery and drugs, holistic medical professionals understand that the root cause of most medical problems can be traced to some type of imbalance in a patient's "attitudes, values, and spiritual outlook, as well as important lifestyle factors such as nutrition, interpersonal relationships, and physical environment."[11] Holistic medical approaches to such imbalances usually involve chiropractic, acupuncture, energy-healing massage, meditation, and other alternative treatments in conjunction with more conventional methods. According to Edmund Bourne, "The new paradigm behind holistic medicine goes far beyond a materialistic universe, stressing fields, subtle energies, and the importance of consciousness in both disease and health."[12]

One indication that holistic medicine is gaining acceptance by medical professionals is the fact that many medical schools in America and elsewhere now offer courses and even whole programs in alternative medicine. Likewise, the National Institutes of Health program in complementary and alternative medicine is expanding dramatically in America.[13] Although holistic methods of combating human diseases and disorders have existed for centuries in Asia, most medical doctors in the West resisted such methods until the latter half of the twentieth century. Therefore, when it comes to the field of medicine, the growing endorsement of holistic medical practices in America and other Western nations in recent decades represents a significant shift toward global interdependence and integration.

Overall, these developments suggest that we are at an important crossroads with regard to the future of human consciousness. The choice is either to move forward toward post-conventional, world-centric ways of thinking and acting or to remain trapped in a world dominated by materialistic, egocentric interests and "survival of the fittest" competition for power and status. And while we make up our minds, there are other signs that a broad shift in human consciousness is occurring.

Development of a Global Electronic Communications Network

Advances in communications technologies that have been made just since the mid-twentieth century have transformed the world in profound ways. Since the introduction of the first working integrated circuit, otherwise known as the microchip, in 1958, microchips have come to be found in every conceivable electronic apparatus, including wristwatches, hand-held calculators, mobile phones, cell phones, scanners, and navigational aids such as global positioning systems.[14] Microchip technology not only has been less expensive, more powerful, and more reliable than earlier methods of communication but has also greatly enhanced information storage. Since huge amounts of information can be stored on microchips in the form of digital "bits," electronic devices have become much smaller and more portable. In his 1998 book, *One Digital Day: How the Microchip Is Changing Our World*, Rick Smolan stressed the far-reaching implications of this invention:

> No invention in history has spread so quickly throughout the world, or revolutionized so many aspects of human existence, as the microchip. Little more than a quarter-century since its invention, there are now nearly 15 billion microchips in use

worldwide—the equivalent of two powerful computers for every man, woman and child on the planet. The microprocessor is not only changing the products we use, but also the way we live, and, ultimately, the way we perceive reality.[15]

Especially significant is the fact that digitization technology has greatly increased the speed of transmitting data. This particular feature was further improved with the introduction of fiber-optics technology in the 1970s, and by the late nineties, worldwide television communication was made possible by communication satellites placed in orbit by space vehicles guided by microchip and digital technology.[16]

This modern means of communicating around the world has diminished, if not eliminated, the previous barriers of time and space. Instant audio and visual communication is now possible between people separated by great distances across the globe, including some of the most remote areas. In fact, these technical advances in communication have the potential of forming what scientist-philosopher Peter Russell describes as a "global brain" with a "central nervous system" of computers, TVs, phones, and countless other communications devices through which "billions of messages continually shuttle back and forth, in an ever-growing web of communication, linking the billions of minds of humanity together into a single system."[17] Howard Bloom, author of *Global Brain: The Evolution of Mass Mind from the Big Bang to the 21st Century*, sees this web of communication in an even larger context:

We are nature incarnate. We are made up of her molecules and cells. We are tools of her probings and if, indeed, we suffer and we fail, from our lessons she will learn which way in the future not to turn. For all that lives and all that ever has is part of a collective brain, a neural net of the most sprawling kind, ... an evolution-driven, worldwide, multibillion-year-old interspecies mind.[18]

The ways this global "central nervous system" is operating, at least at the human level, are worth noting. It has become possible for millions of people around the world to simultaneously witness important social or political events as they happen via satellite TV. The instantaneous reactions to such information are, in effect, made possible by these interconnected, communication "neurons" belonging to what is being called our "global brain," or collective consciousness. Television in particular, with its highly persuasive visual power, has become the world's central nervous system and source of information and understanding. Elgin makes this point in his book *Awakening Earth: Exploring the Evolution of Human Culture and Consciousness*: "Television is at the very heart of our capacity for self-reflective consciousness at a civilizational scale. Television is our social witness—our vehicle for 'knowing what we know' as nations and as a human family." Elgin goes on to say:

> A direct measure of our social intelligence as a species is the intelligence with which we use our social brain—the rapidly evolving telecommunications system. All of the major challenges of the current era are, at their core, communications challenges. The human family will not respond to global warming, ozone depletion, toxic pollution, rain-forest destruction, and other environmental problems until we can visualize their impact through the mass media and thereby mobilize the will of the body politic to bring about changes. Humanity will not respond to homelessness, hunger, and poverty around the world unless we continue to see compelling and persistent images of suffering and need. The visual power of television can lull us into complacency or it can stir us to action.[19]

In addition, satellite communication via the Internet enables the World Weather System to gather and assess weather information from around the world in order to accurately forecast potentially hazardous events in time to make lifesaving preparations. Likewise, satellites and computer databases make it possible for international medical experts to share information instantaneously in an effort to prevent global epidemics.[20]

It is also clear that the new era of global mass communications has had an impact on the world of business. Although the ordinary workplace has usually been located outside the home or in urban centers since the Industrial Revolution, modern communications technology, particularly in Western industrialized nations, has allowed the same work to be accomplished at home or any number of other informal locations that serve particular business goals. This decentralization of labor has led, in turn, to more flexible work hours and reduced commuting costs, at least in the industrialized parts of the world.

Along with this positive development, however, decentralization has encouraged the outsourcing of jobs to foreign countries at the expense of livable-wage jobs once offered to domestic workers. The growing tension between the profit-by-any-means mind-set and the humane treatment of workers is a moral issue that will need to be addressed in the new millennium if the global evolution of human consciousness beyond first-tier thinking is to be achieved. This issue looms as an important moral crossroads for the future of humanity.

The new era of global communications is also changing the face of education. Greater distance-learning opportunities are now possible through university-based undergraduate, graduate, and continuing education programs because of the Internet. This is making adult education and retraining more affordable and accessible. Modern computer technologies are expanding the traditional classroom to the point where a classroom of young children in one country may talk in real time with their counterparts in another part of the world. This development certainly has the potential to increase levels of cross-cultural understanding.

While there will always be a need for traditional classrooms with one-on-one instruction, they will be complemented by more nonlocal experiences and instruction because of present and future advances in communications technologies. Communication via the Internet also makes it possible for the average person who has access to a computer, even beyond a classroom setting, to be exposed to the arts, cultural practices, and intellectual ideas of people, both past and present, throughout the global community.

Modern communications technologies are transforming international politics as well. The ongoing struggle for freedom and against various grievances such as widespread joblessness and a general lack of hope for improvement among the young in the Middle East has largely been fueled by widespread access to handheld communication devices in coordination with around-the-clock television news networks. The growing access to modern communication technologies means that the masses seeking social reforms cannot be silenced entirely by political regimes attempting to stand in the way of this inevitable evolutionary movement toward social justice.

By the same token, these modern means of communication have presented opportunities for individuals and groups to sow the seeds of social disintegration and violence in service to fanatical religious and geopolitical goals. The choice this presents between social harmony and understanding on the one hand and social chaos and destruction on the other brings us to another critical crossroads in the new millennium.

The Rise of Humanitarianism

Today in many parts of the world, there are a variety of organizations that provide aid for victims of natural and man-made disasters. In the West in particular, we have become used to the fact that groups such as the Red Cross and the Salvation Army have the desire and the means, largely provided by public donations, to distribute food, shelter, and medical help for large numbers of people in emergency situations. But what is seldom recognized is that this humanitarian impulse is a relatively new phenomenon when seen against the larger picture of human history.

Even as recently as the sixteenth century, when Martin Luther and the great artists of the Renaissance were alive, most people had no sense of obligation to provide aid for suffering individuals beyond their own families or local communities. Although giving alms to the poor was a common practice, there were no broad-based organizations devoted to serving the needs of poor and suffering people except the Church.[21] The promotion of large-scale outreach programs and social-reform efforts by governments and philanthropic individuals was simply not a cultural norm.

One of the first signs of a new effort to address the problem of human suffering on a large scale in the face of wars and natural disasters was the founding of the Red Cross in 1864. Since that time, the number of public and private humanitarian organizations providing aid to people in need has increased to a remarkable degree.[22]

One of the most important catalysts leading to the unprecedented spread of humanitarian organizations throughout the world was the establishment of the United Nations in October 1945. In response to the ruinous disasters of two world wars, the U.N. was created for the purpose of promoting and maintaining peace among nations throughout the world. Its relatively recent creation is evidence of an emerging evolutionary shift in human consciousness that points toward "second-tier thinking."

Further proof of this shift is found in the fact that the formation of humanitarian organizations known as nongovernmental organizations (NGOs) began to appear subsequent to the establishment of the UN. As a result of their efforts to alleviate suffering and poverty around the world, these nonprofit organizations are promoting peace and understanding among nations and cultures in spite of numerous obstacles. Their common goal is to remove the various political and economic barriers that divide nations and communities in order to deliver aid when and where it is needed. Many of these organizations attract volunteer workers from almost every part of the world. By 2006, a total of forty-five hundred humanitarian-aid organizations were operating around the world.[23] The number has increased considerably since then. Some of the best-known international nonprofit relief organizations are:

The Red Cross & Red Crescent Network
www.redcross.int
Provides disaster relief, health and safety training, and education and vaccination programs in the United States and elsewhere.

Doctors Without Borders
www.doctorswithoutborders.org
Crosses political and religious boundaries to deliver emergency medical aid to those affected by conflict, epidemics, disasters, and exclusion from health care.

CARE International
www.care-international.org
A global confederation of fourteen member organizations working to end poverty.

UN High Commissioner for Refugees (UNHCR)
www.unhcr.org
Involved in repatriation, local integration, and resettlement of

refugees to a third country.

UN International Children's Education Foundation (UNICEF)

www.unicef.org

Focuses its efforts on the rights, survival, development, and protection of children.

The International Rescue Committee

www.rescue.org

Provides emergency relief, post-conflict development and resettlement, and protection of human rights.

Heifer International

www.heifer.org

Works to eliminate poverty and hunger through sustainable holistic community development, animal husbandry, and agricultural training.

FINCA

www.finca.org

Pioneered the "village banking" method of credit delivery. It is a microfinance provider enabling low-income people worldwide to start businesses and gain employment.

During the 1990s, UN observer Clovis Maksoud remarked that the growing number of service-oriented groups was becoming a "constituency of consciousness" in the world. In addition, former UN Secretary General Kofi Annan said in 1998 that the relationship between the various NGOs and the UN's member nations had been "transformed beyond all recognition since 1947."[24] In an address Annan gave in 1999, he even expressed his conviction that the unprecedented growth of humanitarian organizations that occurred during the last half of the twentieth century was at least as important as the rise of the nation-state had been in the past.[25]

Although many of the UN's member nations still have not advanced beyond "first-tier thinking" and the tendency to pursue their own self-interests at the expense of other nations and their own most vulnerable populations, the UN still provides the world's best hope for making a peaceful and cooperative world become a reality. The spiritual evolutionary process continues in this respect, albeit rather slowly.

The Rise of Ecological Movements Worldwide

Among other things, the communications revolution has provided us with views of the Earth and the universe never seen or imagined before humanity's venture into outer space in the late twentieth century. Two of the most enlightening impressions gained from seeing the photographs and television images of Earth from outer space are the planet's breathless beauty and the lack of any visible artificial national borders. The sense of wholeness is unmistakable, and it is now more clearly evident than at any time in the past that the Earth is a fragile living organism. These impressions were vividly brought home to the astronaut Rusty Schweickart years ago as he returned to Earth from a mission to the moon:

> The Earth is so small and so fragile and such a precious little spot in that universe that you can block it out with your thumb, and you realize that on that small spot, that little blue and white thing, is everything that means anything to you—all of history and music and poetry and art and death and birth and love, tears, joy, games, all of it on that little spot out there that you can cover with your thumb. And you realize from that

perspective that you've changed, and there's something new there, that the relationship is no longer what it was.[26]

In his 1979 book, *Gaia: A New Look at Life on Earth*, British biologist James Lovelock proposed that Earth is a living, conscious organism rather than the complex unconscious machine envisioned by conventional science. Since the publication of this book, Lovelock's "Gaia hypothesis" has led to the development of a new field of scientific study known as "earth system science" or geophysiology.[27]

As a consequence, there is a growing awareness within the scientific community and beyond that the health and survival of our planet is in question as a result of the persistent use of nonrenewable energy sources being extracted from the Earth and the polluting effects they've had since the Industrial Revolution. The historic trend, especially among the industrial nations, toward unlimited economic growth and material consumption can no longer be maintained without avoiding catastrophic global climate change and the socioeconomic chaos that could occur as a result of the depletion of fresh water and life-sustaining crops.

However, along with the recognition among most scientists that our global ecology is threatened as never before has come an increasing willingness by people around the world at the grass-roots level to take concrete action in the interest of transforming the world's sources of energy. There are now estimated to be about two million organizations around the globe working to save the environment for future generations.[28] While this could be loosely described as a movement, it does not follow the traditional pattern for movements in the sense that there are no specific leaders or agendas. Paul Hawken describes it this way:

Movements, in short, have followers. This movement, however, doesn't fit the standard model. It is dispersed, inchoate, and fiercely independent. It has no manifesto or doctrine, no overriding authority to check with. It is taking shape in schoolrooms, farms, jungles, villages, companies, deserts, fisheries, slums—and yes, even fancy New York hotels. One of its distinctive features is that it is tentatively emerging as a global humanitarian movement arising from the bottom up.[29]

It is not a liberal or conservative activity; it is a sacred act. It is a massive enterprise undertaken by ordinary citizens everywhere, not by self-appointed governments or oligarchies.[30]

Hawken goes on to suggest that this is the largest social movement in history, largely due to the fact that it is happening in the age of the Internet.[31] Even though the movement consists of countless small groups all over the world, the Internet allows them to be connected as never before.

As the new millennium began, at least five thousand environmental groups in 184 countries brought their collective power to bear on the various government entities around the world.[32] As a result, organizers—ordinary people connected by the Internet in different parts of the world—created what is known as the Earth Day Network. While the Earth Day Network has faced significant opposition from various pseudo-science deniers, heavily funded oil lobbyists, and uncourageous politicians, it continued to build its online base to more than nine hundred thousand community members by the end of the first decade of the new millennium.[33]

The "metamorphosis" continues but is far from complete. The social "immune systems" across the world, in the form of both governmental and nongovernmental institutions, continue to resist such progress. But a progressive evolutionary change in consciousness, even at the highest levels of the political and corporate realms, is growing, principally because the energy and ideas are coming from the bottom up. The survival and progress of humanity hang in the balance—we are clearly at an ecological crossroads.

Decline of Social, Political, and Economic Systems

Another sign that the world is going through a crucial period of transition is seen in many news stories about the disintegration and collapse of governments, banks, and national economic systems, terrorist attacks, regional wars, and extreme political ideological polarization—a very unstable picture at best. It is symptomatic of a dying era of first-tier thinking. Hubbard's metamorphosis analogy seems quite relevant to the present global disintegration and decline of conventional social, political, and economic systems that have failed to serve the common good: "The breakdown of the caterpillar's old system is essential for the breakthrough of the new butterfly."[34]

It seems fair to say that the recent spread of modern communication technologies and the rapid increase in citizen demands for freedom from the suffocating power of old-world dictatorships have come together in a "perfect storm" of divine purpose. The fact that broad-based, initially peaceful protests against the dictatorial leaders of most Middle Eastern countries occurred almost simultaneously is a dramatic demonstration, on a global scale, that the "imaginal disks" of a new world were beginning to link up to hasten the breakdown of the old egocentric and ethnocentric world. Despite subsequent social fragmentation and violence in many parts of the Middle East, the "metamorphosis" toward a more integral world continues as it must. When viewed from a broader perspective, these developments are signs of a new spiritual awakening.

Another sign of a global awakening has been evident in the country of South Africa since Nelson Mandela's release from prison during the last decade of the twentieth century. Only three years after Mandela's release after twenty-seven years of imprisonment, he and South Africa's president, Frederick Willem de Klerk, were awarded the Nobel Peace Prize together for their work to end the long-standing system of apartheid and the establishment of a new democratic South Africa.

Even more remarkable was the establishment of South Africa's Truth and Reconciliation Commission (TRC) after Mandela's eventual election as South Africa's first black president. The commission, which included such tireless peace advocates as Archbishop Desmond Tutu, was put in place according to the terms of the country's new Promotion of National Unity and Reconciliation Act. The commission's purpose was "to bear witness to, record, and in some cases grant amnesty to the perpetrators of crimes relating to human rights violations as well as reparation and rehabilitation."[35]

What was particularly significant about the process undertaken by the TRC was that its emphasis on reconciliation stood in stark contrast with the more conventional emphasis on prosecution in response to crimes committed by nations and organizations in the past. In an attempt to break a potential cycle of vengeful retributions, all sides involved in the apartheid struggle appeared before the commission and were heard in an attempt to find ways to heal the nation's severely divided population.

From their newfound positions of power, the elected black leaders chose to exercise restraint and find forgiveness in cases of freely admitted crimes from all the parties involved. While some criticized the TRC for being ineffective, the process, taken as a whole, marked a significant turning point in the direction of second-tier thinking and an integral world. It is interesting that, since that time, other countries have instituted similar commissions to avoid lingering divisions and recriminations.[36]

A similar awakening occurred in America when, on November 2, 2008, Barack Obama became the first African-American to be elected U.S. president. It is impossible to overestimate the profound shift in consciousness that this election represented in America. While the evil of racial prejudice and division still exists, the transition from a system of apartheid in at least the southern United States as recently as the mid-twentieth century to the comparatively more racially integrated environment that exists today, in which blacks hold important leadership positions in business, politics, the medical profession, and education, is truly remarkable.

This development is a sign of a spiritual awakening, at least among the rising number of Americans who have evolved to a level of consciousness similar to what Beck and Cowan would describe as the sensitive self or the FlexFlow levels we saw in Chapter 8. Of course, for every action there is a reaction, especially when substantial social change is imminent. Nevertheless, it has been estimated that the majority of American citizens will be people of color by the year 2025. This shift in demographics will challenge all Americans to recognize the things we all have in common and that, in the divine sense, we are all one. It seems that the divine purpose in these dramatic social shifts is that we must learn to choose love rather than fear as a driving force.

A spiritual awakening appears to be underway in China as well. As we enter the new millennium, China's economic growth and strength is "trickling down" to more of its citizens than ever before, thus creating greater pressure for social change from within. The frequency in the number of calls for individual freedoms and democratic reforms as well as the courage being prominently demonstrated by some individuals calling for such reforms is becoming more obvious despite all the suppression tactics exercised by the Chinese government. Even while China makes remarkable technological gains and expands its economy, its political leaders remain insecure to the point of extreme paranoia, as demonstrated by their need to completely suppress dissenting opinions.

Despite its growing power on the world scene and its immense intellectual capital, China's leaders desperately cling to the authoritarian beliefs of a dying world. Among the various forces that may prove to hasten China's inevitable sociopolitical metamorphosis are the spontaneous grass-roots efforts within the population to form unofficial, spirit-based Christian communities and the dramatic expansion and availability of social communication technologies. In the latter case, we have already seen the important catalytic role that electronic social communications have had in regard to the growing global ecological movement and in the struggle for human rights being opposed by various authoritarian regimes.

Along with an overall global shift from a decidedly ethnocentric mind-set toward one that is more world-centric, the United States seems to be heading in a direction that focuses on efforts to build and maintain more cooperative relationships with other nations. As we in the United States head toward a more integral world, as we must if we are to survive as a world community, our relationships with other nations will need to be based first on the "moral interest" of the world—the common global good—which in the long run is in the best interests of every nation, including our own. Perhaps America is moving, albeit slowly, toward a state of spiritual maturity that will enable it to adjust gracefully to the emerging global shift with all other nations.

It's becoming increasingly clear as the new millennium progresses that America's economic standing in the world is changing. Some in America view this with alarm, but in his book *The Post-American World*, Fareed Zakaria helps us see the current economic picture from a more instructive international perspective. He points out that from at least the end of the twentieth century until recently, the United States was the most powerful nation in the world since ancient Rome in terms of economics, politics, science, and culture. But now he believes the world is experiencing a major power shift that he calls "the rise of the rest."[37]

According to Zakaria, countries all over the world have been experiencing unprecedented rates of economic growth just since the 1980s.

While Asia is the most prominent among "the rest," other parts of the world have gained economic power as well. He points out that 124 countries grew at a rate of 4 percent or better. Thirty of the countries are in Africa, and among the twenty-five fastest-growing multinational companies, sixteen are located in Brazil, Mexico, South Korea, and Taiwan. The other nine are located in India, China, Argentina, Chile, Malaysia, and South Africa. London has become a leading financial center, and the United Arab Emirates is where the most heavily endowed investment fund is located.[38]

Zakaria also observes that while the world's poorest people live in fifty countries in the world, poverty is slowly dropping in the other 124. In other words, poverty is being reduced to some degree in the areas that are home to as much as 80 percent of the world's population. This is not to say that poverty has been eliminated, but the trend seems to be in a better direction. The net result is that for the first time in history, economic growth is occurring globally. As Zakaria puts it:

> This is creating an international system in which countries in all parts of the world are no longer objects or observers, but players in their own right. It is the birth of a truly global order.
>
> A related aspect of this new era is the diffusion of power from states to other actors. The "rest" that is rising includes many nongovernmental entities. Groups and individuals have been empowered, and hierarchy, centralization, and control are being undermined. Functions that were once controlled by governments are now shared with international bodies like the World Trade Center and the European Union.[39]

From a global standpoint, we are essentially seeing a clash of consciousness levels or worldviews. A rising number of people around the world are demonstrating various degrees of the spiral-dynamics levels of human consciousness referred to earlier as the sensitive Relativistic and integrative Systemic levels, in contrast with the more controlling Purposeful and competitive StriveDrive ways of thinking. As the new millennium progresses, a critical mass of Relativistic and Systemic forms of consciousness will eventually be reached as more and more people become inclined to embrace the values of cooperation, compromise, and openness to new ideas. Just as every nation will be seen as a community of individuals responsible to one another for the common good, so the world community will come to recognize the prime necessity of having a United Nations organization with broader executive, legislative, and judicial power to enable and ensure that all nations are responsible for one another for the common good.

Declining Interest in Fixed Religious Orthodoxies

If there are signs that a new global paradigm is emerging—possibly to be seen in the communications revolution, the rise of ecological movements, and the various social-political and economic upheavals—the same could be said about the growing interest in universal forms of spirituality. It seems clear that a grass-roots spiritual awakening is challenging traditional religious orthodoxies and concepts.

In many parts of the world, a growing number of Christians and followers of other faiths are seeking a relationship with the divine that is more spiritual than religious in the formal sense of the word. This does not necessarily mean the wholesale rejection of organized religions, but it does suggest, particularly for progressive-minded Christians, that the rigidly prescribed dogmas and practices of many conventional churches are too limiting and exclusive for one living in the twenty-first century.

In the minds of some, spirituality simply means a narcissistic process of self-reflection that leads inward and amounts to a retreat from the real world and a lack of concern for the welfare of others. But spirituality has a communal as well as personal dimension. Here we are referring to the kind of spirituality that reaches out and engages others with compassion, humility, and understanding. In other words, it embodies a Christ-like engagement with the world. It is this form of spirituality that is appealing to larger numbers of Christians and non-Christians alike. By the same token, this development does not imply that institutional religion and spirituality are mutually exclusive. It simply means that God's loving presence and saving Grace are accessible with or without unfailing adherence to certain prescribed religious requirements or beliefs.

Harvey Cox refers to this development as the emergence of a new "Age of the Spirit,"[40] and author and theologian Phyllis Tickle describes it as the "Great Emergence" that characterizes the present and future state of Christianity.[41] What, then, are the signs of an emerging spiritual awakening, and what does this mean for the future of Christianity and other organized religions?

Many people in America are forming groups, both within and without established churches, as a way of deepening their spirituality and of finding a community of Christians more interested in new thinking and social-justice initiatives than in following outdated creeds or doctrines. A significant example is the spiritually driven initiative to claim, unequivocally, that gay, lesbian, bisexual, and transgendered people (LGBTs) are worthy in the sight of God and the Church.

Unlike the highly restrictive and exclusivist "family values" of evangelicalism, this spiritually motivated movement within some of the more progressive churches in America supports a set of values that includes the rejection of homophobia and the affirmation of equal rights across lines of gender and sexual orientation.[42] The United Church of Christ, for instance, has officially declared that LGBTs are welcome in its churches, allows its clergy to perform same-sex marriages, and permits the ordination of LGBT clergy.

Likewise, in 1997 the General Convention of the Episcopal Church in America presented an apology "on behalf of the Episcopal Church to its members who are gay or lesbian and to lesbians and gay men outside the Church for years of rejection and maltreatment" and for "its sins committed against lesbian and gay people."[43]

Other churches and organizations have done much the same over the past thirty to forty years. They include the More Light Presbyterians, who consist of individuals and some congregations that "work for the full participation of lesbian, gay, bisexual and transgender people of faith"; the Christian organization Lutherans Concerned/North America, which has been "affirming God's love for people of all sexual orientations and gender identities since 1974"; and Dignity USA, which "works for respect and justice for all gay, lesbian, bisexual and transgender persons in the Catholic Church and the world through education, advocacy and support."[44]

Followers of Dignity USA, in particular, faced stern resistance from the Vatican. In an official Vatican letter to the bishops of the Catholic Church (before Pope Francis's ordination), orders were given to all church officials to "'withdraw all support' from any group that did not condemn 'homogenital acts' as immoral."[45] This resulted in the expulsion of several Dignity USA groups from church properties. Nevertheless, Dignity USA has gone on to form local chapters where LGBTs are welcome and allowed to worship openly.[46]

When it comes to all these groups that are attempting to emulate Jesus's teachings within and beyond conventional Christian churches, it's not so much about what people believe or what their sexual orientation happens to be but who they are spiritually in relation to others. Jesus was not about separating believers from nonbelievers or rejecting "sinners." His focus was on inclusion and serving the poor and the outcasts of society regardless of their religious beliefs or affiliations.

Among other important indicators of a religiously oriented spiritual awakening is the growing interest in worship experiences that cross religious boundaries and encourage cross-cultural understandings. The growing adoption of Asian, Native American, Celtic, Nordic, and other cultural forms of worship by some Christian congregations is a case in point.

Nevertheless, this loosening of liturgical distinctions has been cause for concern to the more conservatively oriented Christian leaders, who tend to see it as a weakening of the Church and a rejection of traditional Christian beliefs.[47] For example, R. Albert Mohler Jr., president of the Southern Baptist Theological Seminary, in Louisville, Kentucky, and Mark Driscoll, former pastor of the Seattle-based Mars Hill Church, believe that Christians should avoid yoga because of what they claim to be its "demonic roots."[48]

The parallel between this type of institutional resistance to more inclusive, less narrowly defined religious practices and the first-century Pharisees' objections to Jesus's alleged lack of religious "purity" is strikingly similar. However, as we move gradually toward a more integral world, it is only natural that such defensiveness should exist.

Another important change of a spiritual nature is the growing interest in experiential forms of spirituality within religious circles, as shown by the rapid expansion of Pentecostalism, as mentioned in Chapter 3. While Christian churches are declining in size and numbers in Europe, Pentecostal Christian churches are spreading rapidly and steadily, especially in Latin America.[49]

Even though Pentecostals are often assumed to be Christian fundamentalists in terms of their beliefs, there are important differences. While fundamentalists tend to be more literal in their interpretations of the Bible, Pentecostals—as we have seen—place a higher value on having a direct experience of the Holy Spirit through ecstatic forms of worship characterized as "speaking in tongues." They also oppose what they perceive to be fundamentalists' rigidity and their "man-made creeds and lifeless rituals"[50] Even so, most white North American Pentecostals tend to be more strongly influenced by Christian fundamentalism than their comparatively more progressive counterparts in Latin America, Africa, and Asia.

There are now more than 279 million Pentecostals throughout the world and the number continues to grow.[51] Tickle points to the fact that by 2006, Pentecostals, and other Christians known as charismatics who believe in the presence of miracles, signs, and the spiritual gifts of prophecy and healing, totaled more than five hundred million around the world. [52] The Latin American, African, and Asian Pentecostals are generally more closely aligned with Jesus's ministry to the poor and are more heavily engaged in social-justice issues and ministries. They are less concerned with being "saved" in preparation for the afterlife than with the needs of the impoverished, the sick, and the social outcasts of this world.

This is not unlike the situation that existed during the earliest phase of Christianity when the followers of Jesus modeled his love and compassion for others even before the existence of formal creeds and requirement for salvation. Cox sees this new move toward experiential spirituality and egalitarianism among Pentecostal Christians as an innate desire to re-connect with the earliest and most authentic phase of Christianity, which occurred before it became imperialized and institutionalized under Constantine in the fourth century.[53]

Tickle also points out the contemporary significance of this phenomenon:

"Pentecostalism by definition assumes the direct contact of the believer with God and, by extension, the direct agency of the

Holy Spirit as instructor and counselor and commander as well as comforter. As such and stated practically, Pentecostalism assumes that ultimate authority is experiential rather than canonical."[54]

This growing desire to go "back to the basics" that has become apparent not only among Pentecostals but also among newer generations of Christians in general is closely related to the whole systematic search for the historical Jesus that has been underway since the beginning of the twentieth century. Meanwhile, other grass-roots Christian movements more closely related in expression to early Christianity are emerging in other areas of the globe as well.

In China there are indications of a growing need within the country's population for a more substantive faith that offers a sense of belonging, stability, and spiritual strength as an alternative to the very impersonal, intrusive, and controlling environment created by the Chinese government over the last several decades.[55] In many places throughout China, various "house churches" have sprung up without encouragement from the Communist government. One of the reasons is that growing numbers of Chinese are yearning to fill the vacuum left by a substantial loss of faith in Marxist ideologies after the destructive Cultural Revolution of 1966 to 1976 and the government's brutal Tiananmen Square crackdown in 1985. Interestingly enough, the government is beginning to realize that the churches are a force for social stability rather than just opposition.[56]

Similar spiritual awakenings are occurring in the other major religions as well. Among the followers of the Islamic faith, there are some who believe that society has a responsibility to respond to the needs of the poor and that Islam is not just a matter of obeying ritual obligations.[57] In 2006 the Egyptian-based Muslim Brotherhood publicly proclaimed that its goal was the establishment of a democratic state as opposed to an Islamic one. Couple this with the fact that in November 2008 an American intelligence report indicated that support for Al Qaeda dropped dramatically among Muslims because of its lack of attention to the problems of poverty, unemployment, and education as well as its use of indiscriminate violence to achieve its ends.[58] Clearly, the beginnings of a shift away from an emphasis on rigidly observed rituals and religious dogmas toward democratic ideals and serving the social needs of others in nonviolent ways is underway not just in Egypt but in other parts of the Islamic world as well. This is occurring despite continuing Islamic terrorist attempts to retreat into extreme religious authoritanianism.

Likewise, a "Buddhist Reformation"—a spiritual shift in priorities—seems to be taking place within various Buddhist communities. Japan's largest denomination, known as the Nichiren Shoshu, has seen the formation of a movement called Soka Gakkai that favors establishment of an educational system that fosters creative thinking rather than the more traditional authoritarian model. Its members, who are now represented in 128 countries, are also dedicated to establishing world peace, women's rights, and interfaith dialogue.[59] Like all forward-thinking movements for change, Soka Gakkai has met with stiff resistance, in this case from the more traditional Buddhist priesthood within the Nichiren Shoshu denomination.

In Israel, increasing numbers of young Jews are losing interest in the rigid orthodoxy of their country's established religion and show great interest in Hasidic, Asian, and Sufi spirituality. In America, some synagogues prefer to call themselves "post-denominational" and reject the older labels of *orthodox, conservative*, and *reform*.[60] Especially significant is the fact that unofficial efforts, if not official ones, are on the rise between Jews and Muslims to engage in dialogue and cooperative efforts toward peaceful reconciliation.

But perhaps the so-called Liberation Theology movement that

began in Latin America has had the greatest spiritual impact on people around the world representing diverse religious communities. Cox refers to it as "the most creative theologian movement of the twentieth century."[60]

Liberation Theology is, first and foremost, a religiously motivated movement rather than a political one even though it has had significant political consequences. It had its beginnings in the 1960s, sparked by the ideas and tireless efforts of Peruvian Catholic priest Gustavo Gutierrez Instead of being a "trickle-down" or "top-down" theology promoted by the church hierarchy, it has sprung to life from the grassroots—the exploited poor and destitute people in Latin America, Asia, Africa, and India. Among its main proponents have been people such as Bishop Desmond Tutu of South Africa.[62]

In his early years, while studying in France, Gutierrez became enthralled with Jacques Maritain's "integral humanism" and the writings of Pierre Teilhard de Chardin, whom the Vatican had blacklisted for his progressive ideas.[63] He was also impressed with Karl Marx's criticisms of ideology, class, and capitalism even while rejecting Marxist ideas about materialism, economic determinism, and atheism. In the end, Gutierrez came away believing that his mission as a Christian was to improve people's lives here and now rather than to simply offer them the prospect of later rewards in heaven. In his book *The Power of the Poor in History*, Gutierrez says, "From the beginning, the theology of liberation posited that the first act is involvement in the liberation process, and that theology comes afterward, as a second act. The theological moment is one of critical reflection from within, and upon, concrete historical praxis, in confrontation with the world of the Lord as lived and accepted in faith."[64]

It is his belief that liberation and salvation are the same thing and that salvation, first and foremost, involves a transformation of society whereby the poor are freed from economic, political, and social oppression. Gutierrez seems to be motivated by Jesus and the ancient

Hebrew prophets who came before him who were willing to become politically involved on behalf of the poor and the dispossessed. Marcus Borg explains:

> Jesus was not the first in Jewish history to criticize conventional wisdom. In the Hebrew Bible, the authors of Ecclesiastes and Job protested against the conventional wisdom represented by the book of Proverbs, that easy confidence that the righteous would prosper and the wicked wither. They were subversive sages who challenged and subverted the popular wisdom of their day. Jesus stood in this tradition of subversive wisdom.[65]

> Just as the ethos of holiness had led to a politics of holiness, so also the ethos of compassion was to lead to a politics of compassion. The ethos of compassion profoundly affected the shape of the Jesus movement.[66]

Again, we should be reminded that Gutierrez and other proponents of Liberation Theology in Latin America were not in favor of assuming that the poor's suffering was the will of a loving God that must be endured. Instead, they saw in Jesus's words and deeds a reason to believe that such suffering should and could be eliminated through positive action. Rather than seeing Jesus as a "personal savior" who came to save them from a fallen world, the poor of many parts of Latin America have come to recognize, with the help of Gutierrez and others, that the Kingdom of God was to come to the world—this world. Liberation Theology as demonstrated and embodied by Gutierrez and others like him is, in essence, a politics of compassion.

All the examples given so far of an evolutionary shift toward spirituality and away from narrowly prescribed religious orthodoxies and institutions suggest that the people who are creating this shift are freely crossing the arbitrary boundaries of Judaism, Christianity, Islam, Buddhism, Hinduism, and other religions around the world. In fact, people of all faiths now live among one another on every continent.

As this happens, religions will become less exclusive, less hierarchical, less dogmatic, less denominational, and more willing to accept women in all leadership roles, along with those of different races, cultures, sexual orientations, and beliefs. This will not happen quickly or easily. The more conservative and fundamentalist elements within the various organized religions will resist this coming evolutionary shift for fear of losing what is familiar, but they are on the wrong side of history. As Cox puts it, "They are attempting to stem an inexorable movement of the human spirit whose hour has come."[67]

It seems to me that Cox's words have relevance far beyond what is happening within the world's religions today. They speak as well to all the other evolutionary developments discussed in this chapter, since they are all spiritually interconnected. In short, they are all interconnected holons of a larger evolutionary holarchy. John Shelby Spong also provides us with a much-needed picture of what these evolutionary developments could, and hopefully will, create. Although he is actually referring to what he calls the "ecclesia of the future" within the context of an evolving Christianity, in his book *A New Christianity for a New World* his description could just as well describe the essence of the new emerging paradigm in its broadest sense:

> The new ecclesia will also offer opportunities for people to grow into a new being—a being not bounded by tribal claims, superiority claims, gender claims, or even religious claims. Having surrendered the security-producing tribal claims which suggest that our way is the only way, we will be freed

to recognize that we do not have to say to another person that his or her way into the holy is wrong. Those who once called themselves Catholic and Protestant, orthodox and heretic, liberal and evangelical, Jew and Muslim, Buddhist and Hindu, will all find a place in the ecclesia of the future. There being and nonbeing, substance and shadow, can be accepted—no, even celebrated. There we will walk together into the meaning of God—the joy, the wonder, the mystery of God—a God not bounded by our formulas, our creeds, our doctrines, our liturgies, or even our Bible, but still real, infinitely real.[68]

The evolution of human consciousness as envisioned by Graves, Beck, Cowan, and Wilber continues despite any immediate evidence to the contrary. Indeed, such evidence as the loss of faith in exclusivist religious orthodoxies; the destabilization and collapse of major financial institutions, economies and political regimes; and an increase in the number of unusually calamitous ecological disasters in many parts of the world, all in quick succession, strongly suggests that in many ways the world as we have known it is dying even as a new world struggles to be born.

Given all that we have discussed, coupled with our own real-world experiences, Barbara Marx Hubbard's earlier description of the caterpillar's metamorphosis into a butterfly seems all the more relevant to our current world situation. We now know that difficulties lie ahead and that they are an inevitable part of the transformation process, but we also know that human thought produces energy that can actually change the world both physically and spiritually. So it becomes a matter of how positive, constructive, and powerful such collective human energy can be going forward.

It is easy to be cynical, fatalistic, and pessimistic in the face of tragic and difficult times, but such negative energy is antithetical to the power of God and leads to temporary spiritual blindness. Faith in God is faith in the supreme power of love and compassion and in the certain knowledge of a future "reign of God" on Earth as in heaven.

Once again I yield to Brian McLaren as he interprets the biblical Exodus narrative within the context of our own time:

> If the Exodus story situates us in the sacred present on a pilgrimage toward external and internal liberation, then the story of the peace-making kingdom ignites our faith with a sacred vision of the future, a vision of hope, a vision of love. It represents a new creation, and a new exodus—a new promised land that isn't one patch of ground held by one elite group, but that encompasses the whole Earth. It acknowledges that whatever we have become or ruined, there is hope for a better tomorrow; whatever we have achieved or destroyed, new possibilities await us; no matter how far we have come or backslidden, there are new and more glorious adventures ahead. And, the prophets aver, this is not just a human pipe dream, wishful thinking, or whistling in the dark; this hope is the very word of the Lord, the firm promise of the living God.[69]

The mounting evidence of an approaching evolutionary leap of human consciousness is, in my view, a significant part of that firm divine promise. This is happening at a critical time in history because of the reality of our spiritual interconnection with God, one another, and all of Creation. Today and in the years to come, new incarnations of ancient souls will come with new insights, knowledge, and spiritual missions shaped by the experiences of previous lives and lessons learned directly from those angelic beings who guide us and love us.

All the while, the veil that has separated us from this world and the next—our spiritual home—is becoming increasingly transparent by virtue of the revelations we have gained from those who have seen and experienced the light firsthand. For those who care to notice with open hearts and minds, the sometimes-painful but ever-hopeful birthing process of a new, more holistic world has begun.

NOTES

INTRODUCTION

1. Harvey Cox, *The Future of Faith* (New York: HarperCollins Publishers, 2010), 37.

2. Ibid.

3. Cox, *The Future of Faith*, 101.

4. John Shelby Spong, *Why Christianity Must Change or Die: A Bishop Speaks to Believers in Exile* (New York: HarperCollins Publishers, 1998), 19-21.

5. Hal Taussig, *A New Spiritual Home: Progressive Christianity at the Grassroots* (Santa Rosa, CA: Polebridge Press, 2006).

6. Diana Butler Bass, *Christianity After Religion: The End of Church and the Birth of a New Spiritual Awakening* (New York: HarperCollins Publishers, 2012), 15.

7. Ken Wilber, *A Theory of Everything: An Integral Vision for Business, Politics, Science and Spirituality* (Boston: Shambhala Publications Inc., 2000), 20.

CHAPTER ONE

1. Victoria LePage, "The God Debate: Monotheism vs. Panentheism in Postmodern Society," the Theosophical Society in America, http://www.theosophical.org/publications/quest-magazine/1572.

2. Ibid.

3. Paul Alan Laughlin, *Remedial Christianity: What Every Believer Should Know about the Faith, but Probably Doesn't* (Santa Rosa, CA: Polebridge Press, 2004), 44.

4. Laughlin, *Remedial Christianity*, 47.

5. Ibid.

6. Thomas Dennis Rock, *The Mystical Woman and the Cities of the Nations* (London: William MacIntosh, 1867), 22-23.

7. Arthur Weigall, *Paganism in Our Christianity* (New York: Garden City Publishing, 1928), 197-198.

8. Laughlin, *Remedial Christianity*, 46-47.

9. "Theism," Wikipedia.org, http://www.en. wikipedia.org/wiki/theism.

10. Marcus Borg, *The God We Never Knew* (New York: HarperCollins Publishers, 1997), 65.

11. Ibid.

12. Ibid., 67.

13. Ibid., 68.

14. Ibid., 32.

15. Timothy Conway, "Panentheism and the Reality of God," Enlightened-Spirituality.org, http://www.enlightened-spirituality.org/panentheism.html.

16. Ibid.

17. Ibid.

18. Laughlin, *Remedial Christianity*, 55-56.

19. LePage, "The God Debate: Monotheism vs. Panentheism in Postmodern Society," http://www.theosophical.org/publications/quest-magazine/1572.

20. Ibid.

21. Conway, "Panentheism and the Reality of God," http://www.enlightened-spirituality.org/panentheism.html.

22. Borg, *The God We Never Knew*, 32.

23. C. Alan Anderson and Deborah G. Whitehouse, *New Thought: A Practical American Spirituality* (Bloomington, IN: AuthorHouse Publisher, revised edition, 2003), 89.

24. Quincy Howe Jr., *Reincarnation for the Christian* (Philadelphia: The Westminster Press, 1974), 20.

25. "Big Bang Theory—an Overview," All about Science, http://www.big-bang-theory.com/.

26. Borg, *The God We Never Knew*, 34.

27. Ibid.,79.

CHAPTER TWO

1. James Orr, "The Apostles' Creed," *International Standard Bible Encyclopedia Online*, 1939 edition, http://www.internationalstandardbible.com/A/apostles-creed-the.html.

2. "Apostles' Creed," Wikipedia.org, http://en. wikipedia.org/w/index. php?title=Apostles%27_creed&printable=yes.

3. "The Apostles' Creed," *International Standard Bible Encyclopedia Online*, 1939 edition, http://www.internationalstandardbible.com/A/apostles-creed-the.html.

4. Ibid.

5. Bart D. Ehrman, *The Orthodox Corruption of Scripture: The Effect of Early Christological Controversies on the Text of the New Testament* (New York: Oxford University Press Inc., 2011), 14-15.

6. "The Trinity in Christian Theology," ReligionFacts.com, http://www.religionfacts.com/christianity/beliefs/trinity. htm.

7. Arthur Cushman McGiffert, *A History of Christian Thought*, Vol. 1 (New York: Charles Scribner's Sons, 1954), 258.

8. "How Ancient Trinitarian Gods Influenced Adoption of the Trinity," United Church of God—an International Association, http://www.ucg.org/booklet/god-trinity/how-ancient-trinitarian-gods-influenced-adoption-trinity/.

9. http://history-christian-church. blogspot.com/2012/03/arian-controversy.html.

10. Ibid.

11. "First Council of Nicaea," Wikipedia.org, http://en. wikipedia.org/wiki/First_Council_of_Nicaea.

12. Karen Armstrong, *A History of God* (New York: Ballantine Books, 1993), 108.

13. "First Council of Nicaea," Wikipedia.org, http://en. wikipedia.org/wiki/First_Council_of_Nicaea.

14. Ibid.

15. Armstrong, *A History of God*, 108-109.

16. "Constantine," *Encyclopedia Britannica*, 1971 edition, vol. 6, 386.

17. Armstrong, *A History of God*, 111.

18. Ibid., 115.

19. "The Surprising Origins of the Trinity Doctrine," United Church of God—an International Association, http://www.ucg.org/booklet/god-trinity/surprising-origins-Trinity-doctrine/.

20. Ibid.

21. "The Trinity in Christian Theology," ReligionFacts.com, http://www.religionfacts.com/christianity/beliefs/trinity. htm.

22. Ibid.

23. Ibid.

24. Stevan Davies, *The Gospel of Thomas: Annotated & Explained*, Ed. Andrew Harvey (Woodstock, VT: Skylight Paths Publishing, 2002), 5.

25. Laughlin, *Remedial Christianity*, 78-79.

26. Ibid.

27. Spong, *Why Christianity Must Change or Die*, 12.

28. Ehrman, *The Orthodox Corruption of Scripture*, 59.

29. Ibid., 60-61.

30. Ibid., 58.

31. Marcus Borg, *Jesus: A New Vision: Spirit, Culture and the Life of Discipleship* (New York: HarperCollins Publishers, 1987), 40-41.

32. Marcus Borg, ed., *Jesus and Buddha: The Parallel Sayings* (Berkeley, CA: Ulysses Press, 1997), vi.

33. Ibid., v-xvii.

34. Ehrman, *The Orthodox Corruption of Scripture*, 16.

35. Ibid., 56-57.

36. Ibid., 16.

37. Robert J. Miller, ed., *The Apocalyptic Jesus: A Debate* (Santa Rosa, CA: Polebridge Press, 2001), 39-40.

38. Miller, *The Apocalyptic Jesus*, 69-70.

39. Ibid., 42.

40. Ibid., 66-67.

41. Borg, *Jesus: A New Vision*, 97.

42. Miller, *The Apocalyptic Jesus*, 70-71.

43. Ibid.

44. Ibid., 75-76.

45. Ibid., 76.

46. Elaine Pagels, *The Gnostic Gospels* (New York: Random House, 1979), 5.

47. Laughlin, *Remedial Christianity*, 194-195.

48. Ibid., 196.

49. Ibid.

50. Matt J. Rossano, "Does Resurrection Contradict Science?" *Huffington Post*, Apr 25, 2013, http://www.huffingtonpost.com/matt-j-rossano/does-resurrec-tion-contrad_b_848577.html.

51. Ibid.

52. J. Denny Weaver, *The Nonviolent Atonement* (Grand Rapids, MI: Wm. B. Eerdmans Publishing Co., 2001), 14.

53. Ibid., 14-15.

54. Ibid., 15.

55. Ibid., 16.

56. Ibid.

57. Ibid.

58. Ibid., 16-17.

59. Ibid., 210.

60. Ibid., 211.

61. Ibid.

62. Borg, *Jesus: A New Vision*, 125-126.

63. James D. Tabor, *Paul and Jesus: How the Apostle Transformed Christianity* (New York: Simon & Schuster, 2012), xviii.

CHAPTER THREE

1. Marcus Borg, *Reading the Bible Again for the First Time: Taking the Bible Seriously but Not Literally* (New York: HarperCollins Publishers, 2001), 39.

2. Ibid., 40-41.

3. Ibid., 22.

4. Phyllis Tickle, *The Great Emergence: How Christianity Is Changing and Why* (Grand Rapids, MI: Baker Publishing Group, 2008), 80-81.

5. Borg, *Reading the Bible Again for the First Time*, 44-45.

6. Borg, *Meeting Jesus Again for the First Time* (New York: HarperCollins Publishers, 1994), 122-125.

7. John Shelby Spong, *Rescuing the Bible from Fundamentalism: A Bishop Rethinks the Meaning of Scripture* (New York: HarperCollins Publishers, 1991), 210-214.

8. Borg, *Reading the Bible Again for the First Time*, 276-278.

9. "Enlightenment," *Stanford Encyclopedia of Philosophy*, http://plato. stanford. edu/entries/enlightenment/html.

10. Ibid.

11. Ibid.

12. Ibid.

13. Ibid.

14. "Fundamentalist-Modernist Controversy," Wikipedia.org, http://en. wiki-pedia.org/wiki/Fundamentalist%E2%80%93Modernist-Controversy.

15. Ibid.

16. "Inspiration, Authority & Criticism in the Thought of Charles Augustus Briggs," Bible.org, http://bible.org/pringt/683.

17. Ibid.

18. Ibid.

19. "Fundamentalist-Modernist Controversy," Wikipedia.org, http://en. wikipedia.org/wiki/Fundamentalist%E2%80%93Modernist-Controversy.

20. Ibid.

21. Ibid.

22. "Inspiration, Authority & Criticism in the Thought of Charles Augustus Briggs," Bible.org, http://bible.org/pringt/683.

23. "Fundamentalist-Modernist Controversy," Wikipedia.org, http://en. wikipedia.org/wiki/Fundamentalist%E2%80%93Modernist-Controversy.

24. "Who Were the Fundamentalists?" *Christianity Today*, October 1, 2006, http://www.christianitytoday.com/ch/2006/issue92/3. 12ahtml.

25. "Fundamentalist-Modernist Controversy," Wikipedia.org, http://en. wikipedia.org/wiki/Fundamentalist%E2%80%93Modernist-Controversy.

26. "Harry Emerson Fosdick: Liberalism's Populizer," *Christianity Today*, August 8, 2008, http://www.christianitytoday.com/ch/131christians/pastorsandpreachers/fosdick.html.

27. R. W. Scribner & C. Scott Dixon, *The German Reformation* (New York: Palgrave MacMillan, 2003), 18.

28. "Five Solas," *Theopedia, an Encyclopedia of Biblical Christianity*, http://www.theopedia.com/Five-Solas.

29. Tabor, *Paul and Jesus: How the Apostle Transformed Christianity*, xviii.

30. Barbara Pitkin, "Calvin's Reception of Paul," Academia. edu, http://www. academia. edu/879076/Calvins_Reception_of_Paul.html.

31. Dave Hunt, "Calvin's Surprising Catholic Connection," TheBereanCall. org, http://www.thebereancall.org/content/july-2012-classic.

32. "The Canons of the Synod of Dordt, 1618-1619," Fordham University: The Jesuit University of New York, http://www.fordham. edu/halsall/ mod/1619dordt. asp.

33. Ibid.

34. Dr. Richard P. Bucher, "Calvinistic Theology," Our Redeemer Lutheran Church, http://www.orlutheran.com/html/calvinisttheology.html.

35. Laughlin, *Remedial Christianity*, 152.

36. Ibid.

37. Ibid., 154.

38. Neale Donald Walsch, *Conversations With God: An Uncommon Dialogue*, Book 1 (New York: G. P. Putnam's Sons, 1995), 55-56.

39. Laughlin, *Remedial Christianity*, 142-143.

40. Ibid., 154.

41. Ibid., 159.

42. Ibid., 141.

43. Ibid., 155.

44. Tabor, *Paul and Jesus*, 135-139.

45. Hunt, "Calvin's Surprising Catholic Connection," TheBereanCall.org, http://www.thebereancall.org/content/july-2012-classic.

46. "The Canons of the Synod of Dordt, 1618-1619," Fordham University: The Jesuit University of New York, http://www.fordham. edu/halsall/ mod/1619dordt. asp.

47. Hunt, "Calvin's Surprising Catholic Connection," TheBereanCall.org, http://www.thebereancall.org/content/july-2012-classic.

48. Dr. H. L. Champion, "What Do Baptists Believe?" Baptist.org, http://www.baptist.org/beliefs/doctrines/html.

49. "The Canons of the Synod of Dordt, 1618-1619," Fordham University: The Jesuit University of New York, http://www.fordham. edu/halsall/mod/1619dordt. asp.

50. "The Canons of the Synod of Dordt, 1618-1619," Fordham University: The Jesuit University of New York, http://www.fordham. edu/halsall/mod/1619dordt. asp.

51. Gene Taylor, "Calvinism v: Irresistible Grace," Centerville Road Church of Christ, http://www.centervilleroad.com/articles/calvinism-5.html.

52. "The Canons of the Synod of Dordt, 1618-1619," Fordham University: The Jesuit University of New York, http://www.fordham. edu/halsall/mod/1619dordt. asp.

53. Hunt, "Calvin's Surprising Catholic Connection," TheBereanCall.org, http://www.thebereancall.org/content/july-2012-classic.

54. David Schaff, *Our Father's Faith and Ours: A Comparison between Protestantism and Romanism* (New York: G. P. Putnam's Sons, 1928), 172.

55. Hunt, "Calvin's Surprising Catholic Connection," TheBereanCall.org, http://www.thebereancall.org/content/july-2012-classic.

56. John L. Jeffcoat III, "English Bible History," Greatsite.com, http://greatsite.com/timeline-english-bible-history/html.

57. Ibid.

58. Hunt, "Calvin's Surprising Catholic Connection," TheBereanCall.org, http://www.thebereancall.org/content/july-2012-classic.

59. H. Wheeler Robinson, *The Bible in Its Ancient and English Versions* (Oxford, England: Clarendon Press, 1940), 186, 206-207.

60. Hunt, "Calvin's Surprising Catholic Connection," TheBereanCall.org, http://www.thebereancall.org/content/july-2012-classic.

61. "Westminster Confession of Faith," Wikipedia.org, http://en. wikipedia. org/wiki/Westminster_Confession_of_Faith.

62. Ibid.

63. Ibid.

64. "Creationism," *Stanford Encyclopedia of Philosophy* (2007).

65. Ibid.

66. "Dispensationalism," *Theopedia, an Encyclopedia of Biblical Christianity*, http://www.theopedia.com/Dispensationalism/html.

67. "Homosexual Behavior Due to Genetics and Environmental Factors," *e!Science News*, http://esciencenews.com/article/2008/06/281/homosexualbehavior. due. genetics. and. environment.

CHAPTER FOUR

1. "The Gospel According to Mary Magdalene," the Gnostic Society Library: Gnostic Scriptures and Fragments, http://www.gnosis.org/library/marygosp. htm.

2. "About the Nag Hammadi Library (The Nag Hammadi Scriptures)," the Gnostic Society Library: the Nag Hammadi Library, http://www.gnosis.org/naghamm/nhl.html.

3. Karen L. King, *What Is Gnosticism?* (Cambridge, MA: The Belknap Press of Harvard University Press, 2005), 20.

4. Ibid., 20-21.

5. Ibid., 6.

6. Ibid., 174-175.

7. Ibid., 27.

8. Ibid., 29.

9. Pagels, *The Gnostic Gospels*, 21.

10. King, *What Is Gnosticism?*, 26.

11. Ibid., 123.

12. Ibid., 26-27.

13. "Gospel of Philip," Wikipedia.org, http://en. wikipedia.org/wiki/ Gospel_of_Philip.

14. "Valentinus (Gnostic)," Wikipedia.org, http://en. wikipedia.org/wiki/ Valentinus_(Gnostic).

15. Ibid.

16. King, *What Is Gnosticism?*, 154-155.

17. "The Gospel of Truth," Robert M. Grant, trans., the Nag Hammadi Library, http://www.gnosis.org/naghamm/got.html.

18. Ibid.

19. Ibid.

20. "Valentinus (Gnostic)," Wikipedia.org, http://en. wikipedia.org/wiki/ Valentinus_(Gnostic).

21. "The Gospel of Philip," Early Christian Writings, http://www.earlychristianwritings.com/gospelphilip.html.

22. "Gospel of Philip," Wikipedia.org, http://en.wikipedia.org/wiki/ Gospel_of_Philip.

23. Ibid.

24. Ibid.

25. Ibid.

26. "Female Disciples of Jesus," Wikipedia.org, http://en. wikipedia.org/wiki/ Female_disciples_of_Jesus.

27. "Jesus's Interactions with Women," Wikipedia.org, http://en. wikipedia. org/wiki/Jesus%27_interactions_with_women.

28. "Mary Magdalene," Wikipedia.org, http://en. wikipedia.org/wiki/ Mary_Magdalene.

29. Karen L. King, *The Gospel of Mary of Magdala: Jesus and the First Woman Apostle* (Santa Rosa, CA: Polebridge Press, 2003), 3.

30. Ibid., 3-4.

31. Ibid., 14-18.

32. Stevan Davies, *The Gospel of Thomas: Annotated & Explained*, (Woodstock, VT: SkyLight Paths Publishing, 2002), 13.

33. Ibid., xxviii-xxxi.

34. Ibid.

35. Miller, ed., *The Apocalyptic Jesus: A Debate*, 72-73.

36. Davies, *The Gospel of Thomas*, 5.

37. Ibid., 4.

38. Ibid., 3.

39. Ibid., 21.

40. Ibid., xxii.

41. Ibid., xxxiv.

42. Ibid., 15.

43. Elaine Pagels, *Beyond Belief: The Secret Gospel of Thomas* (New York: Random House, 2003), 40.

44. Ibid., 39-40.

45. Ibid., 40-41.

46. Davies, *The Gospel of Thomas*, 35.

47. Pagels, *Beyond Belief: The Secret Gospel of Thomas*, 32.

48. Ibid., 58.

49. Davies, *The Gospel of Thomas*, 33.

50. Davies, *The Gospel of Thomas*, xvii-xix.

51. Ibid.

52. "Origen of Alexandria," *Internet Encyclopedia of Philosophy*, http://www. iep. utm. edu/origen-of-alexandria/print.

53. "Origen," Wikipedia.org, http://en. wikipedia.org/wiki/ Origen_of_Alexandria.

54. Ibid.

55. "Origen of Alexandria," *Internet Encyclopedia of Philosophy*, http://www. iep. utm. edu/origen-of-alexandria/print.

56. Ibid.

57. "First Council of Nicaea," Wikipedia.org, http://en. wikipedia.org/wiki/ First_Council_of_Nicaea.

58. "Origen," Wikipedia.org, http://en. wikipedia.org/wiki/ Origen_of_Alexandria.

59. Pagels, *The Gnostic Gospels*, 4.

60. "Origen of Alexandria," *Internet Encyclopedia of Philosophy*, http://www. iep. utm. edu/origen-of-alexandria/print.

61. Ibid.

62. Ibid.

63. "Origen," Wikipedia.org, http://en. wikipedia.org/wiki/ Origen_of_Alexandria.

64. "Origen of Alexandria," *Internet Encyclopedia of Philosophy*, http://www. iep. utm. edu/origen-of-alexandria/print.

65. "Origen," Wikipedia.org, http://en. wikipedia.org/wiki/ Origen_of_Alexandria.

CHAPTER FIVE

1. Cox, *The Future of Faith*, 182.

2. Ibid., 183.

3. "Richard Dawkins," Wikipedia.org, http://en. wikipedia.org/wiki/ Richard_Dawkins.

4. Scott Detwiler, "Carl Sagan's Religion of Science," Detwiler.us (1987), http://www.detwiler. us/sagan.html.

5. James Randerson, "Childish Superstition: Einstein's Letter Makes View of Religion Relatively Clear," *The Guardian*, May 12, 2008, http://www.the-guardian.com/science/2008/may/12/peopleinscience. religion/print.

6. Braden, Gregg, *The Divine Matrix: Bridging Time, Space, Miracles, and Belief* (Carlsbad, CA: Hay House, 2007), 22.

7. Lynne McTaggart, *The Field: The Quest for the Secret Force of the Universe* (New York: HarperCollins Publishers, 2008), xxiv.

8. Bruce Lipton, PhD, "Spontaneous Evolution: New Scientific Realities Are Bringing Spirit Back into Matter," *Noetic Now*, February 2011, http://noetic.org/noetic/issue-7-february/ spontaneous-evolution-new-scientific-realities-are/.

9. Braden, *The Divine Matrix*, 24.

10. Ibid.

11. Ibid., 24, 30.

12. "Science in Quotes: Mind as the Matrix of All Matter," *The Epoch Times*, June 26, 2011, http://www.theepochtimes.com/n2/science-in-quotes-mind-as-the-matrix-of-all-matter.

13. McTaggart, *The Field*, 21.

14. Ibid.

15. Ibid., xxvii.

16. Braden, *The Divine Matrix*, 21.

17. McTaggart, *The Field*, xxviii.

18. Braden, *The Divine Matrix*, 30-31.

19. Ibid., 32.

20. Ibid., 43.

21. Ibid., 43-45.

22. Ibid., 46-48.

23. Ibid., 48-49.

24. Biocommunication is the general field of study of communication between different biological life forms, mostly in nature, sometimes in the laboratory. It involves the use of instrumentation to observe reactive events occurring in all kinds of life—animal, plant, cellular, microscopic, and so on—and includes observational biology, high-quality observational studies, and study of the effect of human thought and intention on life forms in the environment.

25. "Exploring a Sentient World," Franci Prowse with Cleve Backster, *Shift: At the Frontiers of Consciousness*, June-August 2006, http://www.primarhyperception.com.

26. Ibid.

27. Ibid.

28. http://www.heartmath.com/institute-of-heartmath/.

29. Braden, *The Divine Matrix*, 50-51.

30. "Lessons from the Heart," *Body and Soul with Gail Harris*, PBS, January 28, 2011, http://www.pbs.org/bodyandsoul/203/heartmath. htm.

31. Braden, *The Divine Matrix*, 52.

32. Ibid., 53.

33. "How Holograms Are Made," Ask the Van, http://van. physics. illinois. edu/ga/lisgting. php?id=1926.

34. http://www.cosmometry. net/fractal-holographic-synergetic-universe.

35. Alan T. Williams, "Consciousness, Physics, and the Holographic Paradigm" http://hermital.org/book/holoprt7-1. htm.

36. Michael Talbot, *The Holographic Universe*, (New York: HarperCollins Publishers, 1991), 1-2.

37. Ibid., 11-12.

38. Ibid., 12-13.

39. Ibid., 14-17.

40. Ibid., 21.

41. Ibid.

42. Ibid.

43. Ibid., 18-19.

44. Ibid., 20.

45. Ibid.

46. Ibid., 27.

47. Ibid., 35-36.

48. David Pratt, "David Bohm and the Implicate Order" (Theosophical University Press, 1993), 2, http://www.theosophy-nw.org/.

49. Ibid.

50. Ibid.

51. F. David Peat and John Briggs, "Interview with David Bohm," *Omni*, January 1987, 1, http://waw. fdavidpeat.com/interviews/bohm. htm.

52. Ibid., 6.

53. Ibid., 5-6.

54. Pratt, "David Bohm and the Implicate Order," 3, http://www.theosophy-nw.org/theosnw/science/prat-boh. htm.

55. Ibid.

56. Ibid.

57. Peat and Briggs, "Interview with David Bohm," *Omni*, January 1987, 7, http://waw. fdavidpeat.com/interviews/bohm. htm.

58. Ibid.

59. Pratt, "David Bohm and the Implicate Order," 3, http://www.theosophy-nw.org/theosnw/science/prat-boh. htm.

60. Peat and Briggs, "Interview with David Bohm," *Omni*, January 1987, 2, http://waw. fdavidpeat.com/interviews/bohm. htm.

61. Neale Donald Walsch, *Home with God: In a Life That Never Ends* (New York: Atria Books, 2006), 140-141.

62. Talbot, *The Holographic Universe*, 259.

63. Wilma Wake, "George Dole's Hologram: From Influx to Transpersonal Psychology," SwedenborgianCommunity.org, http://swedenborgiancommunity.org/content. cfm?id=2631.

64. David C. Lewis, "The Human Aura," the Hearts Center Community, http://www.heartscenter.org/TeachingsBlogs/FoundationalTeachings/UnderstandingtheHumanAura.

65. "Brennan Healing Science," Barbara Brennan School of Healing, http://www.barbarabrennan.com/page-contents. php?pageId=25.

66. Talbot, *The Holographic Universe*, 167-168.

67. Ibid., 171-172.

68. Cheryl Lavin, "Larry Dossey in 'Healing Words: The Power of Prayer and the Practice of Medicine,'" *Chicago Tribune*, June 26, 1994, http://articles. chicagotribune.com/1994-06-26/features/9406260216_1_dr-larry-dossey-practice.

69. Ibid.

70. Bruce Lipton, "Spontaneous Evolution: New Scientific Realities Are Bringing Spirit Back into Matter," *Noetic Now*, February 2011, 8, http://noetic.org/noetic,issue-7- february/spontaneous-evolution- new-scientific-realities-are/."

CHAPTER SIX

1. Janice Miner Holden, Bruce Greyson and Debbie James, eds., *The Handbook of Near-Death Experiences: Thirty Years of Investigation* (Santa Barbara, CA: Praeger Publishers, 2009), 160.

2. Ibid.

3. Ibid., 164-165.

4. Ibid., 167.

5. Ibid., 168-169.

6. P. M. H. Atwater, *Near-Death Experiences: The Rest of the Story: What They*

Teach Us about Living, Dying, and Our True Purpose (Charlottesville, VA: Hampton Roads Publishing Company, 2001), 3.

7. Kenneth Ring, *Heading toward Omega: In Search of the Meaning of the Near-Death Experience* (New York: William Morrow & Company, 1985), 35.

8. Atwater, *Near-Death Experiences*, 5.

9. Ibid., 4.

10. Pim Van Lommel, *Consciousness beyond Life: The Science of the Near-Death Experience* (New York: HarperCollins Publishers, 2010), viii.

11. P. M. H. Atwater, *The Big Book of Near-Death Experiences: The Ultimate Guide to What Happens When We Die* (Charlottesville, VA: Hampton Roads Publishing Company, 2007), 9.

12. Raymond A. Moody Jr., *Life after Life: The Investigation of a Phenomenon–Survival of Bodily Death*, (Covington, GA: Mockingbird Books, 1975), 25-76.

13. P. M. H. Atwater, *Children of the New Millennium: Children's Near-Death Experiences and the Evolution of Humankind* (New York: Three Rivers Press, 1999), 54.

14. Atwater, *Near-Death Experiences*, 18-19.

15. Atwater, *Children of the New Millennium*, 56.

16. Atwater, *Near-Death Experiences*, 18.

17. Eben Alexander, *Proof of Heaven: A Neurosurgeon's Journey into the Afterlife* (New York: Simon & Schuster, 2012), 29.

18. Ibid., 31.

19. Ibid., 32.

20. George G.. Ritchie, *Return from Tomorrow* (Grand Rapids, MI: Revell Books, 1978), 64.

21. Ibid., 66.

22. Holden, et al., eds., *The Handbook of Near-Death Experiences*, 66-67

23. Ibid.

24. Ibid., 68.

25. Atwater, *The Big Book of Near-Death Experiences*, 24.

26. Holden, et al., eds., *The Handbook of Near-Death Experiences*, 69.

27. Ibid., 73.

28. Ibid., 84.

29. Moody, *Life after Life*, 32.

30. Ibid., 40.

31. Ibid., 37.

32. Kenneth Ring, *Lessons from the Light: What We Can Learn from the Near-Death Experience* (Needham, MA: Moment Point Press, 2000), 65-66.

33. Ibid., 81.

34. Ibid., 75-77.

35. Ring, *Heading Toward Omega*, 57-59.

36. Van Lommel, *Consciousness beyond Life*, 27-28.

37. Ring, *Lessons from the Light*, 37.

38. Van Lommel, *Consciousness beyond Life*, 32-33.

39. Ibid., 33.

40. Ibid., 36.

41. Ring, *Lessons from the Light*, 156.

42. Moody, *Life after Life*, 50-51.

43. Ring, *Lessons from the Light*, 28-30.

44. Ibid., 37-38.

45. http://www.nde. net. au/transformativeProcess. htm.

46. Atwater, *The Big Book of Near-Death Experiences*, 102.

47. Ring, *Heading toward Omega*, 74.

48. Ibid., 72.

49. Ring, *Lessons from the Light*, 288.

50. Van Lommel, *Consciousness beyond Life*, 22-23.

51. Kevin Williams, "Dr. Melvin Morse," NearDeath.com, http://www.near-death.com/experiences/experts06.html.

52. Ibid.

53. Atwater, *The Big Book of Near-Death Experiences*, 229-232.

54. Moody, *Life after Life*, 109-110.

55. Van Lommel, *Consciousness beyond Life*, 159.

56. Ibid., 194.

57. "Is Your Brain Really Necessary?" *Science*, December 12, 1980, 1232-1234, http://www.sciencemag.org/content/210/4475/1232. extract.

58. Van Lommel, *Consciousness beyond Life*, 199.

59. Ibid., 194.

60. Moody, *Life after Life*, 112-113.

61. Holden, et al., eds., *The Handbook of Near-Death Experiences*, 7.

62. Moody, *Life after Life*, 119.

63. Ibid., 116.

64. Ibid., 117.

65. Van Lommel, *Consciousness beyond Life*, 47.

66. Holden, et al., eds., *The Handbook of Near-Death Experiences*, 46-47.

67. Atwater, *The Big Book of Near-Death Experiences*, 103.

68. Van Lommel, *Consciousness beyond Life*, 52-53.

69. Ring, *Lessons from the Light*, 131.

70. Van Lommel, *Consciousness beyond Life*, 58-61.

71. Ibid., 58.

72. Atwater, *The Big Book of Near-Death Experiences*, 106.

73. Van Lommel, *Consciousness beyond Life*, 59.

74. Holden, et al., eds., *The Handbook of Near-Death Experiences*, 49.

75. Dannion Brinkley, *Saved by the Light: The True Story of a Man Who Died Twice and the Profound Revelations He Received* (New York: HarperCollins Publishers, 2008), 122.

76. Ring, *Lessons from the Light*, 140.

77. Cherie Sutherland, "Psychic Phenomena Following Near-Death Experiences: An Australian Study," *Journal of Near Death Studies* 8, no. 2 (winter 1989): 99.

78. Barbara Harris and Lionel C. Bascom, *Full Circle: The Near-Death Experience and Beyond* (New York: Pocket Books, 1990), 103.

79. Harris and Bascom, *Full Circle*, 43.

80. Ring, *Lessons from the Light*, 219.

81. P. M. H. Atwater, "Aftereffects of Near-Death States," International Association for Near Death Studies, http://iands.org/aftereffects-of-near-death-states.html.

82. Ring, *Heading toward Omega*, 231.

83. Van Lommel, *Consciousness beyond Life*, 61.

84. Atwater, *Near-Death Experiences*, 77-78.

85. Atwater, *Children of the New Millennium*, 36.

86. Ibid., 116.

87. Atwater, *The Big Book of Near Death Experiences*, 283-284.

88. Ring, *Lessons from the Light*, 201.

89. Ibid.

90. Ring, *Lessons from the Light*, 213.

CHAPTER SEVEN

1. Silvia Cranston, *Reincarnation: The Phoenix Fire Mystery* (Pasadena, CA: Theosophical University Press, 1994), 188-189.

2. Ibid., 192-193.

3. Ibid., 195-196.

4. Ibid., 196.

5. Ibid.

6. Ibid., 197.

7. Ibid., 198-201.

8. Ibid., 203-204.

9. Silvia Cranston and Carey Williams, *Reincarnation: A New Horizon in Science, Religion and Society* (Pasadena, CA: Theosophical University Press, 1999), 180.

10. Elizabeth Clare Prophet, *Reincarnation: The Missing Link in Christianity* (Corwin Springs, MT: Summit Publications, 1997), 55.

11. Ibid., 56.

12. Ibid., 57.

13. Ibid., 66.

14. Cranston, *Reincarnation: The Phoenix Fire Mystery*, 135.

15. Prophet, *Reincarnation: The Missing Link in Christianity*, 102.

16. Ibid., 107.

17. Cranston, *Reincarnation: The Phoenix Fire Mystery*, 141-152.

18. Benjamin Crème, "Emperor Responsible for Ban on Rebirth Doctrine," Share International (2005), http://share-international.org/archives/ AgelessWisdom/aw_bannned. htm.

19. Cranston, *Reincarnation: The Phoenix Fire Mystery*, 144.

20. Prophet, *Reincarnation: The Missing Link in Christianity*, 179.

21. Ibid., 184.

22. Ian Stevenson, *Twenty Cases Suggestive of Reincarnation*, Second Edition (Charlottesville, VA: University of Virginia Press, 1974), 1.

23. Tom Schroder, *Old Souls* (New York: Simon & Schuster Paperbacks, 1999), 14.

24. "Scientific Proof of Reincarnation: Dr. Ian Stevenson's Life Work," reluctant-messenger.com, http://www.reluctant-messenger.com/reincarnation-proof. htm.

25. Stevenson, *Twenty Cases Suggestive of Reincarnation*, xii-xiv.

26. Ibid., 20.

27. Ibid., 23.

28. Ibid., 20.

29. Ibid., 22.

30. Ibid., 32.

31. Ibid., 31.

32. Ibid., 324.

33. "Interview with Ian Stevenson," *Omni*, January 1988, 116.

34. Ibid.

35. Paul Von Ward, *The Soul Genome: Science and Reincarnation* (Tucson, AZ: Fenestra Books, 2008), 38.

36. "Interview with Ian Stevenson," *Omni*, January 1988, 78, 80.

37. Ibid., 110.

38. Ibid.

39. Ibid.

40. Ibid., 118.

41. Ibid., 110.

42. Ward, *The Soul Genome*, x.

43. Ibid., xii.

44. Ibid., xii-xiii.

45. Ibid., 11.

46. Ibid., 5.

47. Ibid., 5-7.

48. Ibid., 59.

49. Ibid., 78-80.

50. Ibid., 86-89.

51. Ibid., 3-4.

52. J. Allen Danelek, *Mystery of Reincarnation: The Evidence & Analysis of Rebirth* (New York: Authors Choice Press, 2005), 29-30.

53. Ibid.

54. Ibid., 30-31.

55. Ibid.

56. Ibid., 32.

57. Michael Newton, PhD, *Destiny of Souls: New Case Studies of Life between Lives* (St. Paul, MN: Llewellyn Publications, 2004), 116-118.

58. Hans TenDam, *Exploring Reincarnation: The Classic Guide to the Evidence of Past-Life Experiences* (London: Random House, 2003), 311-314.

59. Ibid., 314.

60. Ibid., 311.

61. Ibid., 330.

62. Ibid.

63. Gary Zukav, *The Seat of the Soul* (New York: Simon & Schuster, 1990), 122.

64. Newton, *Destiny of Souls*, 117-118.

65. TenDam, *Exploring Reincarnation*, 331.

66. Cranston, *Reincarnation: The Phoenix Fire Mystery*, 10.

67. Daneleke, *The Mystery of Reincarnation*, 248.

68. TenDam, *Exploring Reincarnation*, 335.

69. Prophet, *Reincarnation: The Missing Link in Christianity*, 182.

70. Ibid., 221-222.

71. Quincy Howe Jr., *Reincarnation for the Christian* (Philadelphia: The Westminster Press, 1974), 20.

72. Crème, "Emperor Responsible for Ban on Rebirth Doctrine," Share International, http://share-international.org/archives/AgelessWisdom/aw_bannned. htm.

73. Prophet, *Reincarnation: The Missing Link in Christianity*, 193-195.

74. Ibid., 196.

75. Howe, *Reincarnation for the Christian*, 81.

76. The Rev. Gerald DuPont, "Do Catholics Believe in Reincarnation?" Faithleap.org (2003), http://www.faithleap.org/reincarnation. htm.

77. Mike Aguilina, "Come Again?" CatholicCulture.org, http://www. catholicculture.org/culture/library/view. cfm?recnum=198.

78. Cranston and Williams, *Reincarnation: A New Horizon in Science, Religion and Society*, 207.

79. Ibid.

80. Daneleke, *Mystery of Reincarnation*, 113.

81. Robert H. Brom, bishop of San Diego, "Reincarnation," Catholic.com (2004), http://www.catholic.com/tracts/reincarnation.

82. Ibid.

83. DuPont, "Do Catholics Believe in Reincarnation?" Faithleap.org (2003), http://www.faithleap.org/reincarnation. htm.

84. Daneleke, *Mystery of Reincarnation*, 267.

85. Raymond A. Moody, *Coming Back: A Psychiatrist Explores Past-Life Journeys* (New York: Bantam Books, 1991), 57-58.

86. Cranston and Williams, *Reincarnation: A New Horizon in Science, Religion and Society*, 302-303.

87. Atwater, *The Big Book of Near-Death Experiences*, 74-75.

CHAPTER EIGHT

1. Teilhard de Chardin, *The Phenomenon of Man* (New York: Harper & Row Publishers, 1959), 180-182.

2. Ibid., 239-240, 250-252.

3. Barbara Marx Hubbard, *Conscious Evolution: Awakening the Power of Our Social Potential* (Navato, CA: New World Library, 1998), 18-19.

4. Dr. Richard Maurice Bucke, *Cosmic Consciousness: A Study in the Evolution of the Human Mind* (Philadelphia: Inness & Sons, 1901), 7-8.

5. Nancy Seifer and Martin Vieweg, *When the Soul Awakens: The Path to Spiritual Evolution and a New World Era,* second edition (Reston, VA: Gathering Wave Press, 2009), 134.

6. Bucke, *Cosmic Consciousness*, 1.

7. Seifer and Vieweg, *When the Soul Awakens*, 134.

8. Bucke, *Cosmic Consciousness*, 2.

9. Ibid., 14.

10. Ibid., 4.

11. Ibid., 2.

12. Ibid., 3.

13. Ken Wilber, *The Theory of Everything: An Integral Vision for Business, Politics, Science and Spirituality* (Boston: Shambhala Publications, 2000), 5-6.

14. Don Edward Beck and Christopher Cowan, *Spiral Dynamics: Mastering Values, Leadership, and Change* (Malden, MA: Blackwell Publishing, 1996), 40.

15. Ibid., 31.

16. Ibid., 31-32.

17. Ibid., 61-64.

18. Hubbard, *Conscious Evolution*, 10.

19. Wilber, *The Theory of Everything*, 6.

20. Ibid., 8.

21. Beck and Cowan, *Spiral Dynamics*, 274.

22. Ibid., 197.

23. Steve Dinan, "Summary of Spiral Dynamics, by Don Beck and Christopher Cowan," Esalen Institute (1999), http://www.spiraldynamics. com/book/SDreview_Dinan. htm.

24. Beck and Cowan, *Spiral Dynamics*, 203.

25. Dinan, "Summary of Spiral Dynamics, by Don Beck and Christopher Cowan," Esalen Institute (1999), http://www.spiraldynamics.com/book/ SDreview_Dinan. htm.

26. Beck and Cowan, *Spiral Dynamics*, 215.

27. Dinan, "Summary of Spiral Dynamics, by Don Beck and Christopher Cowan," Esalen Institute (1999), http://www.spiraldynamics.com/book/ SDreview_Dinan. htm.

28. Beck and Cowan, *Spiral Dynamics*, 229.

29. Dinan, "Summary of Spiral Dynamics, by Don Beck and Christopher Cowan," Esalen Institute (1999), http://www.spiraldynamics.com/book/ SDreview_Dinan. htm.

30. Beck and Cowan, *Spiral Dynamics*, 244.

31. Dinan, "Summary of Spiral Dynamics, by Don Beck and Christopher Cowan," Esalen Institute (1999), http://www.spiraldynamics.com/book/ SDreview_Dinan. htm.

32. Beck and Cowan, *Spiral Dynamics*, 260.

33. Dinan, "Summary of Spiral Dynamics, by Don Beck and Christopher Cowan," Esalen Institute (1999), http://www.spiraldynamics.com/book/ SDreview_Dinan. htm.

34. Beck and Cowan, *Spiral Dynamics*, 275.

35. Dinan, "Summary of Spiral Dynamics, by Don Beck and Christopher Cowan," Esalen Institute (1999), http://www.spiraldynamics.com/book/SDreview_Dinan. htm.

36. Beck and Cowan, *Spiral Dynamics*, 287.

37. Dinan, "Summary of Spiral Dynamics, by Don Beck and Christopher Cowan," Esalen Institute (1999), http://www.spiraldynamics.com/book/SDreview_Dinan. htm.

38. Wilber, *The Theory of Everything*, 8.

39. Ibid., 13-14.

40. Ibid., 7.

41. Ibid., 33.

42. Ibid., 38.

43. Ibid., 40.

44. Ibid.

45. Brian McLaren, *A New Kind of Christianity: Ten Questions That Are Transforming the Faith* (New York: HarperCollins Publishers, 2010), 232.

46. Ibid., 237.

47. Ibid.

CHAPTER NINE

1. Edmund J. Bourne, *Global Shift: How a New Worldview Is Transforming Humanity* (Oakland, CA: New Harbinger Publications, 2008), 53.

2. Hubbard, *Conscious Evolution*, 11-12.

3. Carter Phipps, *Evolutionaries: Unlocking the Spiritual and Cultural Potential of Science's Greatest Idea* (New York: HarperCollins Publishers, 2012), 50.

4. Ibid.

5. Ibid., 52-53.

6. Ibid., 59.

7. Duane Elgin with Coleen LeDrew, *Global Consciousness Change: Indicators of an Emerging Paradigm* (San Anselmo, CA: Millennium Project, 1997), 4.

8. Hubbard, *Consciousness Evolution*, 10-11.

9. Bourne, *Global Shift*, 60.

10. Ibid., 61.

11. Ibid., 63.

12. Ibid.

13. Ibid., 64.

14. "Integrated Circuit," Wikipedia.org, http://en. wikipedia.org/wiki/Microchip.

15. Rick Smolan, *One Digital Day: How the Microchip Is Changing Our World* (New York: Times Books, 1998), 13.

16. "History of Fiber Optics," http://www.hpcomminc.com/history-of-fiber-optics/.

17. Elgin and LeDrew, *Global Consciousness Change*, 8.

18. Bloom, Howard, *Global Brain: The Evolution of Mass Mind from the Big Bang to the 21st Century* (New York, NY, John Wiley & Sons, Inc., 2000), 216.

19. Elgin, Duane, *Awakening Earth: Expanding the Evolution of Human Culture and Consciousness* (New York, NY, William Morrow & Co., Inc.,

1993), 140-141.

20. Elgin and LeDrew, *Global Consciousness Change*, 6.

21. Seifer and Vieweg, *When the Soul Awakens*, 140-141.

22. Ibid., 141.

23. Ibid., 142.

24. Ibid.

25. Ibid.

26. Elgin, *Awakening Earth*, 136.

27. Bourne, *Global Shift*, 58.

28. Paul Hawken, *Blessed Unrest: How the Largest Social Movement in History Is Restoring Grace, Justice and Beauty to the World* (New York: Penguin Group, 2007), 2.

29. Ibid., 3.

30. Ibid., 5.

31. Ibid., 4.

32. http://www.earthday.org/earth-day-history-movement.

33. Ibid.

34. Hubbard, *Conscious Evolution*, 10.

35. http://en. wikipedia.org/wiki/Truth_and_Reconciliation_commission_ (South Africa).

36. Ibid.

37. Fareed Zakaria, *The Post-American World* (New York: Norton & Company, 2008), 2.

38. Ibid., 2-3.

39. Ibid., 3-4.

40. Cox, *The Future of Faith*, 8.

41. Tickle, *The Great Emergence*, 13-16.

42. Taussig, *A New Spiritual Home*, 35.

43. Ibid., 35-36.

44. Ibid., 37-38.

45. Ibid.

46. Ibid.

47. Cox, *The Future of Faith*, 13.

48. Janet I. Tu, "Yoga 'Demonic'? Critics Call Minister's Warning a Stretch," *Seattle Times*, October 8, 2010 (modified October 11, 2010).

49. Cox, *The Future of Faith*, 199.

50. Ibid., 200-201.

51. "Pentecostalism," Wikipedia.org, http://en. wikipedia.org/w/index. php?title=Pentacostalism&printable=yes.

52. Tickle, *The Great Emergence*, 83-84.

53. Cox, *The Future of Faith*, 203.

54. Tickle, *The Great Emergence*, 85.

55. Jane Macartney, "One Billion Souls to Save," *The Times*, March 28, 2009.

56. Ibid.

57. Cox, *The Future of Faith*, 214-215.

58. Ibid., 215-216.

59. Ibid., 216.

60. Ibid., 217-218.

61. Ibid., 177.

62. Ibid., 191-192.

63. Ibid., 193.

64. Austin Cline, "Catholic Liberation Theology in Latin America: Fighting Poverty with Marx and Catholic Social Teachings," About.com, http://atheism. about.com/od/theology/a/lib_Catholic. htm?p=1.

65. Borg, *Jesus: A New Vision*, 115.

66. Ibid., 131.

67. Cox, *The Future of Faith*, 223.

68. John Shelby Spong, *A New Christianity for a New World: Why Traditional Faith Is Dying and How a New Faith Is Being Born* (New York: HarperCollins Publishers, 2001), 214.

69. McLaren, *A New Kind of Christianity* (New York: HarperCollins Publishers, 2010), 65.

LIST OF REFERENCES

"About the Nag Hammadi Library (The Nag Hammadi Scriptures)," the Gnostic Society Library: the Nag Hammadi Library, http://www.gnosis.org/naghamm/nhl.html.

Aguilina, Mike, "Come Again?" CatholicCulture.org, http://www.catholicculture.org/culture/library/view.cfm?recnum=198.

Alexander, Eben, *Proof of Heaven: A Neurosurgeon's Journey into the Afterlife,* New York: Simon & Schuster, 2012.

Anderson, C. Alan and Deborah G. Whitehouse, *New Thought: A Practical American Spirituality,* Bloomington, IN: AuthorHouse Publisher, revised edition, 2003.

"Apostles' Creed," Wikipedia.org, http://www.en.wikipedia.org/w/index.php?title=Apostles%27_creed&printable=yes.

Armstrong, Karen, *A History of God,* New York: Ballantine Books, 1993.

Atwater, P. M. H., "Aftereffects of Near-Death States," International Association for Near Death Studies, http://iands.org/aftereffects-of-near-death-states.html.

_____. *Children of the New Millennium: Children's Near-Death Experiences and the Evolution of Humankind,* New York: Three Rivers Press, 1999.

_____. *Near-Death Experiences: The Rest of the Story: What They Teach Us About Living, Dying, and Our True Purpose,* Charlottesville, VA: Hampton Roads Publishing Company, 2001.

_____. *The Big Book of Near-Death Experiences: The Ultimate Guide to What Happens When We Die,* Charlottesville, VA: Hampton Roads Publishing Company, 2007.

Bass, Diana Butler, *Christianity After Religion: The End of Church and the Birth of a New Spiritual Awakening*, New York: HarperCollins Publishers, 2012.

Beck, Don Edward and Christopher Cowan, *Spiral Dynamics: Mastering Values, Leadership, and Change*, Malden, MA: Blackwell Publishing, 1996.

"Big Bang Theory—an Overview," All About Science, http://www.big-bang-theory.com/.

Bloom, Howard, *Global Brain: The Evolution of Mass Mind from the Big Bang to the 21st Century*, New York, NY, John Wiley & Sons, Inc., 2000.

Borg, Marcus, *Jesus and Buddha: The Parallel Sayings*, Berkeley, CA: Ulysses Press, 1997.

_____. *Jesus: A New Vision: Spirit, Culture and the Life of Discipleship*, New York: HarperCollins Publishers, 1987.

_____. *Meeting Jesus Again for the First Time*, New York: HarperCollins Publishers, 1994

_____. *Reading the Bible Again for the First Time: Taking the Bible Seriously but Not Literally*, New York: HarperCollins Publishers, 2001.

_____. *The God We Never Knew*, New York: HarperCollins Publishers, 1997.

Bourne, Edmund J., *Global Shift: How a New Worldview Is Transforming Humanity*, Oakland, CA: New Harbinger Publications, 2008.

Braden, Gregg, *The Divine Matrix: Bridging Time, Space, Miracles, and Belief*, Carlsbad, CA: Hay House, 2007.

"Brennan Healing Science," Barbara Brennan School of Healing, http://barbarabrennan.com/page-contents. php?pageId=25.

Brinkley, Dannion, with Paul Perry, *Saved by the Light: The True Story of a Man Who Died Twice and the Profound Revelations He Received*, New York: HarperCollins Publishers, 2008.

Brom, Robert H., bishop of San Diego, "Reincarnation," Catholic.com (2004), http://www.catholic.com/tracts/reincarnation.

Bucher, Dr. Richard P., "Calvinistic Theology," Our Redeemer Lutheran Church, http://orlutheran.com/html/calvinisttheology.html.

Bucke, Dr. Richard Maurice, *Cosmic Consciousness: A Study in the Evolution of the Human Mind*, Philadelphia: Inness & Sons, 1901.

Champion, Dr. H.L., "What Do Baptists Believe?" Baptist.org, http://www.baptist.org/beliefs/doctrines/html.

Chardin, Teilhard de, *The Phenomenon of Man*, New York: Harper & Row Publishers, 1959.

Cline, Austin, "Catholic Liberation Theology in Latin America: Fighting Poverty with Marx and Catholic Social Teachings," About.com, http://atheism.about.com/od/theology/a/lib_Catholic.htm?p=1.

"Constantine," *Encyclopedia Britannica*, 1971 edition, vol. 6, 386.

Conway, Timothy, "Panentheism and the Reality of God," Enlightened-Spirituality.org, http://www.enlightened-spirituality.org/panentheism.html.

Cox, Harvey, *The Future of Faith*, New York: HarperCollins Publishers, 2010.

Cranston, Silvia and Carey Williams, *Reincarnation: A New Horizon in Science, Religion and Society*, Pasadena, CA: Theosophical University Press, 1999.

Cranston, Silvia, *Reincarnation: The Phoenix Fire Mystery*, Pasadena, CA: Theosophical University Press, 1994.

"Creationism," *Stanford Encyclopedia of Philosophy* (2007), http://plato.stanford.edu/entries/creationism/html.

Crème, Benjamin, "Emperor Responsible for Ban on Rebirth Doctrine," Share International (2005), http://share-international.org/archives/AgelessWisdom/aw_bannned.htm.

Danelek, J. Allen, *Mystery of Reincarnation: The Evidence & Analysis of Rebirth*, New York: Authors Choice Press, 2005.

Davies, Stevan, *The Gospel of Thomas: Annotated & Explained*, Ed. Andrew Harvey, Woodstock, VT: Skylight Paths Publishing, 2005.

Detwiler, Scott, "Carl Sagan's Religion of Science," Honesty.com (1987), http://www.detwiler. us/sagan.html.

Dinan, Steve, "Summary of Spiral Dynamics, by Don Beck and Christopher Cowan," Esalen Institute (1999), http://www.spiraldynamics.com/book/ SDreview_Dinan. htm.

"Dispensationalism," *Theopedia, an Encyclopedia of Biblical Christianity*, http:// www.theopedia.com/Dispensationalism/html.

Dodds, The Rev. James, D. D., "Exposition of the Apostles' Creed," http:// www.reformed.org/documents/index.html?mainframe=http://www.reformed. org/documents/apostles_creed.html.

Ehrman, Bart D., *The Orthodox Corruption of Scripture: The Effect of Early Christological Controversies on the Text of the New Testament*, New York: Oxford University Press Inc., 2011.

Elgin, Duane, with Coleen LeDrew, *Global Consciousness Change: Indicators of an EmergingParadigm*, San Anselmo, CA: Millennium Project, 1997.

Elgin, Duane, *Awakening Earth: Exploring the Evolution of Human Culture and Consciousness*, New York, NY, William Morrow and Company, Inc., 1993.

"Enlightenment," *Stanford Encyclopedia of Philosophy*, http://plato.stanford. edu/entries/enlightenment/html.

"Exploring a Sentient World," Franci Prowse with Cleve Backster, *Shift: At the Frontiers of Consciousness*, June-August 2006, http://primarhyperception.com.

"Female Disciples of Jesus," Wikipedia.org, http://en. wikipedia.org/wiki/ Female_disciples_of_Jesus.

"First Council of Nicaea," Wikipedia.org, http://en. wikipedia.org/wiki/First_Council_of_Nicaea.

"Five Solas," *Theopedia, an Encyclopedia of Biblical Christianity*, http://www.theopedia.com/Five-Solas.

"Fundamentalist-Modernist Controversy," Wikipedia.org, http://en.wikipedia.org/wiki/Fundamentalist%E2%80%93Modernist-Controversy.

"Gospel of Philip," Wikipedia.org, http://en.wikipedia.org/wiki/Gospel_of_Philip.

Harris, Barbara and Lionel C. Bascom, *Full Circle: The Near-Death Experience and Beyond*, New York: Pocket Books, 1990.

"Harry Emerson Fosdick: Liberalism's Populizer," *Christianity Today*, August 8, 2008, http://www.christianitytoday.com/ch/131christians/pastorsandpreachers/fosdick.html.

Hawken, Paul, *Blessed Unrest: How the Largest Social Movement in History is Restoring Grace, Justice and Beauty to the World*, New York: Penguin Group, 2007.

"History of Fiber Optics," http://hpcomminc.com/history-of-fiber-optics/.

Holden, Janice Miner, Bruce Greyson and Debbie James, eds., *The Handbook of Near-Death Experiences: Thirty Years of Investigation*, Santa Barbara, CA: Praeger Publishers, 2009.

"Homosexual Behavior Due to Genetics and Environmental Factors," *e!Science News*, http://esciencenews.com/article/2008/06/281/homosexualbehavior.due.genetics.and.environment.

"How Ancient Trinitarian Gods Influenced Adoption of the Trinity," United Church of God—an International Association, http://www.ucg.org/booklet/god-trinity/how-ancient-trinitarian-gods-influenced-adoption-trinity/.

Howe, Quincy Jr., *Reincarnation for the Christian*, Philadelphia: The Westminster Press, 1974.

"How Holograms Are Made," Ask the Van, http://van.physics.illinois.edu/ga/lisgting.php?id=1926.

Hubbard, Barbara Marx, *Consciousness Evolution: Awakening the Power of Our Social Potential*, Navato, CA: New World Library, 1998.

Hunt, Dave, "Calvin's Surprising Catholic Connection," TheBereanCall.org, http://www.thebereancall.org/content/july-2012-classic.

http://en. wikipedia.org/wiki/Truth-and-Reconciliation_commission_(SouthAfrica).

http://history-christian-church. blogspot.com/2012/03/arian-controversy.html.

http://nde. net. au/transformativeProcess. htm.

https://www.ccel.org/creeds/nicene. creed.html.

http://www.cosmometry. net/fractal-holographic-synergetic-universe.

http://www.earthday.org/earth-day-history-movement.

http://www.heartmath.com/institute-of-heartmath/.

"Inspiration, Authority & Criticism in the Thought of Charles Augustus Briggs," Bible.org, http://bible.org/pringt/683.

"Integrated Circuit," Wikipedia.org, http://en. wikipedia.org/wiki/Microchip.

"Interview with Ian Stevenson," *Omni*, January 1988.

"Is Your Brain Really Necessary?" *Science*, December 12, 1980, http://www. sciencemag.org/content/210/4475/1232. extract.

Jeffcoat, John L. III, "English Bible History," Greatsite.com, http://greatsite. com/timeline-english-bible-history/html.

"Jesus's Interactions With Women," Wikipedia.org, http://en. wikipedia.org/wiki/Jesus%27-interactions-with_women.

King, Karen L., *What Is Gnosticism?*, Cambridge, MA: The Belknap Press of Harvard University Press, 2005.

_____. *The Gospel of Mary Magdala: Jesus and the First Woman Apostle*, Santa Rosa, CA, Polebridge Press, 2003.

Laughlin, Paul Alan, *Remedial Christianity: What Every Believer Should Know about the Faith, but Probably Doesn't*, Santa Rosa, CA: Polebridge Press, 2004.

Lavin, Cheryl, "Larry Dossey in 'Healing Words: The Power of Prayer and the Practice of Medicine,'" *Chicago Tribune*, June 26, 1994, http://articles. chicagotribune.com/1994-06-26/features/9406260216_1_dr-larry-dossey-practice.

LePage, Victoria, "The God Debate: Monotheism vs. Panentheism in Postmodern Society," the Theosophical Society.org, http://www.theosophical. org/publications/quest-magazine/1572.

"Lessons from the Heart," *Body and Soul with Gail Harris*, PBS, January 28, 2011, http://www.pbs.org/bodyandsoul/203/heartmath. htm.

Lewis, David, "The Human Aura," the Hearts Center Community, http://www.heartscenter.org/TeachingsBlogs/FoundationalTeachings/UnderstandingtheHumanAura.

Lipton, Bruce, PhD, "Spontaneous Evolution: New Scientific Realities Are Bringing Spirit Back into Matter," *Noetic Now*, February 2011, http://noetic.org/noetic/issue-7-february/spontaneous-evolution-new-scientific-realities-are/.

Macartney, Jane, "One Billion Souls to Save," *The Times*, March 28, 2009.

"Mary Magdalene," Wikipedia.org, http://en. wikipedia.org/wiki/Mary_Magdalene.

MacLaren, Brian, *A New Kind of Christianity: Ten Questions That Are Transforming the Faith,* New York: HarperCollins Publishers, 2010.

McTaggart, Lynne, *The Field: The Quest for the Secret Force of the Universe*, New York: HarperCollins Publishers, 2008.

Miller, Robert J., ed., *The Apocalyptic Jesus: A Debate*, Santa Rosa, CA: Polebridge Press, 2001.

Moody, Raymond A. Jr. with Paul Perry, *Coming Back: A Psychiatrist Explores Past-Life Journeys*, New York: Bantam Books, 1991.

_____. *Life After Life: The Investigation of a Phenomenon-Survival of Bodily Death*, Covington, GA: Mockingbird Books, 1975.

Newton, Michael, PhD, *Destiny of Souls: New Case Studies of Life between Lives*, St. Paul, MN: Llewelyn Publications, 2004.

"Origen of Alexandria," *Internet Encyclopedia of Philosophy*, http://www.iep. utm. edu/origen-of-alexandria/print.

"Origen," Wikipedia.org, http://en. wikipedia.org/wiki/ Origen_of_Alexandria.

Orr, James, "The Apostles' Creed," *International Standard Biblical Encyclopedia*, 1939 edition, vol. 1

Pagels, Elaine, *Beyond Belief: The Secret Gospel of Thomas*, New York: Random House, 2003.

_____. *The Gnostic Gospels*, New York: Random House, 1979.

Peat, David F., and John Briggs, "Interview with David Bohm," *Omni*, January 1987.

"Pentacostalism," Wikipedia.org, http://en. wikipedia.org/w/index. php?title= Pentacostalism&printable=yes.

Phipps, Carter, *Evolutionaries: Unlocking the Spiritual and Cultural Potential of Science's Greatest Idea*, New York: HarperCollins Publishers, 2012.

Pitkin, Barbara, "Calvin's Reception of Paul," Academia. edu, http://academia. edu/879076/Calvins_Reception_of_Paul.html.

Pratt, David, "David Bohm and the Implicate Order," Theosophical University Press, 1993.

Prophet, Elizabeth Clare, *Reincarnation: The Missing Link in Christianity*, Corwin Springs, MT: Summit Publications, 1997.

Randerson, James, "Childish Superstition: Einstein's Letter Makes View of Religion Relatively Clear," *The Guardian*, May 12, 2008.

"Richard Dawkins," Wikipedia.org, http://en. wikipedia.org/wiki/Richard_Dawkins.

Ring, Kenneth, *Heading toward Omega: In Search of the Meaning of the Near-Death Experience*, New York: William Morrow & Company, 1985.

_____. *Lessons from the Light: What We Can Learn from the Near-Death Experience*, Needham, MA: Moment Point Press, 2000.

Ritchie, George G., with Elizabeth Sherrill, *Return from Tomorrow*, Grand Rapids, MI: Revell Books, 1978.

Robinson, H. Wheeler, *The Bible in Its Ancient and English Versions*, Oxford, England: Clarendon Press, 1940.

Rock, Thomas Dennis, *The Mystical Woman and the Cities of the Nations*, London: WilliamMacIntosh, 1867.

Rossano, Matt J., "Does Resurrection Contradict Science?" *Huffington Post*, April 25, 2013, http://www.huffingtonpost.com/matt-j-rossano/does-resurrection-contrad_b_848577.html.

Schaff, David, *Our Father's Faith and Ours: A Comparison between Protestantism and Romanism*, New York: G.P. Putnam's Sons, 1928.

Schroder, Tom, *Old Souls*, New York: Simon & Schuster Paperbacks, 1999.

"Science in Quotes: Mind as the Matrix of All Matter," *The Epoch Times*, June 26, 2011, http://theepochtimes.com/n2/science-in-quotes-mind-as-the-matrix-of-all-matter.

"Scientific Proof of Reincarnation: Dr. Ian Stevenson's Life Work," reluctant-messenger.com, http://www.reluctant-messenger.com/reincarnation-proof.htm.

Scribner, R. W. and C. Scott Dixon, *The German Reformation*, New York: Palgrave MacMillan, 2003.

Seifer, Nancy and Martin Vieweg, *When the Soul Awakens: The Path to Spiritual Evolution and a New World Era*, second edition, Reston, VA: Gathering Wave Press, 2009.

Smolan, Rick, *One Digital Day: How the Microchip Is Changing Our World*, New York: TimesBooks, 1998.

Spong, John Shelby, *A New Christianity for a New World: Why Traditional Faith is Dying and How a New Faith Is Being Born*, New York: HarperCollins Publishers, 2001.

_____. *Rescuing the Bible from Fundamentalism: A Bishop Rethinks the Meaning of Scripture*, New York: HarperCollins Publishers, 1991.

_____. *Why Christianity Must Change or Die: A Bishop Speaks to Believers in Exile*, New York: HarperCollins Publishers, 1998.

Stevenson, Ian, MD, *Twenty Cases Suggestive of Reincarnation*, second edition, Charlottesville, VA: University of Virginia Press, 1974.

Sutherland, Cherie, "Psychic Phenomenon Following Near-Death Experiences: An Australian Study," *Journal of Near Death Studies*, 8, no. 2 (winter 1989).

Tabor, James D., *Paul and Jesus: How the Apostle Transformed Christianity*, New York: Simon & Schuster, 2012.

Talbot, Michael, *The Holographic Universe*, New York: HarperCollins Publishers, 1991.

Taussig, Hal, *A New Spiritual Home: Progressive Christianity at the Grassroots*, Santa Rosa, CA: Polebridge Press, 2006.

Taylor, Gene, "Calvinism V: Irresistible Grace," Centerville Road Church of Christ, http://www.centervilleroad.com/articles/calvinism-5.html.

TenDam, Hans, *Exploring Reincarnation: The Classic Guide to the Evidence of Past-Life Experiences*, London: Random House, 2003.

"The Canons of the Synod of Dordt, 1618-1619," Fordham University: The Jesuit University of New York, http://www.fordham.edu/halsall/mod/1619dordt.asp.

"The Gospel According to Mary Magdalene," the Gnostic Society Library: Gnostic Scriptures and Fragments, http://gnosis.org/library/marygosp.htm.

"The Gospel of Philip," Early Christian Writings, http://earlychristianwritings.com/gospelphilip.html.

"The Gospel of Truth," Robert M. Grant, trans., the Nag Hammadi Library, http://www.gnosis.org/naghamm/got.html.

"Theism," Wikipedia.org, http://en.wikipedia.org/wiki/theism.

"The Surprising Origins of the Trinity Doctrine," United Church of God—an International Association, http://www.ucg.org/booklet/god-trinity/how-ancient-trinitarian-godsinfluenced-adoption-trinity/.

"The Trinity in Christian Theology, ReligionFacts.com, http://religionfacts.com/christianity/beliefs/trinity. htm.

Tickle, Phyllis, *The Great Emergence: How Christianity Is Changing and Why*, Grand Rapids, MI: Baker Publishing Group, 2008.

"Valentinus (Gnostic)," Wikipedia.org, http://en.wikipedia.org/wiki/Valentinus_(Gnostic).

Van Lommel, Pim, *Consciousness Beyond Life: The Science of the Near-Death Experience*, New York: HarperCollins Publishers, 2010.

Wake, Wilma, "George Dole's Hologram: From Influx to Transpersonal Psychology," SwedenborgianCommunity.org, http://swedenborgiancommunity.org/content. cfm?id=2631.

Walsch, Neale Donald, *Conversations With God: An Uncommon Dialogue*, Book 1, New York: G.P. Putnam's Sons, 1995.

_____. *Home With God: In a Life That Never Ends*, New York: Atria Books, 2006.

Ward, Paul Von, *The Soul Genome: Science and Reincarnation*, Tucson, AZ: Fenestra Books, 2008.

Weaver, J. Denny, *The Nonviolent Atonement*, Grand Rapids, MI: Wm. B. Eerdmans Publishing Co., 2001.

Weigall, Arthur, *Paganism in Our Christianity*, New York: Garden City Publishing, 1928.

"Westminster Confession of Faith," Wikipedia.org, http://en. wikipedial.org/wiki/Westminster_Confession_of_Faith.

"Who Were the Fundamentalists?" *Christianity Today*, October 1, 2006, http://www.christianitytoday.com/ch2006/issue92/3. 12ahtml.

Wilber, Ken, *A Theory of Everything: An Integral Vision for Business, Politics, Science and Spirituality*, Boston: Shambhala Publications Inc., 2000.

Williams, Alan T., "Consciousness, Physics, and the Holographic Paradigm," http://hermital.org/book/holopr7-1. htm.

Zakaria, Fareed, *The Post-American World*, New York: Norton & Company, 2008.

Zukav, Gary, *The Seat of the Soul*, New York: Simon & Schuster, 1990.